Towards Greater

992

A Continent without an Iron Curtain

Towards Greater Europe?

A Continent without an Iron Curtain

Edited by

Colin Crouch and David Marquand

Blackwell Publishers

Copyright © The Political Quarterly Publishing Co. Ltd.

ISBN 0–631–18551–8

First published 1992

Blackwell Publishers
108 Cowley Road, Oxford, OX4 1JF, UK.

and
3 Cambridge Center,
Cambridge, MA. 02142, USA.

British Library Cataloguing in Publication Data
Towards Greater Europe? A Continent
without an Iron Curtain. I. Crouch, Colin
II. Marquand, David 320.94
ISBN 0–631–18551–8

Library of Congress Cataloguing in Publication Data
Towards greater Europe? : a Continent without an Iron Curtain/edited
by Colin Crouch and David Marquand.
p. cm.
ISBN 0–631–18551–8 (pbk.)
1. Europe—Politics and government—1989- 2. Europe, Eastern—
Politics and government—1989- I. Crouch, Colin.
II. Marquand, David.
D2009.T68 1992 940.55—dc20 92–7812 CIP

Typeset by Joshua Associates Ltd., Oxford
Printed in Great Britain by Whitstable Litho, Kent.

CONTENTS

INTRODUCTION

EUROPEAN history is now moving so fast that it is impossible to keep up with it. When this book was conceived, an entity known as the Soviet Union was still a super-power (albeit only just) and was still ruled by the party of Lenin, Stalin and Brezhnev. The book was completed before the abortive anti-Gorbachev coup of August 1991, before the Baltic states recovered their independence and before the flag of the Russian Republic flew over the Kremlin. It went to press before the European Community's intergovernmental conferences at the end of that year. By the time these words are read, new developments—unpredictable at the time of writing—will have taken place, both in the little-Europe of Brussels, Strasbourg and Luxembourg, and in the wider Europe that extends to as yet undetermined areas to the east.

All this, however, gives extra urgency to the issues encapsulated in the notion of greater Europe which we have used for our title. As William Wallace's chapter brings home, a paradoxical consequence of the cold war was that the integration of the little-Europe of the west—in some ways, the greatest political achievement the continent has known since the days of Charlemagne—took place in a kind of definitional vacuum. Monnet, Schuman, de Gasperi and the rest could talk of European union, without having to confront the question of what Europe meant: so long as most of central and eastern Europe were, in practice, part of the empire which the Bolsheviks had inherited from the Romanovs, and whose western frontiers had been settled at Yalta and Potsdam, the question was of academic interest only.

In any case, the integration of little-Europe took place in the economic domain far more than in the political. Though the developing European Community always proclaimed a political goal, and had a proto-federal institutional structure to match, it was tacitly accepted that political union was for tomorrow, or the day after tomorrow, not for today. The European Community was first and foremost a customs union, secondly (and less completely) a common market, and thirdly a trading *bloc*. By virtue of the last of these three roles, it had growing clout in the fora where the economic relationships of the non-Communist world were managed, insofar as they were managed at all. But although this gave it a political role of sorts, politics followed economics, and not the other way around. And because its functions were overwhelmingly economic rather than political, the fact that its boundaries did not correspond with any particular cultural, religious, ethnic or other historical boundaries posed no problems. For its central geo-political achievement—the reconciliation of France and Germany—marked the transcendence of an historical

1

division, not the expression of a common identity that might be set against others. Indeed, it was not even a comprehensive European rich man's club. Britain, Scandinavia and Switzerland were all outside; Italy, then poor, was within.

To be sure, the enlargements of the 1970s and 1980s did raise issues of identity and commonality. In the 1970s, the British, and to a lesser extent the Danes, anguished over the implications of Community membership, partly because they were unsure how far they gave precedence to a European identity, as opposed to identities of some other kind—'English-speaking' or 'Atlantic' in the British case; Scandinavian in the Danish. In the 1980s, much the same was true of Greece. But these debates were internal to the countries concerned. The British were not sure whether they wanted to be Europeans, but once de Gaulle was out of the way no one in the rest of the Community disputed their right to be so if they wished. As for Denmark and Greece, no one ever called their European identities into question—though, in the Greek case, there was some concern over the economic implications of Community entry.

The position now is quite different. Before long, the European Community is likely to include the whole of western Europe; only Norway and Switzerland have yet to commit themselves to the search for membership. The Community would then include all of *non-Slav* Europe. Poles, Czechs and Russians would be stopped at an essentially Germanic border. But to define such an entity as 'Europe'—to suggest that Prague and Warsaw are not European cities—would be to deny the facts of history as well as of geography. Then suppose, as Wallace does, that the Community is widened to include Poland, Hungary and Czechoslovakia, and perhaps Slovenia, Croatia and the Baltic states as well. In that case, it would have become (with the exception of Greece within and Romania and parts of the Ukraine without) *non-Orthodox* Europe. But unless the division between Rome and Byzantium were, for some reason, considered to be as critical for the twenty-first century as it was for the eleventh, that definition would be equally hard to defend. If culture, language and history are treated as the defining characteristics of a European identity, there is no case for regarding St Petersburg as less European than Prague (or, for that matter, than Lisbon or Liverpool) or Moscow than Warsaw or Warrington. If being European has anything to do with contributing to the continent's common civilisation, the land of Pushkin, Tolstoy and Solzhenitsyn is as European as France, or Italy, or Germany. Politically, it is true, the Bolshevik *Putsch* took Russia out of Europe for seventy years. But even Stalin could not write her out of the civilisation which her writers and musicians had done so much to enrich; and, in any case, the real meaning of the fourth Russian revolution which is now in progress is that the Bolshevik aberration has come to an end: that whatever western Europe may wish, the Russians have reasserted their European identity as the Greeks, Portuguese and Spanish reasserted theirs when they threw off totalitarianism in the 1970s. Yet, if Russia is part of Europe, Europe's boundaries extend, not merely to the Urals, as de Gaulle famously proclaimed, but to the Pacific.

The thorny questions of where 'Europe' ends, of what 'Europe' means, and of how the various possible meanings should relate to each other are, in short, on the table. It will be some time before they are answered. Already, however, one or two points are reasonably clear. The first and most obvious is that the completion of the Community's internal market—soon to be followed by rapid steps towards monetary union—will give a massive new boost to the economic integration of little Europe. Together with the United States and Japan, it will be one of the three great power-houses of the advanced industrial world. This opens huge opportunities for those in a position to reap the benefits of extended markets, but the price of entry will be high: a capacity to grapple with international competition, and to develop firms that can make and sell the goods and services that a Europe-wide market can buy. With the possible exception of Hungary and Czechoslovakia, none of the formerly Communist countries of eastern and central Europe will be able to pay that price for years to come; and what is true of them will be doubly true of whatever successor-states emerge from the carcase of the old Soviet Union. If events are left to take their own course, we are likely to see the emergence of a strong, increasingly tightly defined, European Community, fringed, on its eastern borders, by weak and dependent economies which cannot compete, except at the lower end of the markets they enter, and whose citizens will be unwelcome if they seek to resolve their economic problems by migration.

This leads on to a more speculative point. Weak and dependent economies are unlikely to sustain strong and flourishing polities. Eastern and south-eastern Europe did not, to put it mildly, enjoy happy histories in the days before they were overrun by the Red Army. Democratic, or even constitutional, politics have in most cases been weak; ethnic tensions have frequently been acute; past regimes, non-Communist as well as Communist, have left a dreadful legacy of low trust among citizens. This is equally true, though in a more complicated way, of the former Soviet Union. All of the non-Russian republics have large Russian minorities; Russia has a large non-Russian minority, some of it in autonomous republics with their own national claims, and some of it in the Russian heartland itself. As became clear in the turmoil surrounding the abortive coup of 1991, virtually all the republics have territorial claims against their neighbours. And although pre-revolutionary Russia was beginning to develop along constitutional lines, it did not get far enough to develop traditions of political civility or pluralist give-and-take. Even stable democracies, with long traditions of constitutional government, might find it hard to cope with the economic hardships which the former Communist countries are likely to encounter in the short and medium term. Societies with no such traditions are likely to find it harder still.

This is not to belittle the recent revolutions in eastern Europe and what

3

used to be the Soviet Union. They are among the most hopeful events of this dreadful century, and no one should fail to pay tribute to the courage and idealism that made them possible. By the same token, no one should forget that, in most of the countries concerned, Communism did at least achieve an unprecedented expansion of educational opportunity—of which the anti-Communist revolutions were, at least in part, the para-doxical fruit—and that in consequence democratic institutions have a better chance of taking root than they did in the inter-war period. Western Europe must not talk itself into a mood of despair about the human resources and political capacities of its eastern neighbours. The brave young men and women who manned the flimsy barricades around the Russian parliament building last August, like the crowds that thronged the squares of eastern Europe a couple of years before, represent a hope for the future which it would be foolish, as well as mean-spirited, to denigrate. The fact remains that the revolutionaries' inheritance is not a comfortable one. Subject to two crucial provisos, the eastern lands of the new 'greater Europe' are better placed to make a successful passage to political stability and democratic governance than they have ever been before. But the provisos are that they enjoy at least a modicum of economic fair weather and that the European identities which they have all, in different ways, re-asserted are not denied by inward-looking responses from the little-Europe of the west. On present trends, both provisos will be hard to meet.

Future possibilities

There is no way of telling what the detailed consequences will be if they are not met. It is not difficult, however, to foresee the broad outlines. Sharp economic differences between regions lead to migration, or at least to pressure to migrate. And, as the US and the major European economies have already learned, migrating labour is not a set of de-personalised labour units, but human beings with cultural and ethnic identities, whose encounter with other such identities can generate serious tensions. Countries under pressure from inward migration either receive the influx and then try to come to terms with the tensions; or they erect barriers and try to cope both with the problems of policing and illegal movement that ensue, and with the instability that results in the countries that would-be immigrants have reached before encountering the barrier. Specifically, for western Europe this would mean, at present, coping with a Poland in which hundreds of thousands of unemployed Poles, Balts and Russians had gathered in an attempt to reach the west, or with a Hungary with a similar influx of Romanians and Bulgarians.

Part of eastern Europe, it is worth remembering, has already been brought within the bounds of the Community—namely, the old DDR. German unification serves as a microcosm of the larger European dilemma. The initial collapse of the iron curtain led to large population movements from eastern to western Germany. Finding it impossible to ban these movements, the west Germans faced a choice: either build up the eastern economy, so that people would not wish to leave, or accept massive migration. The former would entail major investment programmes that could be achieved only within the framework of political unification. And the unification would have to be rapid to give the easterners confidence that it was worth staying in their part of the country. In the event, westerners find it difficult and costly to reshape the eastern economy, while the westward movement of population still continues.

The implications are not encouraging. The 'German solution' was made possible by a shared ethnic identity on both sides of the old border; and even so its success is problematic. The Slav lands have no such identity to appeal to; and their economies are, in most cases, less competitive than the eastern German one. This suggests that, in the absence of firm countervailing policies, the closest analogy to the likely pattern of relationships between the Community and eastern Europe will become that between the United States and Latin America. It is not a happy precedent. Massive illegal immigration goes hand in hand with resentment at the dominance over local economies of US multi-national capital, leading in turn to anti-American and anti-capitalist populist movements. One result is that the US has supported some of the world's nastiest non-Communist dictatorships, so as to protect itself against these populist pressures. Meanwhile, many Latin American economies are left to odd niches of illegality, such as the narcotics trade, in order to find an outlet for local entrepreneurship.

At present, no doubt, anti-capitalist movements of this sort seem a remote prospect in eastern Europe, whose peoples are eagerly discarding the residues of decades of anti-capitalist rhetoric. But this may lead to a false sense of security, both on the part of the new regimes in the area, and on the part of western business. Indeed, there are signs that, in their understandable anti-socialist fervour, some east European governments may be tempted to encourage the kind of unregulated capitalism which is no longer to be found in advanced western societies. After the euphoria, however, the day after tomorrow might well see a very different attitude towards a western Europe that dominated eastern economies while also erecting effectively ethnic barriers to population movements. And, quite apart from anti-western or anti-capitalist feelings, a 'Latin American' answer to the question of how the two halves of Europe should relate to each other would also encourage the kind of territorial and ethnic conflicts which have already led to bloodshed in Yugoslavia and the Caucasus.

Yet early accession to the Treaty of Rome is not a satisfactory answer either. Optimists may point to the success of Spanish, Portuguese and Greek entry. But those countries joined the Community when it was itself much looser. Accession now would mean joining a single-market Community. Unless extended transitional arrangements were made, this would mean accepting exposure to the full force of competition from many of the world's most efficient companies at a time when ramshackle former state enterprises are in the throes of major re-structuring. As the east Germans are again discovering, accepting the economic regime of an efficient and powerful country can threaten the viability of much of the domestic economy. Even in the United Kingdom and southern Europe, it is worth remembering, some have doubts about the initial impact of the single market. To be sure, being an insider means having a chance to help shape the development of the new European economy, as well as being eligible for the assistance that poorer regions will receive to offset some of the dislocation that the single market will bring. That, however, provides a further reason why the existing member states may not be in a hurry to accept impoverished new members in the east, as opposed to prosperous ones in the west.

All in all, the best short-term alternative to the 'Latin American' solution is therefore a Europe with 'fuzzy' boundaries and a range of special arrangements, essentially transitional in character, though in some cases destined to last for a comparatively long time, binding the nations on the Community's eastern and south-eastern borders to its core. The whole of non-Community Europe—including the European republics of the former Soviet Union—could be admitted to the Council of Europe, on condition that the governments concerned accepted its commitment to human rights and demonstrated their acceptance by their actions. There would be a series of trade agreements, in which the Community would have to accept the 'infant industries' argument on behalf of the eastern economies; and by the same token, there would be deals that enabled the economies concerned to maintain tariffs against the Community which were not reciprocated. Meanwhile, the Community countries would strengthen their programmes of technology transfer, know-how assistance and straightforward economic aid, so as to facilitate the necessary transformation of the eastern economies. By implication, at any rate, the little-Europe of the Community would have acknowledged that it is only a part of greater Europe, and that greater Europe must have an institutional framework of some kind. The question of whether the tighter framework of little Europe would ultimately be extended to cover the whole of greater Europe—and not just the parts of it on little Europe's eastern borders—would be left open.

Europe's wider role

It is already becoming clear that the EC is bound to become a force in international affairs in its own right. The achievements of such a role are to date rather minor: an ill-starred peace initiative in Yugoslavia, a commitment to a small Franco-German army; joint positions of EC states on certain problem areas. But the tendency of the British to mock such ventures and contrast them unfavourably with the achievements of the Anglo-American alliance is likely before long to seem like yet another piece of imperial nostalgia riding on the USA's back. The pressures towards concerted foreign, and therefore defence, policies among EC members are overwhelming. Relations with eastern Europe and the old USSR, once the main force behind US hegemony over western Europe, now primarily generate issues affecting the EC as such. The sheer economic power of the Community as it integrates its economies and currencies requires it to become an actor on the world stage at a time when foreign policy is increasingly driven by the politics of international trade. Already states in many parts of the world address the EC as a political entity.

Europe's internal political momentum combines here with the implications of the end of the cold war to produce a growing autonomy of the EC countries as a group from the USA; not an hostility, but an autonomy, and one that is rich in irony. It was the old Communist regime of the Soviet Union that sustained US dominance within Europe; western Europeans must accept that, in return for their new autonomy, they must start paying for their own defence; and Americans must reconcile themselves to relinquishing a role in Europe that they in fact entered only very reluctantly and 'temporarily' after 1942.

The inevitability of a growing European world role means that it is foolish to try to retard it by propping up the institutions of the rigid cold-war world, as, for example, British insistence that all European defence developments must be subordinate to NATO seems at times to do. Nevertheless, the development of the new role will be hard and slow. Establishing a new partnership with a USA increasingly uncertain whether it encounters more ingratitude among the nations it helped after World War II when it looks at the world across the Atlantic or the Pacific is an issue beyond the scope of this volume, but it is highly relevant to the character of Europe's future.

Closer to home—geographically, but not in most other respects—are relations with the heterogeneity of Moslem countries to the south. The significance of oil, the position of Israel, the importance of Islam in providing a defence against western economic and cultural imperialism and the problems of Islamic minorities in France, Germany, the UK and elsewhere have given the old confrontation across the northern and southern shores of the Mediterranean a lease of life far more real and dangerous than that between Western and Orthodox Christianity that might be coming to constitute Europe's eastern frontier.

It is however that eastern edge, the main theme of this volume, that is providing Europe's most immediate proving ground. A major issue here will be the role of Germany, not only the EC's dominant state, but in particular the one most significantly placed both economically and geopolitically for policy towards the east. For many years the former western Federal Republic avoided, for obvious reasons, any strong foreign-policy role, concentrating on economic links alone. In particular, the 'old soldiers' generation' of German politicians, such as the former Chancellor,

Helmut Schmidt, who had fought on the eastern front in the Second World War, maintained the strong maxim that Germany had no role meddling in the affairs of Poland and the rest of eastern Europe, except in order to break down the barriers within the then divided Germany. As that generation passes, will we see a brash new age of German politicians that lacks such inhibitions—just as, in domestic politics in Britain and elsewhere, the passing of the generation that said 'never again mass unemployment' after the 1930s ushered in the governments of the 1980s that viewed the prospect with equanimity?

Not only in Germany but elsewhere in Europe there have been disturbing signs in recent years that old tensions between the peoples of western Christendom and Slavs, Moslems and Jews had not been so securely buried in history's graveyard as had been assumed in more confident post-war years. Large-scale migration, the return of unemployment and economic insecurity, and the collapse of the iron curtain—three diverse forces—have curiously combined to act as ghouls. The new Europe is bound to be on the move, and much optimism attends its journey. But it will need to tread softly; there are many ghosts that should not be wakened.

* * *

Since its foundation in 1930, *The Political Quarterly* has tried to explore issues of emerging public importance in both Britain and elsewhere, mainly but by no means exclusively from a left-of-centre point of view. It does this primarily through its regular quarterly pages, but also through occasional conferences and seminars or, as in the present case, through a book devoted to a question of particular topicality and importance.

In preparing the present volume the editors were also able to take advantage of a symposium on the extension of Europe organised by the Andrew Shonfield Association in Oxford in March 1991. A version of William Wallace's paper was presented there, and discussion at the symposium informed part of this Introduction. The editors are grateful to all participants in the symposium, though none of them is responsible for what we have said.

CC
DM
The Editors,
The Political Quarterly

THAWING HISTORY: EUROPE IN THE 1990s AND PRE-COLD WAR PATTERNS

DAVID REYNOLDS*

'PEACE on earth would mean the end of civilisation as we know it', observed novelist Joseph Heller in 1989 about the Soviet–American relationship. These two systems, he claimed, had become organised around mutual hatred and mutual assured destruction. 'The government of each was helpless without the threat from the other. It is impossible to imagine either nation functioning so smoothly without the horrifying danger of annihilation by the other.'[1]

Writing in 1991, there seems little danger of peace on earth. Yet Heller's sarcastic dictum encapsulates the new sense of uncertainty and drift that has been created by the Gorbachev revolution, the collapse of bipolar Europe and the demise of the Soviet Union itself in December 1991. Are we entering a new age—the so-called post-Cold War order—with Europe 'liberating itself from the legacy of the past', as the 'Charter of Paris' signed on 21 November 1990 affirmed?[2] Or is the 'whirligig of time' going to 'bring in its revenges', to borrow Shakespeare's phrase, as the warming of East–West relations thaws out old historical problems that had been frozen for a generation in the icy grip of the Cold War?

First, I want to outline certain historical trends which had indeed been frozen by the Cold War and which, now thawing out, are on the move again. But then I also wish to direct attention to some of the ways in which Europe has changed fundamentally in the last half-century. Consequently old problems take shape in a new context and amid new developments which alter their character and salience. These are the two main sections of my essay. I preface them, however, with a word about concepts. For a contribution that all scholars can make to intellectual debate is to use their greater opportunity for reflection to propose clarifications of terms that are widely used and abused.

* David Reynolds is a Fellow of Christ's College, Cambridge. His most recent book is *Britannia Overruled: British Policy and World Power in the Twentieth Century*, Longman, London, 1991. This article was originally presented in March 1991 as a paper for a series of seminars on 'Europe in the 1990s' organised by the Royal Institute of International Affairs in conjunction with the Economic and Social Research Council. The author is grateful for comments from members of the seminar, especially its convenor William Wallace, and from Cambridge colleagues Niall Ferguson and Geoffrey Edwards.

[1] Joseph Heller, *Picture This*, Picador, London, 1989, p. 100.
[2] *New York Times*, 22 Nov. 1990, p. A16.

Concepts and confusions

The Cold War: In Paris in November 1990 President George Bush asserted that 'the cold war is over'—a pronouncement which he had studiously avoided hitherto.[3] Among Soviet spokesmen and international commentators, however, it had already become a common-place, reflected in constant talk about the 'post-Cold-War era'. This tendency to equate the Cold War with the whole of history since 1945, or even with Soviet–American relations back to 1917, is a regrettable one. It denies the term 'Cold War' any real precision and thus utility.

It is therefore worth noting that in recent years many historians have preferred to talk of several Cold Wars in the post-1945 era. 1947–53, 1958–62, 1979–85 are among the candidates.[4] The precise number and dating of these remain debatable and, after a certain point, the debate becomes of dubious value. What is useful is the idea of oscillations between cold war and détente which reminds us that post-war history is not a unity. Both the years immediately after Stalin's death and also the early 1970s surrounding the SALT 1 and CSCE agreements were demonstrably different in tone and substance from what came before and after. One might say that the late 1980s appears to have brought to an end a long period of Soviet–American antagonism (because of a fundamental change in Soviet philosophy, the demise of the Soviet empire in Eastern Europe and finally the disintegration of the USSR as we knew it). But it is wiser to term that period the 'era of cold wars' rather than the Cold War *per se*. Otherwise 1945–91 becomes a crude monolith.

Bipolarity: This is another term often used to cover the whole post-war era, or alternatively the period up to the early 1970s when 'multipolarity' begins to emerge.[5] Its usage is obviously more justifiable than the concept of a single Cold War—for forty years from 1949 there were clearly two opposed fields of force in Europe, each centred on a rival superpower. Yet, on closer inspection, the period again exhibits a richer texture. Recent scholarship on the 1940s shows how the crucial divisions of Europe were shaped as much by intra-European forces as by Soviet–American antagonism. Of these the persistence of the German question was the most significant, so much so that the First Cold War could be described as a struggle for mastery of Germany. Recent work has also highlighted the

---

[3] *New York Times*, 22 Nov. 1990, p. A1.

[4] For examples of different periodisations see D. C. Watt, 'Rethinking the Cold War: A Letter to a British Historian', *Political Quarterly*, 49, 1978, p. 450; Fred Halliday, *The Making of the Second Cold War*, Verso, London, 1989, ch. 1.

[5] As, for example, in President Richard Nixon's concept of a pentapolar world: 'It would be a safer world and a better world if we have a strong, healthy United States, Europe, Soviet Union, China, Japan; each balancing the other, not playing one against the other, an even balance.' Comments of Jan. 1972, quoted in Seyom Brown, *The Faces of Power: United States Foreign Policy from Truman to Reagan*, Columbia University Press, New York, 1983, pp. 328–9.

influence of Britain—not to be written off as a great power in the first post-war decade—in the origins of the Cold War and of NATO, while France played a decisive role both in promoting European integration and in determining its peculiar character and limitations.[6] Even at mid-century, therefore, bipolarity was by no means total.

East versus West: One consequence of the division of Europe into two blocs was the tendency to talk crudely about Western Europe and Eastern Europe. These were the only divisions that seemed to matter—divisions defined by ideology or even by race ('Asia stands on the Elbe', as Konrad Adenauer put it in 1946).[7]

The result was some very strange packaging. Through NATO 'the West' came to include the Mediterranean regions of Italy and Greece—very different in character from the northwest European core of Britain, France and the Benelux—and also the almost totally Islamic country of Turkey, whose demand to be treated as Western in matters economic as well as military has now become a matter of acute embarrassment to the European Community. As for the concept of Eastern Europe, this cut across the historically momentous divide of Slavs and non-Slavs, lumping a country such as Bulgaria (Slavic and predominantly Orthodox, cherishing strong historic links to Russia) with Hungary (non-Slavic, largely Catholic, and self-defined as the historic 'bastion of the West' against Tartars, Turks or Russians). Moreover, the notion of central or Middle Europe drawing in Hungary, western Czechoslovakia and Austria, where ethnic, cultural and economic links to Germany had been strong, disappeared down the bipolar chasm.

Mention of Austria reminds us, however, that significant parts of Europe did escape inclusion in one or other bloc. Apart from Austria after 1955, and also traditional neutrals such as Sweden and Switzerland, one should remember Finland and Yugoslavia—both intriguing cases whose Cold War histories raise searching questions about the rigidity of Stalin's policy and the inevitability of a tight Soviet bloc (as distinct from a Soviet sphere of influence).[8]

Capitalism versus Communism: The collapse of the Soviet bloc in 1989 evoked paeans of praise in some quarters about the triumph of capitalism/liberalism and even claims for 'the end of history'.[9] While it is

---

[6] I have discussed these themes and the supporting literature more fully in 'The "Big Three" and the Division of Europe, 1945–48: An Overview', *Diplomacy and Statecraft*, 1, 1990, pp. 111–36.

[7] Konrad Adenauer to William Sollmann, 16 March 1946, in Adenauer, *Briefe, 1945–1947*, ed. Hans Peter Mensing, Siedler, Berlin, 1983, p. 191.

[8] For suggestive discussions of the Austrian and Finnish cases see Günter Bischof and Josef Leidenfrost (eds), *Die bevormundete Nation: Österreich und die Alliierten, 1945–1949*, Haymon-Verlag, Innsbruck, 1988; Tuomo Polvinen, *Between East and West: Finland in International Politics, 1944–1947*, edited and translated by D. G. Kirby and Peter Herring, University of Minnesota, Minneapolis, 1986.

[9] Cf. the astonishing essay by Francis Fukuyama, 'The End of History?', *The National Interest*, Summer 1989, pp. 3–18.

demonstrably true that Comecon/Warsaw Pact was 'the bloc that failed',[10] it was never a monolithic economic unit. Of course, state-ownership and worship of 'the plan' were ubiquitous, yet considerable diversity remained under surface uniformity. In Poland, for instance, the collectivisation of agriculture virtually stopped in 1956, while in East Germany a substantial private sector of small businesses continued to operate discreetly. In Hungary after 1968 the New Economic Mechanism, though intermittently enforced, did see a significant degree of economic devolution and the enhancement of living standards.[11]

As for Western Europe, capitalism there was hardly the pure version beloved by liberal economists. This was a corporatist structure, in which the market was weighted by the power of key elements—especially big businesses, banks and unions. Mention of the latter also reminds us of the popularity of redistributive economics and the provision of welfare programmes—both of which differentiated much of western Europe from the USA. These were responses to pressure from unions and socialist movements and also from the new Christian Democracy in the wake of the Second World War. Undoubtedly the principal distinction between the USA and Western Europe on the one hand and Eastern Europe on the other was the market, yet the Western European version of capitalism was generally a *social* market economy with corporatist overtones. On closer examination, therefore, the East-West economic divide was less sharp than the ideological rhetoric of capitalism and communism would suggest.

Nationalism: This concept lies at the heart of discussion about Europe, old and new. The nation-state is, after all, the basic building bloc of inter-*national* affairs—the 'United Nations', etc. After the First World War, amid the ruins of the old Ottoman, Habsburg and Romanov empires, Western European concepts of the nation-state were applied to Eastern Europe, where they fell foul of the ethnic diversity of the region. Czechoslovakia, for example, was more accurately 'Czecho-Germano-Polano-Magyaro-Rutheno-Roumano-Slovakia', as Mussolini called it in 1938.[12] In post-war Western Europe attempts to move ostensibly in the opposite direction to foster a supranational European Community have been challenged by advocates of a 'Europe of the states', notably Charles de Gaulle and Margaret Thatcher.

It needs to be emphasised, therefore, that nationalism is not an expression of historical fact but 'a theory of political legitimacy, which requires that ethnic boundaries should not cut across political ones'. Indeed 'it is nationalism which engenders nations, and not the other way round'.[13] There is no necessary reason why the political unit and the

---

[10] Charles Gati, *The Bloc that Failed: Soviet-East European Relations in Transition*, Indiana University Press, Bloomington, 1990.

[11] For a useful overview see L. P. Morris, *Eastern Europe since 1945*, Heinemann, London, 1984, ch. 4.

[12] Quoted in Iain Macleod, *Neville Chamberlain*, Frederick Muller, London, 1961, pp. 229–30.

[13] Ernest Gellner, *Nations and Nationalism*, Basil Blackwell, Oxford, 1983, pp. 1, 55.

national unit should be congruent, as nationalism posits. Rather, the European nation-state should be seen as a product of a phase of human history. It emerged in reaction to dynastic empires when and where the impact of capitalism and print technology had made it credible for people to feel part of a political community formed by a distinct language group.[14] That happened much earlier in Western Europe (from the sixteenth century in the case of 'the English' and 'the French'), than in much of eastern Europe where it is a phenomenon of the late nineteenth and twentieth centuries. In the Soviet Union, which should be seen as an old dynastic empire under new leadership, the process of nation-building has recently begun anew and is now entering an explosive phase.

If nationalism is seen as a product of time and circumstance, rather than the goal of history, then it is easier to recognise that the extension of capitalism and communication in the electronic age make possible larger political communities. This is not to prejudge the supranational versus national debate about European identity. It is simply to suggest that, just as monarchs and empires are no longer political absolutes, so the nation-state may not be the end of history.[15]

Taken together, these conceptual points suggest a larger conclusion. Stated simply: 1945 was not 'year zero', 'Nullpunkt', 'the end of an era', or any such definitive statement of historical novelty.[16] Although there is a neat symmetry about dividing our century to date in 1945 and again in 1989–91, to do so risks underestimating the complexity of the post-war era and over-stating the break with patterns from the past. Rather than thinking of 1945 as a blank slate we should see the post-war era as a palimpsest, with new layers of historical script superimposed on the old, which still nonetheless show through. 1945–91 was not simply a period of superpower domination, for which we must now suddenly find alternatives. Bipolarity coexisted with other, if temporarily weaker forces, generated by pre-war history. The next part of this essay tries to identify some of these and, in particular, to come to terms with Hitler's legacy.

Recurrent problems

The end of the era of cold wars enables us better to appreciate the enormity of what we call World War Two. In the broad sweep of twentieth-century history, its true significance has often been masked.

[14] Benedict Anderson, *Imagined Communities: Reflections on the Origins and Spread of Nationalism*, Verso, London, 1983, esp. ch. 5.

[15] E. J. Hobsbawm, *Nations and Nationalism since 1780: Programme, Myth, Reality*, Cambridge University Press, Cambridge, 1990, esp. ch. 6.

[16] John Lukacs, *1945: Year Zero*, Doubleday, New York, 1978, esp. p. 13. For a succinct critique of such an approach, see Alfred Grosser, *The Western Alliance: European-American Relations since 1945*, trans. Michael Shaw, Macmillan, London, 1980, ch. 1.

Looking backward it is linked too closely with the war of 1914–18; looking forward it has often become almost the prologue to the Cold War and bipolarity—the accident of history that finally ushered in the inevitable and long-predicted dominance of the superpowers, America and Russia.[17]

Yet the events of 1939–45 (or more exactly 1940–5) deserve to be seen in their own appalling uniqueness. In particular, the war of 1914–18, though involving a long struggle in the Middle East over the carcass of the Ottoman empire and also sporadic fighting in East Asia, was not a truly world war. By contrast, the total upset in the European balance of power in 1940, caused by Hitler's defeat of France, had global ramifications.[18] With the Western European imperial powers nearly impotent, it gave Italy and Japan undreamt-of opportunities to seek their own spheres of influence. This opened up fronts in the Mediterranean in 1940–1 and the Western Pacific in 1941–2, each of which became the focus of long and bloody fighting for Anglo-American forces. In Europe, Hitler's remarkable victories gave him the chance to attack the USSR years earlier than expected and, from June 1941, Germany's Eastern Front became the decisive theatre of Hitler's war. The Anglo-American invasion of France in June 1944 came almost a year after the Red Army had turned the tide against the Wehrmacht.

What we call 'the Cold War' in Europe was to a large degree the legacy of the World War and the way it was fought. Soviet victories in 1942–4 made it virtually certain that Stalin would enjoy a sphere of influence in Eastern and East-Central Europe. What was at issue was the nature of the sphere—how open? how 'Stalinist'?—and whether it would conform to Anglo-American preferences. Above all, the wartime allies had to agree on their treatment of Germany—the source of two great wars and perhaps a third, if peacemaking was not handled properly this time. Meanwhile, in Asia, the Japanese victories had shaken the foundations of colonial rule. Although the Europeans regained much of their territory in the wake of the Japanese surrender, the French, Dutch and British found themselves on the defensive against a potent cocktail of nationalism and communism that made Southeast Asia and then the Middle East areas of acute instability in the post-war decade—instability exacerbated by the spreading Soviet–American rivalry. In short, rather than seeing World War as prologue to Cold War, one might with as much justice view the era of Cold Wars as a gradual overcoming of Hitler's legacies. Although perhaps overstated, that approach helps us view our century in a different light. The Cold War and bipolarity become a *distortion* as much as a *reflection* of the broad lines of modern history. This can be seen at several points, each of

[17] On the nineteenth-century predictions see Geoffrey Barraclough, 'Europa, Amerika und Russland in Vorstellung und Denken des 19. Jahrhunderts', *Historische Zeitschrift*, 20, 1966, pp. 280–315.
[18] I have developed this argument more fully in '1940: Fulcrum of the Twentieth Century?', *International Affairs*, 66, 1990, pp. 325–50.

which exposes continuities that Hitler's war and its Cold War consequences temporarily obscured but did not ultimately destroy.

Multipolar Europe

We have already seen that, even in the first post-war decade, Europe was never as completely bipolar as sometimes thought. From the vantage point of 1991, it is also clear that the extent of the dominance of the superpowers was artificial.

Bearing in mind the maxim that power is relative—one country's strength is directly proportionate to the weakness of its rivals—we can see that the influence of the Soviet Union and even the United States in post-war Europe had much to do with the continent's temporary eclipse by Hitler and his eclipse in turn by the Soviet and American forces. The USSR gained a formal empire of conquest in Eastern Europe, the USA an informal empire of commerce in the West. The Soviets maintained their empire through large armed forces, based on a substantial military-industrial complex, which was sustained in turn by a command polity that was able to divert a vast proportion of GDP (15–20 per cent, or even more?) for these purposes. Unlike the American sphere of influence, it was not the result of an efficient productive system, as became clear when the Gorbachev revolution took hold.

Yet the American economy had its own limitations. In 1945 it produced about one-half of the world's manufactured goods—a degree of pre-eminence that owed much to the temporary ruin of all its rivals, especially Germany and Japan. By 1980, however, its share of world production was 31.5 per cent, almost exactly the same as in 1938 and, indeed, in 1913.[19] Likewise, the unquestioned pre-eminence of the dollar reflected America's productive advantage backed by control of two-thirds of the world's gold reserves. The latter allowed it to peg the dollar to gold and to run substantial payments deficits for a decade from the late 1940s in the interests of international reflation and Cold War containment. By the early 1970s, with America controlling little more than one quarter of the world's gold reserves, those deficits were unsustainable and automatic gold-dollar convertibility (the 'Bretton Woods system') was suspended in 1971.[20] The impressive exertions of American power in the last decade—the Reagan defence build-up, SDI and the Gulf War—should not mask the fact that this has been done on global credit. Without the willingness of foreign investors, especially from Japan and Britain, to fund America's $300 billion budget deficit, the assertion of American power on this scale would have been impossible.

[19] Paul Bairoch, 'International Industrialization Levels from 1750 to 1980', *Journal of European Economic History*, 11, 1982, esp. pp. 301, 304.
[20] Paul Kennedy, *The Rise and Fall of the Great Powers: Economic Change and Military Conflict, 1500–2000*, Unwin Hyman, London, 1988, p. 434.

There was, then, an element of artificiality about the degree of bipolarity in post-war Europe. Pre-1940 Europe was a complex of various forces; so, too, will be post-1990 Europe. Of these forces, one of the most important will be created by

The German question

Between 1870 and 1945 this was the underlying problem of European history. Until the 1860s Prussia, to quote the historian Theodor Mommsen, had been 'the fifth wheel on the wagon of Europe', whereas the defeat of France and the creation of a unified German empire in 1870 'put Europe's centre of gravity in its right place', in the words of his colleague Heinrich von Treitschke.[21] With the rapid industrialisation of the country in the last third of the century, the double-edged character of the German question had been clearly posed.

On the one hand, Germany was the economic powerhouse of Europe, passing Britain in total GNP by the start of the First World War. The instability of its currency lay at the heart of Europe's economic problems in the 1920s and recent historians have stressed the crisis of its financial sector as much as American withdrawal of loans in explaining the Central European depression of the early 1930s.[22] Its neighbours, especially France and the Low Countries, were dependent upon it for coal, iron and industrial goods. After 1945 the economic stability and recovery of Germany became a priority of British and American policy. This was one side of the question—Germany as the locomotive of the European economy.

Yet, as Germany's neighbours were all too painfully aware, economic power could be translated into military might. This had happened in 1914 and again in 1939. After both wars the dominant instinct of French policy was to castrate Germany—amputating its vital parts, the Ruhr and Saar, to make the old enemy militarily impotent. In 1945 the Soviets' aim was massive reparations to rebuild their own shattered country. Neither France nor the USSR in 1945 was anxious to see rapid German economic recovery, for fear of a third German war. Here was the other side of the German question—Germany as the engine of European warmaking.

The Cold War was a struggle for mastery of Germany, animated by competing views of the German question. By 1947 the British and Americans were fearful above all of another German-centred slump, from which only communism could gain. The Soviets and, for a while, the French feared another German War, of which they (and not the 'Anglo-Saxons') would again be the prime victims. By 1949 the French had,

[21] Quoted in Carsten Holbraad, *The Concert of Europe: A Study in German and British International Theory, 1815–1914*, Longman, London, 1970, pp. 69, 93.
[22] Cf. Harold James, *The German Slump: Politics and Economics, 1924–1936*, Oxford University Press, Oxford, 1986.

reluctantly, come round to the Anglo-American sense of priorities. And although the four occupying powers could not agree on a German peace settlement, the result of their disagreement—a divided Germany—proved an acceptable *de facto* 'solution' of the German question for a generation. German economic recovery took place, but in partial form and under superpower control. 'I love Germany so much that I am glad there are two of them'—François Mauriac's *bon mot*—expressed a tacit European consensus.[23]

The revolution of 1989–90 re-opened the German question for many observers. To what extent would the enhanced economic and political strength of the united country be translated into international assertiveness? On a crude level, this could be seen in the argument, suggested by Nicholas Ridley's *Spectator* interview, that there was 'a German racket designed to take over the whole of Europe' and that in this connection it was 'useful to remember . . . the Second World War'.[24] More sophisticated is the argument, propounded by historian Paul Kennedy, that *in the long run* 'military power is usually needed to acquire and protect wealth'.[25] In other words, will Germany, whatever its current reluctance, gradually have to assume a larger international role—bringing the wheel full circle? This is an issue to which I will return, but there can be no dispute that there is once more a German question to which answers are required.

The black hole of Eastern Europe

The disintegration of Comecon and the Warsaw Pact has reopened another historic European problem—the instability of Eastern and Southeastern Europe. A battleground for several centuries between the Ottoman and Habsburg empires, this region threw off imperial rule in the late nineteenth century and World War One. Various states emerged, largely legitimised rather than created by the peacemakers at Paris in 1919. These were usually based on a predominant ethnic group (Czechs, Serbs, Magyars) but included many rival minorities, not least Germans and Jews who often formed the commercial classes. Internal divisions were exacerbated by ethnic and territorial disputes between the new states. Of these, the position of Poland was perhaps the worst, re-created at the expense of Austria, Germany and Russia. The latter two in particular refused to accept this new order. Most of these successor states adopted democratic constitutions, modelled on the French Third Republic, with weak executives and strong legislatures, but their socio-economic circumstances were ill-suited to democratic politics and, during

---

[23] Harold James, *A German Identity: 1770–1970* (2nd edn), Weidenfeld and Nicolson, London, 1990, p. 208.
[24] *The Spectator*, 14 July 1990, pp. 8–10.
[25] Paul Kennedy, *op. cit.*, p. xvi.

the Depression, all but Czechoslovakia collapsed in some form of military autocracy.[26]

During the late 1930s the region fell anew under the influence of an imperial power, this time Nazi Germany, as Hitler's influence pushed east and south, swallowing Austria, Czechoslovakia and Poland in 1938–9 and reaching the Aegean and Black Seas by 1941. But from 1943 Nazi power began to recede against the Soviet counter-offensive. In 1944–5 Eastern Europe and the Balkans now fell into Moscow's empire. After a confused period of political pluralism in the mid-1940s Stalinist controls were imposed at the end of the decade. Despite various mutations, Soviet influence remained the fundamental fact of life until the revolutions of 1989.

For East and Southeast Europe, therefore, the 1990s have certain similarities with the 1920s. Again we see independent states, based on dominant national groups, trying to embrace Western European liberalism in its social market form. In some respects the situation is more favourable than seventy years ago. The states are ethnically less polyglot— the hated Jewish and German minorities, in particular, have largely disappeared through holocaust and 1945 migrations. The old enmity between landowners and peasants is a thing of the past and all these countries have an industrial base. Nevertheless, ethnic rivalries remain acute in places (Serbs and Croats in the old Yugoslavia, Hungarians in Romania, Turks in Bulgaria and the Slovak problem in Czechoslovakia). The industrial base is antiquated and the environmental problems that forced industrialisation have created are appalling. And, with some exceptions, such as Czechoslovakia, the capacity for democratic politics remains limited. Achieving political stability, economic prosperity and regional cooperation will not be an easy task.

The hegemon-less political economy

The conditions of multipolarity under which the German and East-European problems have re-emerged also affect the European economy. The multilateral global economy that was emerging in the last third of the nineteenth century collapsed into competing economic blocs in the Depression of the 1930s. It was recreated, albeit slowly, within 'the Western world' in the 1940s and 1950s and may now be enlarged to include the old Soviet bloc in the wake of the Gorbachev revolution. In the extent of international trade and especially in the liquidity and velocity of capital movements, our own era is of course very different from that of the 1920s. The electronic revolution has created almost instantaneously international money markets and in consequence the destabilising effects of capital flows are felt far more quickly than, say, in the period 1929–31.

---

[26] Antony Polonsky, *The Little Dictators: A History of Eastern Europe since 1918*, Routledge and Kegan Paul, London, 1975, still provides a valuable overview.

Yet there are grounds for thinking that this is a difference of degree rather than kind. For it can be argued that the basic predicament in managing the international financial system may well be the same in the 1920s and the 1990s.

Stated crudely, in the eras from roughly 1870 to the First World War and again from 1945 to the early 1970s a single hegemonic power held sway.[27] In the first case it was Britain (though this can be exaggerated[28]); in the second the United States, through what was known as the 'Bretton Woods system'.[29] Hegemonial leadership applied both to the private and the public sectors. In the private sphere, the City of London and then Wall Street were the principal sources of global investment capital. In the public sphere, the British and later the US governments operated policies geared to maintain international liquidity and promote world trade—through counter-cyclical lending, low tariffs and the like. For Britain, the interests of the City were often congruent with those of the country, given the latter's economic reliance on overseas trade in goods and services (though the cost in neglect of domestic investment may well have been enormous).[30] For the USA, its greater self-sufficiency as a continent-wide common market was offset by its willingness in the 1940s and 1950s to rebuild commercial rivals on credit in the interests of containing communism.

By contrast, the 1920s, like the period since the early 1970s, saw a largely open international economy but one in which there was no unequivocal leader. After World War One, New York and later Paris emerged to challenge London's preeminent financial role. Today we have several major financial centres—led by New York, Tokyo, London and, increasingly, Frankfurt—who compete frenetically in the marketing of money. And, in the public sphere, the dominance of a single currency (sterling or the dollar) and of supporting governmental policies, gave way to a plurality—pound, dollar, franc and mark in the inter-war years; the dollar, yen and Deutschmark regimes of today. Neither the various central banks of the inter-war years nor our present mix of national and transnational organisations (the latter including G7, ERM and IMF) constitute a single source of direction.

Whether or not the international monetary system needs a single

[27] For this argument see e.g. Charles P. Kindleberger, *The World in Depression, 1929–1939*, University of California Press, Berkeley, 1973; Arthur A. Stein, 'The Hegemon's Dilemma: Great Britain, the United States, and the International Economic Order', *International Organization*, 38, 1984, pp. 355–86.

[28] See David Reynolds, *Britannia Overruled: British Policy and World Power in the Twentieth Century*, Longman, London, 1991, esp. ch. 1.

[29] Cf. Michael J. Hogan, 'Revival and Reform: America's Twentieth-Century Search for a New Economic Order Abroad', *Diplomatic History*, 8, 1984, pp. 287–310.

[30] Geoffrey Ingham, *Capitalism Divided?: The City and Industry in British Social Development*, Macmillan, London, 1984; Michael H. Best and Jane Humphries, 'The City and Industrial Decline', in Bernard Elbaum and William Lazonick (eds), *The Decline of the British Economy*, Clarendon Press, Oxford, 1986, pp. 223–39.

hegemonic power remains a matter of debate.[31] It is also legitimate to ask whether such leadership is now possible given the degree of international-isation achieved. Nevertheless, I feel that current problems are part of clear historical patterns and that reflection on the problems of inter-national financial management in the 1920s may well be particularly profitable.

The crisis of 'democracy'

Behind these recurrent problems of stability and prosperity lies an endur-ing struggle to achieve civil rights and representative government. By stating it in that way one is in danger of sounding Whiggish or teleological—as if history were a long march towards democracy.[32] That would be misleading, not least because it obscures the fragility of demo-cratic institutions in Europe (supposedly their home) for much of this century. Contempt for party politicians—historically the main vehicle of democracy—and the yearning for a strong leader were evident in the histories of Italy, Germany, Spain, Portugal and much of eastern Europe after World War One. But they have also been recurrent motifs in, say, the history of modern France—supposedly the progenitor of democratic politics. (Lest these observations encourage an exaggerated sense of British exceptionalism, one might ponder the role of the Commons as largely a legitimiser of the will of the majority party or consider how little the existing UK voting system represents popular aspirations.)

In the end all this only highlights the irrelevance of much democratic theory to the political realities of modern governance. 'Government of the people, by the people, for the people' exists only in the pages of Lincoln's Gettysburg address. The practical problem is not so much democracy as accountability—how to create forms of government that are at once efficient and yet tolerably responsible and in which periodic changes of leadership can be accomplished peacefully under the potentially chaotic conditions of universal suffrage. In the inter-war years, that balance of stability and change, within the framework of a new mass politics, proved unattainable in much of Europe. Since 1945 it has been tenuously estab-lished in the core of Western Europe and extended in the 1970s 'south-ward' to Greece, Spain and Portugal. (Indeed their inclusion within the EC had much to do with the desire of the existing Nine to strengthen the pro-democratic forces within these states as they threw off military rule.[33])

---

[31] See the debate in Benjamin M. Rowland (ed.), *Balance of Power or Hegemony: The Interwar Monetary System*, New York University Press, New York, 1976.

[32] Cf. Raymond Carr, *Modern Spain, 1875–1980*, Oxford University Press, Oxford, 1980, p. 97, who observed that the period 1923–77, during which Spain abandoned, only finally to revive, a parliamentary monarchy based on universal suffrage, 'might be considered a waste of historical time'.

[33] Stephen George, *Politics and Policy in the European Community*, Oxford University Press, Oxford, 1985, pp. 154–5.

The problem takes on two new dimensions in the 1990s. One is to foster civil society and democratic political institutions in the newly independent nation states of Eastern Europe, in often shallow soil and after some sixty years of neglect. This can perhaps be considered an extension of the Western European political story. The other problem is truly novel, namely to correct the 'democratic deficit' within a trans-national grouping—the European Community—currently run largely by a mixture of intergovernmental bargaining (the European Council and Council of Ministers) and bureaucratic fiat (the Commission, which is only tenuously accountable to a weak Parliament). The Community's need simultaneously to develop more efficient and more responsive decision-making has been at the centre of continental debate since the mid-1980s—prompted particularly by the Stuttgart Council's Solemn Declaration of 1983 and the Parliament's Draft Treaty of 1984.[34] Those imperatives pull in potentially opposite directions—towards greater élitism and greater accountability—and they have to be handled on a scale of participatory politics never yet seen in human history.

In some ways, then, the inter-war era invites comparison with our own: elements of multipolarity, concern about Germany, the instability of East and Southeast Europe, the undirected international political economy and the crisis of liberal democracy. This comparability reflects the re-emergence of underlying problems as the impact/distortions of Depression, World War and Cold War have waned. The continuities seem particularly apparent with the 1920s—which some recent historians insist should be portrayed as a distinct period of incipient stability rather than 'an era of illusions' within a thirty-year war.[35] Of course, the fact that the 1920s were followed by the 1930s—with economic slump and renewed conflict—is not an encouraging precedent, but before we go further we should remember my prefatory remarks about continuity and change. Similar or subsisting problems take on very different forms as their context changes. Or, to pit cliché against cliché—if history seems to repeat itself, time also marches on.

Changes and contrasts

In certain profound respects the 1990s are fundamentally different from the period before 1945.

---

[34] Cf. Roy Pryce, 'Relaunching the European Community', *Government and Opposition*, 19, 1984, pp. 486–500.

[35] E.g. Jon Jacobson, 'Is There a New International History of the 1920s?', *American Historical Review*, 88, 1983, pp. 617–45; cf. Sally Marks, *The Illusion of Peace: International Relations in Europe, 1918–1933*, Macmillan, London, 1976. Some of these themes are explored in the essays on the period in Rolf Ahmann (ed.), *Problems of West European Security, 1918–57*, Oxford University Press, Oxford, forthcoming.

Management of (post-) industrial economies

The half-century after World War One saw the demise of agriculture as Europe's major employer and productive activity. In this sense the continent changed more in fifty years than in the previous five hundred. In a few countries this transformation had already occurred by 1914. Britain's industrial revolution had been largely the result of a wholesale transfer of population from farming into labour-intensive industries and by the 1840s only a quarter of the labour force was still in agriculture and mining.[36] By 1920 only 8 per cent of the 'active population' was in agriculture; in some other advanced countries the pattern was similar if less extreme—around 25 per cent in the Netherlands and Switzerland. But in Scandinavia and the Iberian peninsula the shift came later; likewise, to a somewhat lesser degree, in the 'core' EC countries of Germany, France and Italy where the 1920 percentages were respectively 31, 42 and 56. France did not reach 25 per cent until around 1960,[37] and the problems of large, inefficient yet politicially important agricultural sectors, especally in France and Germany, have plagued the EC throughout its history.

Thus, even in parts of developed 'Western Europe' the industrial/urban revolution is of recent occurrence. This is overwhelmingly the case in Eastern Europe. As the figures in the note indicate,[38] East Germany and Czechoslovakia were the most industrialised but the shift in the Balkan states from roughly three-quarters to one-quarter of the work force in agriculture (1950 to 1980) is particularly striking—although the contrast with the British figures reminds us of the profound socio-economic differences between all these countries and the UK.

Stalin's version of Marxism–Leninism was the mechanism by which Eastern Europe was driven into the industrial and urban age. Develop-

---

[36] Cf. N. F. R. Crafts, *British Economic Growth during the Industrial Revolution*, Clarendon Press, Oxford, 1985, p. 62.

[37] Figures from Carlo Cipolla (ed.), *The Fontana Economic History of Europe*, vol. 5, Part 2, Harvester Press edn., Brighton, 1977, ch. 8, esp. pp. 409–15.

[38] Percentage of the workforce employed in agriculture:

	1950	1980
Czechoslovakia	38	12.6
GDR	24	10.0
Hungary	49	20.6
Poland	56	26.1
Bulgaria	73	23.8
Romania	74	29.8
Yugoslavia	70	33.4
UK	5.5	1.6

(Figures from L. P. Morris, *op. cit*. p. 115.)

ments that took some eighty years in Britain (1760–1840) were accomplished in a quarter-century in many of these countries, though the human and environmental costs of such forced industrialisation are notorious. What deserves to be underlined, in addition, is that Stalinist socialism brought Eastern Europe into the industrial age just in time for the latter's demise. Marxism–Leninism was a 'heavy metal ideology', which reacted to but was also modelled on the nineteenth-century West European class-economy centred on coal, iron, steel and other heavy industries. By the time Eastern Europe had achieved those forms of economic development, their products were on the scrap-heap of history. In the 1970s all of Europe was facing the challenge of the electronic revolution, transforming information and communication systems and requiring major upheavals in industrial organisation and practice. In addition, even in traditional industries, such as textiles, steel and automobiles, European products were being undercut by those from countries with lower labour costs. In both areas of production—new and old—the main challenge came from the Pacific Rim countries centred on Japan. 'Advanced' Western Europe found it hard to meet that challenge. For Eastern Europe, tied rigidly to outmoded forms of ideology, economic organisation and political structure, adaptation was virtually impossible. Indeed the system was kept alive in many 'Soviet-bloc' countries from the 1970s by massive Western investment. Thus the crisis of communism was the crisis of capitalism as a whole—or more exactly the crisis of European industrial society—for which Marxism–Leninism was particularly ill-suited.[39]

Thus, whatever the analogies with the 1920s, the European economy is now totally transformed. We are talking about countries that, for all their differences, are basically industrialised, yet whose forms of industrialisation are often profoundly inadequate for the current let alone future state of technology and who are weighed down by the rusting remains of heavy-metal industrialisation. The management of these post-industrial economies is a novel and demanding problem, and, as indicated in my earlier remarks about 'capitalism versus communism', it is unlikely that classical liberalism will provide an all-sufficient guide. The logic of the market, left to itself, points to economic and social costs on a scale politically inconceivable in corporatist, welfare states.

Informal patterns of integration

What is also novel about contemporary Europe is the degree to which it is becoming truly integrated. The term 'integration' is often used exclusively to refer to formal political structures. The limitations of these, particularly the European Community, may distract from the reality of *informal*

---

[39] I follow in this paragraph the stimulating argument of Charles S. Maier, 'The Collapse of Communism: Approaches for a Future History', *History Workshop*, 31, Spring 1991, pp. 34–59.

integration—that created by 'the dynamics of markets, technology, communications networks and social exchange, or the influence of religious, social or political movements'.[40]

If we look at the human dimension of this, it becomes clear just how far Europe, and more particularly Western Europe, has moved in the post-war period.[41] Literally. One indicator is tourism. In 1950 there were 25 million global cross-border tourist movements, in 1985 the figure was 333 million. Of the latter, 148.6 million, or a remarkable 45 per cent, were tourist movements *within* Western Europe. Another measure is migration statistics. Since 1945 there has been a threefold increase in the number of foreign residents in Europe. The largest constituencies are in (West) Germany, 4.4 million out of 62 million in 1986, and France, 3.7 million out of 55 million in 1982. Until the first oil crisis of 1973 the main flow was 'guestworkers' from southern Europe into the booming northern economies. After this tailed off, there has been a substantial influx of illegal immigrants from Mediterranean Africa and Asia into southern Europe. They are estimated conservatively as totalling 2 million in 1985—half of them in Italy. Western Europe has also welcomed numerous refugees from Africa, Asia and recently Eastern Europe, and there are also significant intra-regional flows, particularly the movement of skilled workers and professionals within northern Europe and the growing tide of northerners establishing residence in the 'European Sunbelt', notably Spain. These massive and sustained population flows make Europe, particularly its western half, an integrated area in a way never true in previous history. At the centre of all of them—tourism, student exchanges, guestworkers, refugees—is Germany.

Economic dimensions of integration should also be noted. The interdependence of the international monetary system, dominated by private rather than governmental wealth, has already been mentioned. In many ways this was a revival and enlargement, albeit on a technologically revolutionary scale, of patterns already apparent in the 1920s which were disrupted by depression and war. More truly novel, it seems to me, has been the post-war dependence of Western Europe on the Middle East for crucial supplies of oil. Although commodities from Africa and Asia had long been important to many European economies, particularly Britain, the reliance of all European economies on one source of energy from another region of the world was a sharp break with the past. Moreover, it occurred very rapidly. In 1950 Western Europe relied on solid fuel for 82.5 per cent of energy consumption. Twenty years later the proportion was only 29.2 per cent. Meanwhile reliance on petroleum soared from

<hr />

[40] William Wallace, *The Transformation of Western Europe*, RIIA/Pinter, London, 1990, p. 54.

[41] This paragraph is based on the chapter by Federico Romero, 'The Human Dimension: Cross-Border Population Movements', in William Wallace (ed.), *The Dynamics of European Integration*, RIIA/Pinter, London, 1990.

14 per cent of energy consumption to 60.2 per cent.[42] During roughly the same period the Middle East became the main single source of oil—rising from 7 per cent of world production in 1945 to 38 per cent in 1973, while North America dropped from 65 per cent to 21 per cent.[43] The oil shocks of 1973 and 1979 dramatised Western Europe's dependence and, although the oil weapon seemed less impressive in the 1980s, the 1991 Gulf War is a striking reminder of just how important it is for Western Europe and the USA to have a stable, secure and relatively cheap flow of oil from the Middle East. The lesson of oil is that informal integration has not made Europe independent of the wider world—on the contrary, in one crucial commodity it is dangerously dependent on perhaps the most volatile region of the globe.

Formal integration—the European Community

On the level of formal integration the most striking innovation is the European Community. Here 'European' of course means predominantly Western European—the movement for European union, which in the closing days of the war was truly continent-wide, became another casualty of the first Cold War.[44] The limitations of the Community in other respects than geographical are also readily apparent. Thanks to Franco–German compromises made to facilitate its foundation, it became a device to protect inefficient, backward yet politically important agricultural sectors at great cost. The Common Agricultural Policy consumes the bulk of Community spending—70 per cent in 1985.[45] Despite periodic 'relaunches', the Community has failed to develop into an effective political unit and efforts at a common foreign policy have had limited practical, as distinct from rhetorical, success.

Nonetheless, what surely stands out in historical perspective are the achievements rather than the failures of the Community. In its first decade it created a genuine customs union; by the mid-1990s (if not exactly by the end of '1992') it will have eliminated most non-tariff barriers to the movement of goods, currency and people. This is integration of a unique character for advanced national economies. The effect on trade flows has been marked. The economies of the original 'Six' were already highly interdependent—that was part of the rationale for the EEC. But the enlargement of the Community and the related development of EFTA have had striking consequences. Of the 18 countries that made up the EC and EFTA in 1987, only four (Iceland, Switzerland, Finland and the UK) send as much as one-third of their exports beyond this combined

---

[42] Carlo Cipolla, op.cit. vol. 5, part 1, p. 227.

[43] Fiona Venn, Oil Diplomacy in the Twentieth Century, Macmillan, London, 1986, p. 11.

[44] Cf. Walter Lipgens, A History of European Integration, vol. 1, 1945–1947, Clarendon Press, Oxford, 1982, esp. Introduction.

[45] Hugh Arbuthnott and Geoffrey Edwards, A Common Man's Guide to the Common Market (2nd edn), Macmillan, London, 1989, p. 150.

European Economic Space (EES). Even Britain, historically oriented outside Europe, now sells 57 per cent of its exports within the EES, compared with 30 per cent in the mid-1950s.[46]

And on the sensitive issue of 'sovereignty', the word has lost its historic meaning for all the member states of the EC. These are still separate states, with their own elected governments, yet large areas of their national life are no longer fully under their own control. The most contentious area in recent years in Britain was of course exchange rate and currency policy. Sterling was defined by prime minister Margaret Thatcher a few days before her demise as 'the most powerful expression of sovereignty you can have'.[47] Membership of the European Monetary System has been a major substantive and symbolic issue for all British political parties over the last decade and a half—only recently resolved. But behind the scenes, Community jurisdiction over much of national life has been inexorably enlarged. The most striking indicator of this is the way that every Whitehall department, and not merely the Foreign Office, now has a 'foreign policy', a European dimension. The Home Office, Transport and Environment are no less Brussels-oriented than Agriculture or Trade and Industry. The same is true for every member government of the EC.

Politically as well as economically, then, the formal integration of the European Community has taken shape, making governmental decisions a novel mixture of domestic and EC imperatives. The context of national policy-making has thereby been fundamentally transformed. The problems of Europe, old and new—be they the financial markets, Eastern Europe or the management of post-industrial economies—are all addressed within this new framework. Indeed some of the problems have also been transformed. Nowhere is this more evident than in the case of the German question.

From a Ridleyesque standpoint one can view the new Europe as a vehicle for renewed German domination. In the late 1980s—even before unification—West Germany, with about 20 per cent of the EC's population, accounted for nearly 40 per cent of its manufacturing output, 35 per cent of its manufactured exports and 40 per cent of its manufactured exports to the outside world. The EC has therefore been represented as the 'German Co-Prosperity Sphere'—a sinister echo of Japan's name for its putative sphere of influence in World War Two.[48]

Yet, instead of seeing the EC as posing the German question in a new if peaceful form, from another standpoint one can see it as a new answer to the old question. Indeed, that was very much the aim of Jean Monnet and Robert Schuman as they took up the ideas of functional integration in the 1950s. Theirs was a response to the failure of French attempts—after both German wars—to dismember Germany and thus destroy German power.

[46] William Wallace, *The Transformation of Western Europe, op. cit.*, pp. 23–4.
[47] *The Guardian*, 29 October 1990, p. 1.
[48] Tony Cutler *et al.*, *1992—The Struggle for Europe: A Critical Evaluation of the European Community*, Berg, Oxford, 1989, ch. 1, especially pp. 12, 15.

Faced with a new West German state, economically revived under Anglo-American direction, the French decided that if German power could not be tamed, it should be harnessed to European ends. This required a mutual sacrifice by Germany and its neighbours of sovereignty over their economies and thus of their war-making capabilities. The Coal and Steel Community of 1952 and the EEC of 1958 were therefore not merely devices for economic recovery; they were attempts to resolve the Franco-German problem—and as such they have proved strikingly successful. An antagonism which lay at the roots of three foundation-shaking wars in seventy years (1870, 1914 and 1939) was resolved within this new framework.[49]

And at the same time the internal character of Germany has been reshaped. One of the insidious effects of nationalist ideology is the idea that there is a discrete national character—an unchanging essence within each 'people'. Such theories, the product in part of social Darwinist ideas about the competition of the races at the turn of this century, are hard to establish on any scientific footing. For one thing, the idea that Germany was a special case in the history of European economic and political development because it failed to undergo a liberal, bourgeois revolution on the model of Britain has now been seriously contested.[50] At the same time, questions have been asked about the degree to which Britain itself was radically industrialised in the nineteenth century. Instead of the German *Sonderweg* we now have the peculiarities of Britain's 'gentlemanly capitalism'—all of which should call into question existing models of liberal, capitalist democracy.[51]

Germany's problems were as much political as psychological. Specifically, there was nothing 'natural' or 'inevitable' about the 'Prussian' answer to the German question in the 1860s—namely the creation of a unified German empire out of most of the Germanic states under the aegis of Prussian militarism. This was indeed the product of 'blood and iron'.[52]

---

[49] E.g. Pierre Gerbet, 'Les origines du plan Schuman', in Raymond Poidevin (ed.), *Histoire des débuts de la construction européenne*, Bruylant, Brussels, 1986, pp. 199–222; in English see Alan S. Milward, *The Reconstruction of Western Europe, 1945–51*, Methuen, London, 1984, esp. chs 4, 12–13; John W. Young, *Britain, France and the Unity of Europe, 1945–1951*, Leicester University Press, Leicester, 1984, esp. chs 14–15.

[50] The classic text is David Blackbourn and Geoff Eley, *The Peculiarities of German History: Bourgeois Society and Politics in Nineteenth-Century Germany*, Oxford University Press, Oxford, 1984.

[51] As noted by Wolfgang Krieger, 'Die britische Krise in historischer Perspektive', *Historische Zeitschrift*, 247, 1988, pp. 585–602. The locus classicus here is Martin J. Wiener, *English Culture and the Decline of the Industrial Spirit, 1850–1980*, Cambridge University Press, New York, 1981. On 'gentlemanly capitalism' see the two articles by P. J. Cain and A. G. Hopkins covering the periods 1688–1850 and 1850–1945, 'Gentlemanly Capitalism and British Expansion Overseas', *Economic History Review*, 2nd series, 39, 1986, pp. 501–25 and 40, 1987, pp. 1–26. All this work has, of course, generated its own scholarly controversies.

[52] Cf. James J. Sheehan, *German History, 1770–1866*, Clarendon Press, Oxford, 1989, esp. p. 913.

And in the succeeding three-quarters of a century the new German state proved both too rigid and too fragmented to cope with the pressures of frenzied and erratic industrialisation, amid the cycles of the world economy, building into its political fabric a propensity for external and internal violence. Arguably Germany's geopolitical predicament as *die verspätete Nation*—'born encircled' to quote David Calleo[53]— encouraged this development. Since mid-century, however, 'the social forces which favour the institutionalisation of conflict, compromise politics and a policy between revolutionary radicalism and conservative immobilism have been slowly gaining the upper hand'.[54] In shorthand, militarism had faded, democracy has taken root. No society breaks totally with its past, but the novelty of the new Germany deserves as much attention as the persistence of the old German question. And the integration of post-war Germany into Europe—encirclement transcended—is at the heart of that novelty.

The Soviet dis-Union

While the integration, both informal and formal, of western Europe is proceeding erratically if inexorably, at the far edge of the continent the Russian empire has finally broken apart. For the last quarter-millennium a powerful Russia has been an integral part of the European states system, while in the nineteenth century the Romanovs pushed their empire farther south—reinforcing the country's Janus-like character as both a European and an Asian power. Yet this was a polyglot empire, of numerous ethnic and national groups, resistant to the efforts at Russification imposed by Alexander III and his successors after 1881. And at the end of World War One the Romanov empire—like that of the Ottomans and the Habsburgs—very nearly broke apart amid Revolution and Civil War. At times in 1919 the Red Army controlled little more than the extent of Muscovite Russia in the sixteenth century.

Yet the Russian empire survived, albeit under new leadership. Arguably that is as important a legacy of the Bolshevik revolution as the coup of 1917. And in 1923 a new federation of Soviet republics came into existence, prior, supposedly, to the eventual merger (*sliyanie*) of the various national proletariats. Russification was renewed during and after the 'Great Patriotic War' of 1941–5 and the maintenance of Stalin's system, with modifications, by his successors kept the lid on the nationality question.

But Gorbachev's reform programme opened Pandora's box. Pere-

---

[53] David Calleo, *The German Problem Reconsidered: Germany and the World Order, 1870 to the Present*, Cambridge University Press, Cambridge, 1978, p. 206. *Die verspätete Nation* ('the belated nation') is the title of an influential book by Helmuth Plessner published in 1959.

[54] V. R. Berghahn, *Modern Germany: Society, Economy and Politics in the Twentieth Century*, Cambridge University Press, Cambridge, 1982, p. 248.

stroika meant in practice *de*construction—the old order was dismantled, without a new one taking its place. At the same time glasnost allowed vent to the pent-up frustrations. Officially the old USSR comprised 140 nationalities (more inclusive estimates suggest 400 or even 800), of which 20 formed about 90 per cent of its 286 million people. Fractionally over 50 per cent of the population is Russian, compared with 72 per cent in 1923. The next largest groups are Ukrainian (15.4 per cent) and Uzbeks (5.8 per cent).[55] None of these 'national groups' fits neatly into the member republics—all have minority problems, witness the friction over the substantial Russian elements in Estonia and Latvia or the Karabakh crisis of 1988–9 between Armenia and Azerbaijan. In fact, more than 60 million former Soviet citizens (nearly 21 per cent) live outside their 'own' republic and Kazakhstan alone has more than one hundred different nationalities.[56]

Historically, the crisis of the Russian empire is not novel. It echoes those of the Ottoman and Habsburg empires before. Yet neither precedent is encouraging, if one thinks of both the duration and the magnitude of their death-throes. We are still wrestling with their legacies today. And, in terms of international implications, the Russian case is novel, for neither of these other old empires could be catagorised as the equivalent of a modern, nuclear superpower extending over such a vast geographical area. What polities will succeed the old Russian empire is unclear, though some form of inter-relationship seems likely in the long run, given the republics' economic interdependence. Managing international change (for instance nuclear arms control) against the background of upheavals in so vast a part of the world is hardly an attractive prospect. And the refugee problem, if one takes German fears seriously, is likely to strain severely a European core already hard pressed to cope with the existing degree of population mobility.

The security dimension—America's role

The spectacular internal disintegration of one superpower in the last few years has left the other looking extremely impressive by comparison. That contrast is enhanced by the American success in mobilising some 400,000 military in a matter of months for war in the Persian Gulf.

The projection of American power abroad is one of the most striking differences between the post-1918 era and the period after 1945. In the inter-war period the United States was not totally 'isolationist'—the term 'independent internationalism' has been used to describe the 1920s phenomenon of private financial investment in Germany and France to

---

[55] Graham Smith (ed.), *The Nationalities Question in the Soviet Union*, Longman, London, 1990, esp. p. v, 363–4.

[56] Stephen White, *Gorbachev in Power*, Cambridge University Press, Cambridge, 1990, p. 147.

promote European stability.[57] Nevertheless, the lack of political and military commitments made America an unstable and unreliable element in European politics—'you will get nothing from the Americans but words, big words but only words', as Stanley Baldwin summed up conventional wisdom in Britain in 1932.[58] After World War Two the big words were matched by big actions. By 1984 Washington had military alliances with fifty nations and stationed 1.5 million troops in 117 countries.[59] The first and in many ways most important of these entangling alliances was the North Atlantic Treaty of 1949 on which the security policy of Western Europe has rested ever since.

NATO has shown remarkable durability. Every few years there have been warnings of its collapse—think of the Korean war rearmament crisis, the furore over the French withdrawal, the rows over Kissinger's 'Year of Europe' in 1973, the strains over détente, the protests over the Cruise/Pershing deployments. In each case the pundits were breezily penning NATO's obituaries. And well before 1960 the cost of the European commitment was a matter of concern for the US Treasury, as the 'artificiality' of America's post-war economic supremacy wore off and payments deficits emerged. Although troop numbers declined from the Berlin crisis level of 417,000 in 1961, they have remained around 300,000 to 320,000 since the 1970s—despite persistent US budgetary concerns and pressures from Congress (the perennial Mansfield and Nunn resolutions).[60] From an historical perspective, therefore, it should be said that such an integrated alliance has never existed for so long in peacetime.[61] Strains have been present from its creation and one should be wary of saying now that the transatlantic alliance is doomed.

Yet there are grounds for thinking that *this* crisis is significantly different from its predecessors. For one thing it strikes at the *raison d'être* of the Alliance, namely the existence of a substantial Soviet conventional and nuclear threat in Europe. Although not eliminated, that threat is now on a wholly different level following the collapse of the Warsaw Pact and the considerable success of arms reduction agreements since 1987. Secondly, the US budget problems are now on an historically novel scale. Since the Reagan defence build-up of the early 1980s, financed on foreign credit because of the President's dedication to tax cuts, the deficit has been running at $200–300 billion annum. Even before the Gulf War, it was

[57] Joan Hoff Wilson, *Herbert Hoover: Forgotten Progressive*, Little, Brown and Co., Boston, 1975, p. 168.

[58] Keith Middlemas and John Barnes, *Baldwin: A Biography*, Weidenfeld and Nicolson, London, 1969, p. 729.

[59] Stephen E. Ambrose, *Rise to Globalism: American Foreign Policy since 1938* (4th edn), Penguin, Harmondsworth, 1985, p. xiii.

[60] Phil Williams, *US Troops in Europe*, RIIA/Routledge and Kegan Paul, London, 1984, p. 19.

[61] Cf. Simon Duke, *United States Military Forces and Installations in Europe*, Oxford University Press, Oxford, 1989, p. 374: 'In historical terms the hosting on a voluntary basis of such a range and number of foreign military facilities is quite unprecedented.'

unlikely that the USA could remain indefinitely a superpower on tick. The costs of the war and the erosion of domestic wealth and stability made radical rethinking of US foreign commitments very likely.

So the remarkable durability of the Atlantic alliance and the distinctive features of the current crisis each need to be given adequate weight. On balance, one would judge that the case for a new European security structure, with a reduced US role, is now stronger than at any time in recent history. Yet the uncertainties of the current situation still invite caution. The Gulf war has reopened the debate of the early 1980s about NATO's interest in 'out-of-area' problems—those beyond the geographical boundaries of the Treaty which nevertheless impinge on significant Alliance interests (especially oil). With the Gulf War likely to produce fall-out to occupy diplomats for many years to come (the analogy with previous great wars this century is not far-fetched), the case for the Alliance will remain compelling. And within Europe, the looming civil war of the Soviet succession makes it unlikely that either the USA or the Western Europeans will want to sever the connection between American and European security. Both these concerns, however, suggest a very different kind of Alliance from that of the four decades from 1949.

Concluding thoughts

In such a fluid situation, in which what is written can often be outdated by the time it is published, no 'conclusions' would be appropriate. But an effort should be made to pull together the threads of this essay. For the purposes of analysis, I have tried, somewhat artificially, to distinguish some of the persisting and some of the novel features of Europe's current situation. I have stressed the complex role of World War Two as both an accelerator and a distorter of long-term trends, so that issues such as the German question and the post-Habsburg problem, apparently 'settled' by the Cold War division of Europe, have now been reopened within a more multipolar economic and security system akin to that of the 1920s. But I have also emphasised that even abiding problems now exist in a new context, formed by post-industrialism, informal integration and the reality of the European Community—all set against uncertainties about the place of the old USSR and the USA in world politics.

It might be objected that my historical frame of reference is too narrow. Going back beyond the 1920s to, say, the end of the last century might prompt doubts about the novelty of the present. Thus, the modern migrations have their analogues in the huge demographic disturbances of late nineteenth-century Europe. The strains these created in East Central and Southeastern Europe have been postulated as an important underlying cause of World War One.[62] Likewise, current Western dependence

[62] Z. A. B. Zeman, *Pursued by a Bear: The Making of Eastern Europe*, Chatto and Windus, London, 1989, esp. ch. 2.

31

on mineral energy from the Middle East might be compared with Europe's sudden and substantial reliance on overseas, especially North American, sources of human energy (grain) from the 1870s when the USA 'emerged as a great food power'.[63] In these ways one might argue that interdependence is a less novel phenomenon than sometimes claimed. Nevertheless, it seems to me that the extent, intensity and immediacy of integration—both formal and informal—is a qualitatively different phenomenon, creating a new arena in which old struggles are played out.

Tentatively, one might postulate the emergence of three Europes, each in its own way facing the problem of relating *nation*, *state* and *democracy* against the background of *post-industrial* crisis. Europe 1 is formed around the EC core. Here the challenge will be to build a trans-state political grouping, in a way that accommodates national distinctiveness and also deals with the democratic deficit. This massive task will be complicated by the issue of the EC's relationship with the developed EFTA group, the continued absorption of the recent southern European members, the demands of other Mediterranean applicants (especially Turkey), and also Germany's assimilation of the old GDR.

Europe 2 is Eastern Europe, meaning the former Soviet bloc apart from Germany. In places the national question remains critical—the Yugoslavian federation (a creation of World War One Serbian imperialism cemented by Tito's personal rule) has now fallen apart—but in comparison with the inter-war period, national and ethnic tensions are generally less prevalent. Most of these states are ethnically viable in a way that was not true in the 1920s and 1930s. The huge challenge for them is to develop democratic institutions and to cope with the appalling strains of adjustment to market forces in unfavourable economic conditions. In their response to this challenge one may predict that older patterns will re-emerge. It is likely that the more developed states of Central Europe, especially Hungary and Czechoslovakia, will be changed more easily than their eastern neighbours—evidence of the old Mitteleuropa reasserting itself. And, linked with this, one must expect both the revival of German economic influence and of consequent resentment against it. More speculatively, one can envisage former Habsburg Eastern Europe adjusting better than the more profoundly Ottomanised areas farther south and east, particularly Albania. Such historical distinctions may be relevant to a new policy of 'differentiation' by the EC.

Thirdly, one might isolate the European part of the old USSR (Europe 3)—which of course begs the question about Russia's Janus-like identity straddling Europe and Asia. Here all the challenges must be faced at once. New state structures have to be created and the nationality question is being posed on a scale that makes post-Habsburg Europe or the post-Ottoman Middle East seem child's-play by comparison. Unlike

[63] A point suggested by Avner Offer's provocative book *The First World War: An Agrarian Interpretation*, Clarendon Press, Oxford, 1989, quotation from p. 81.

Eastern Europe, the people lack even vestigial democratic traditions or the experience of any kind of mixed economy. In the process, however, one might expect that the historically disputed parts of Russia's western empire—notably the Baltic states and perhaps Belorussia—will reassert their links with East Central Europe and move more into the orbit of Europe 2. How the European Community, or more generally G7, handles all this is a fraught question. Aside from the issue of aid, there is the problem of dealing with an increasingly fragmented governmental structure as the republics vie with the weak Commonwealth for control over the economy, armaments and natural resources of the country.

Economically, Europe 3 remains relatively separate from Europe 1. Yet, purely on grounds of self-interest, we cannot be indifferent to its fate. The potential influx of refugees is one reason; another is the grotesque Soviet environmental crisis, graphically symbolised by Chernobyl. More profoundly, the Europe-wide problem of security in a nuclear age makes the Soviet Union's metamorphosis an issue of vital concern to Western and Eastern Europe alike.

The underlying, perhaps abiding, problem for those euphemistically called 'policymakers' is to manage the process of change. For what we call 'stability is a special case of change, not the natural order of things'.[64] The demise of the Soviet Union will be doubly threatening—involving not only the passing of a major international manager but also chaotic change among a significant proportion of the earth's population. As Joseph Heller suggested, the Cold War era had its compensations.

---

[64] A. W. DePorte, *Europe between the Superpowers: The Enduring Balance*, Yale University Press, New Haven, 1979, p. xiii—a warning that perhaps he might have taken more seriously in the writing of his stimulating book.

FROM TWELVE TO TWENTY FOUR? THE CHALLENGES TO THE EC POSED BY THE REVOLUTIONS IN EASTERN EUROPE

WILLIAM WALLACE*

Now that the immediate euphoria over the dismantling of the Wall and the collapse of authoritarian socialism has passed, the European Community and its member governments have begun to appreciate the enormity of the challenges which the reintegration of their eastern neighbours into the European system present. In many ways, the cold war had come to serve Western Europe fairly well. It neatly defined its eastern boundaries. It provided a stable security framework. It kept a number of awkward questions off the explicit European agenda: defence, dominated by the USA and managed within NATO; the question of Germany, contained by its division between the blocs; the definition of 'Europe's place in the world', resolved at the end of successive transatlantic crises by West European acceptance that it was safer to follow the American lead in defining global order than to risk a confrontation over a distinctive European 'identity' or foreign policy.

The confrontation between East and West held Western Europe in place, within the Western Alliance. The Community was able to define itself as a 'civilian power', dealing in the business of 'low' politics while the USA led on 'high' politics. Community interests and American went together in accepting Spain, Portugal and Greece into membership— though motives were rather different on each side of the Atlantic. The Greeks and the Spaniards sought to lessen their dependence on the USA by increasing their political integration into the Western European political system, while the USA sought to bind them more closely into the 'Western' camp through full participation in its European 'pillar'. And the EC *was*, uncomfortable as it has been for many to admit it, a pillar of the Western system, under American leadership. Eleven of its twelve current member states are members of the Atlantic Alliance—Ireland, the exception, a historical neutral against the United Kingdom more than against the broader East-West conflict. We have all grown up within an Atlantic world: a mental map of political relationships within which

* William Wallace is the Walter F. Hallstein Fellow at St Antony's College, Oxford.

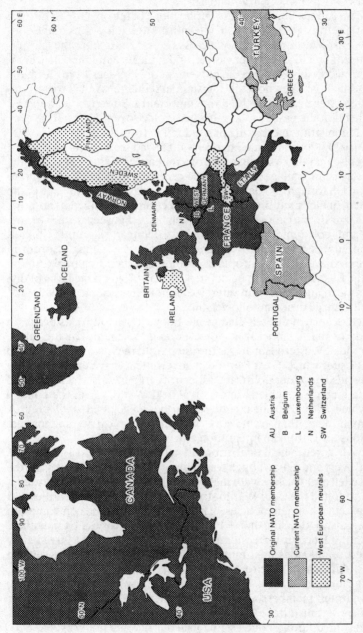

Source: William Wallace, *The Transformation of Western Europe*, published by Pinter for the Royal Institute of International Affairs, London, 1990.

Map 1. Euratlantica.

Washington seemed closer to Western Europe than Prague, New York than Warsaw (Map One: Euratlantica).

Before we can take on board the implications of the opening to Eastern Europe, therefore, we have to note the enormous implications of the ending of the East-West confrontation across central Europe for the EC. It is extremely difficult to assess them as yet, under the further immediate complications of the Gulf War and the movement of US forces from Germany to the Middle East. We know that substantial reductions in US troops stationed in Western Europe—the most important US foreign land and air commitment for the past 45 years—will take place over the next five years. The US administration is talking of a reduction from the current 300,000 to around 100,000; some in Congress want to reduce even more sharply. We recognise that the disappearance of a military Soviet threat across the central European plain at once ends the centrality of the European commitment in US foreign and defence policy *and* ends the dependence of the government of Germany on American protection and goodwill. The 'post-war transatlantic bargain'—with its close linkage between security partnership and economic cooperation—is no longer relevant; US and European interests in Mediterranean security, in containing disorder in eastern and south-eastern Europe, in promoting a stable regional order in the Middle East, now have to be defined and managed on the basis of distinct European and American interests, not of American leadership and (often reluctant) European followership.

The significance of this sea-change has not yet been fully considered on either side of the Atlantic. It is, however, as problematic for the future organisation of Western Europe as the opening to the East, in throwing up awkward issues which West European governments have until now been able to avoid. The wider political and security framework which emerged out of the incomplete allied victory in World War Two set the context within which West European integration has developed until now. A transformation of that framework will therefore carry fundamental implications for European integration as a whole.

The Cold War also held the European neutrals in place: self-defined as 'between' West and East, though for so many purposes clearly part of the West. Sweden and Austria, with highly-developed doctrines of neutrality, in effect exploited the Cold War to strengthen their national identities and to justify active foreign policies. The central European confrontation gone, they are now leading their EFTA partners towards full EC membership; with the European Economic Area negotiations of 1990–91 now recognised on all sides as a mutual learning process which has set the context within which at least four of the six EFTA states (seven if we include the mini-state of Liechtenstein, as we are now formally asked to do) will move to full membership within the next three to six years. Further enlargement is thus already on the agenda, with all its implications for Community institutions, policies, financial balance and political coalition-building, before the Commission and the member governments have had

36

the leisure to consider East European entry as more than a distant prospect—and is on the agenda partly because the political block which the EC's dependence on the US for military protection was seen to impose on neutral membership has now gone (Map Two: the European Economic Space).

Source: as Map One.

Map 2. The European Economic Space.

The scale of the challenge

On top of the detailed issues of completing the 1992 programme, the continuing—and still largely fruitless—struggle to reform the CAP and reduce the gross imbalance of Community expenditure between the agricultural sector and other areas, the efforts of governments to catch up with the explosion of cross-frontier movement through defining common rules for cooperation among law and enforcement agencies and for entry

37

into the 'common European space', and the efforts to foster European collaboration in research and high technology, the Community and its governments are thus faced with the need to redefine their partnership with their transatlantic sponsor and protector and to rethink the structure and organisation of *Western* Europe itself. Small wonder that comparatively little effort has yet been devoted to the long-term implications of the opening to Eastern Europe.

The speed of change has been remarkable in the two years since the socialist regimes began to collapse across eastern Europe; the second anniversary of the breach of the Berlin Wall was reached only in November 1991. The process of change is still uncertainly under way, most painfully in Yugoslavia, Albania, Romania, and above all in the former Soviet Union itself. 'Fire-fighting' has—hardly surprisingly—characterised most of the West European response so far, with task forces handling immediate assistance and rapidly convened teams producing reports on what to do next. Policy has unavoidably been driven by events more than by strategy. Riots in Tirana, conflict in Yugoslavia, require rapid adjustment of aid priorities and agendas for intergovernmental consultation. Economic assistance to Romania is suspended and resumed according to changing assessments of domestic political circumstances. Political difficulties in Poland, or deteriorating relations between Czechs and Slovaks, could pose new problems for West European policy-makers. Developments in the Ukraine, or in Russia itself, could yet drive us all off our intended course.

Nevertheless, the outlines of a future Europe—and a future structure for Europe—can be discerned. Just as we could in the early 1980s anticipate the collapse of Soviet domination in Eastern Europe and the reorientation of those states towards their western neighbours, without knowing within what timescale or how such a development was likely to happen, so now we can see the unavoidable expansion of the EC within the next ten to fifteen years to some twenty to thirty member states, without seeing how that transformation of Europe's political and economic structure will be managed (Map Three: the Expanding European Community). The rest of this paper is devoted to considering the issues which the current EC and its members will have to face in attempting to manage this process, and to assessing the likelihood that they will succeed in managing the transformation of a West European Community into a European 'System' without producing a structure as unwieldly as the 18th century Polish Constitution or an economy so inadequately managed that it cannot bear the burdens of adjustment which have to be faced.

Where does 'Europe' stop?

The first, and most fundamental, question is: where do we draw the line in this eastward and southern expansion? Article 237 of the Treaty of Rome

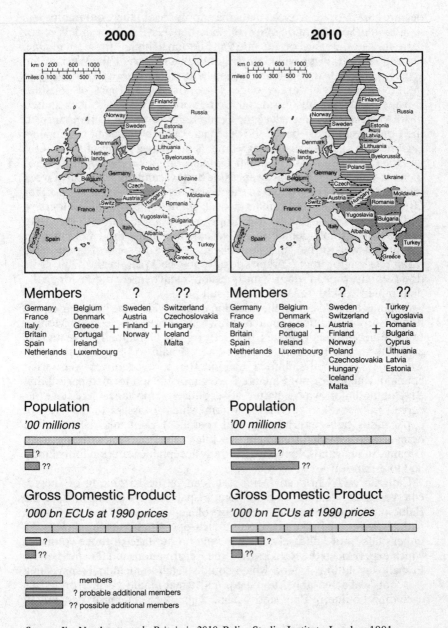

2000

2010

Members ? ??

Germany	Belgium	Sweden	Switzerland
France	Denmark	Austria	Czechoslovakia
Italy	Greece +	Finland +	Hungary
Britain	Portugal	Norway	Iceland
Spain	Ireland		Malta
Netherlands	Luxembourg		

Members ? ??

Germany	Belgium	Sweden	Turkey
France	Denmark	Switzerland	Yugoslavia
Italy	Greece +	Austria +	Romania
Britain	Portugal	Finland	Bulgaria
Spain	Ireland	Norway	Cyprus
Netherlands	Luxembourg	Poland	Lithuania
		Czechoslovakia	Latvia
		Hungary	Estonia
		Iceland	
		Malta	

Population
'00 millions

?
??

Population
'00 millions

?
??

Gross Domestic Product
'000 bn ECUs at 1990 prices

?
??

Gross Domestic Product
'000 bn ECUs at 1990 prices

?
??

members
? probable additional members
?? possible additional members

Source: Jim Northcott *et al.*, *Britain in 2010*, Policy Studies Institute, London, 1991.

Map 3. The Expanding European Community.

declares that 'Any European state may apply to join the Community'. As long as the Soviet Union drew the line between Eastern and Western Europe, the question of Europe's institutional limits was containable. Greece and Turkey provided the major difficulty: part of 'the West' by the accident of post-war demarcation (and British and American intervention in the Greek civil war), though self-evidently not part of Western Europe—and arguably outside the framework of 'Western' values, shared history and culture which gave the Community a sense of community. But the Commission had opened the prospects of eventual membership in its eagerness to sign association agreements at the beginning of the 1960s; and the Commission's more sober *Opinion* on the Greek application for membership of 1975–6 was swept aside by governments swayed by Greek lobbying, desire to consolidate a fragile democracy, American support for Greek membership, and romantic ideas about 'the cradle of democracy' and 'the Greek contribution to European civilisation'. Turkey's failure to re-establish a stable democratic government enabled the EC to avoid a definite answer to the Turkish application then. In spite of heavy hints from Washington that Turkey's loyalty to 'the West' in the Gulf crisis deserves a European reward, the question is still being avoided, for all the determined Turkish renewal of their suit.

So far as I can discover, the question of how widely the boundaries of a future European Union should be drawn never preoccupied Jean Monnet or the other 'founding fathers' of the European Community.[1] He and his associates wanted France, Germany and Britain to be drawn together, with their neighbours, into a Union. The core countries were what counted: whether or not Finland, Portugal or Ireland formed part of that developing union was a matter of secondary importance. We have *no* agreed framework of definition within which to assess the priority of applications between Bulgaria and (perhaps) Lithuania, between the demands for special treatment we might find ourselves facing from Albania and Iceland. Nor do we have any acceptable criterion for calling a halt to expansion.[2]

Catholic and Christian Democrats can be heard talking of the re-emergence of Western Christendom: a space which would include the Baltic states and the northern republics of Yugoslavia, but exclude Greece and the rest of the Balkans (Map Four: Europe without the Superpowers). Others talk, more diffusely, of the common heritage of those countries which experienced the Renaissance, the Reformation, and the ideas of the French Revolution: criteria which could stretch to include Transylvania (but not Wallachia and Moldavia), and which could be interpreted as excluding southern Italy and Spain. There are immense dangers in

[1] Jean Monnet, *Mémoires*, Fayard, Paris, 1976, pp. 316–23, 331–40. I have also consulted several of Monnet's former associates on this point.
[2] This question is discussed at greater length in William Wallace, *The Transformation of Western Europe*, Pinter, London, 1990, ch. 2.

defining 'Europe' as Christian, in implicit contradistinction to the Muslim world: though there is considerable popular appeal in doing so, and good historical justification as well. Contradistinction between 'Europe' and 'Asia' is as dangerous, and a good deal more indeterminate. Metternich saw Asia beginning on the Landstrasse (as you left Vienna for the East).

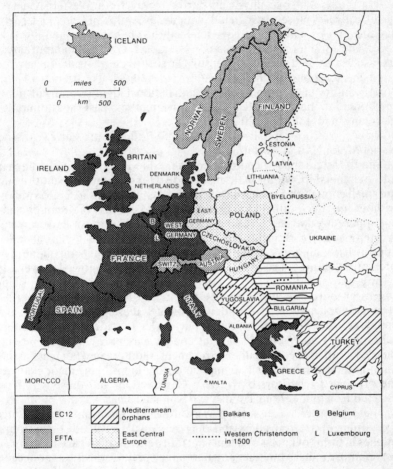

Source: as Map One.

Map 4. Europe without the Superpowers.

Adenauer, like so many others, identified Communism and Soviet power with Asia. Stalinism was placed into a historical and cultural context, as promoting 'the Asiatic system of production'—a phrase which was intended to imply forced labour, which today might be taken as implying quality circles and 'just in time' provision of components.

We are left with a series of groups with differing claims to be accepted as fully 'European'. It may help to list them:

1. Poland, Czechoslovakia and Hungary—the three prime candidates, with established claims to be 'rejoining the West'.

2. 'The Balkans'—Romania, Bulgaria, Yugoslavia (as one unit, or as several), and Albania: physically further away from Western Europe, historically less closely associated (with the exception of Catholic Croatia and Slovenia), politically and economically less hopeful.

3. 'The Mediterranean orphans'—Malta and Cyprus (unimportant in themselves, though potentially sensitive in security terms), and Turkey: too large and too poor for the EC to absorb, too much like Russia, a Euro-Asian country in geography, culture and national identity, and with a rate of population increase which will carry its numbers past those of unified Germany before the year 2000.

4. The Western republics of the old USSR: the Baltic states, Ukraine, Soviet Moldavia and Byelorussia.

The EC is gradually becoming committed to accepting the first group into membership, within the next decade. Hungary and Czechoslovakia are small enough and economically resilient enough for the EC to swallow without too much difficulty. Poland, with a population of 38 million and an apparently weaker economy, gives West European governments greater pause for thought; but the political arguments for a concerted approach to all three countries are likely to prove compelling. The pressures they are successfully exerting might well be followed in twelve to twenty-four months' time by impoverished but newly-independent Baltic states: far more difficult for the EC to handle, given the highly uncertain strategic implications of such a development. If these were taken on board, could the other Western Soviet republics be left outside, or granted only a subordinate status? The Romanians and Bulgarians are already pressing their case for more sympathetic treatment—and greater financial assistance; and complaining that an implicit distinction is being made between the privileged inheritors of Western Christendom and those who have escaped from under both Turkish and Russian rule.

There is a whole succession of awkward choices to be made here. Once the border between insiders and outsiders—with all the distinction that implies in terms of access and financial transfers—is moved eastwards, can we reimpose a sharp boundary? Alternatively, can we devise some acceptable gradation of privilege and access (and subsidy) to satisfy Western Europe's client states (which is what all these are now becoming)? We may prefer a multi-tier Europe, with the former socialist countries constituting the outer and lower tiers. But the experience of Greek entry—and of Spanish and Portuguese—suggests that it is not easy to satisfy the returning prodigal with half a fatted calf.

Widening and deepening

Whether we like it or not, the aim of almost all those states which are in the process of 'returning to Europe' will be to join the European Community: not to become outside associates, grouped in an institutionalised periphery, but full participants in Europe's institutional and political structures. We are witnessing a shift in interpretation of Article 237, in which 'may apply' is becoming 'must apply': for political reasons, above all, as a reassertion of a country's 'rightful place' in the European political system, overriding economic weakness and administrative incapacity. The example of the Mediterranean applicants is compelling: the strength of Spanish determination to demonstrate its European commitment and credentials indeed carried it past EC membership into an initially unwelcome application to join WEU, and most recently into pressing its case to accede to the Schengen Agreement.

It will be politically difficult for the major EC governments to put successive applicants off with arguments for delay or for the acceptance of lesser status. Newly democratic states, unlike the self-confident states of EFTA, need the reassurance and the added domestic and international legitimacy which acceptance into the EC is seen to bring. We are already seeing in the 'Mixed Agreements' with East European countries and in the management of conditional EC aid the emergence of the EC as assessor of democratic and libertarian standards—using economic leverage according to political criteria.[3]

The EC, it should be noted, has not yet definitely refused any application for membership. It took Britain and its fellow applicants twelve years from first application to full membership, after two French vetoes: but persistence brought entry. The Turkish application, it is true, is being tactfully put to one side, amidst widespread hopes that it can be left there until the Turks have come to understand that the objective is mistaken in terms of their own national needs. The political (and economic) damage an outright refusal might give to a fragile East European democracy, struggling to make the transition to a market economy, would be severe. Active diplomacy on a concerted basis will thus be vital in giving the 'right' signals to these emerging democracies about what sort of approaches to the EC would be welcomed, and what sort likely to meet with delay. And that—again—will require EC member governments to develop a far more explicit consensus on their long-term objectives for enlargement than is yet evident.

Insiders feared on each previous enlargement that widening implied dilution—a broader but shallower EC. Thus the careful package deal of the Hague Summit of December 1969, in which 'completion' and 'deepen-

[3] The 'Mixed Agreements' were under negotiation in the first half of 1991, against a background of conflicting economic and political pressures on both sides.

ing' were preconditions for enlargement. Thus also part of the impetus for the Single European Act, to make it easier for a Council of Ministers expanding from nine to twelve states to take decisions. The evidence of two successive rounds of enlargement on the balance between widening and deepening is inconclusive: but it is not certain that the Community would necessarily have been a far closer union if it had stayed a group of six. The British grievance on budgetary transfers and agricultural imbalances made successive governments difficult partners until the 1984 Fontainebleau Settlement—but the assimilation of British ministers and officials into most of the assumptions and working practices of EC negotiations was nevertheless striking long before that point. The Spanish, and to a lesser extent the Portuguese, passed rapidly from novice to loyal enthusiast—with initiatives from Madrid for the agendas of the inter-governmental conferences, most particularly on the development of European 'citizenship'. New entrants from Eastern Europe would suffer acutely on entry from lack of familiarity with multilateral European bargaining, from poor preparation for meetings and from the weak capacity of their national administrations to apply and enforce Community rules. But the Hungarians, in particular, see the Spanish as their model—and with that in mind deny that early entry would necessarily slow the Community's evolution down in any significant way.

So a simple 'drawing of a line in the soil', beyond which EC membership is unlikely to be offered and looser affiliation preferred, is not an option. A move towards a more explicitly multi-tier Community, with a tighter inner core and a looser outer periphery, is. The origins of the split between 'little Europe' and 'wider Europe', after all, reflect the willingness of the 'Six' to move ahead on a core group basis rather than wait for the most reluctant members of the Council of Europe and OEEC. A paper from the German Chancellor's Office in 1989 explicitly floated a strategy for a smaller and tighter core, within a wider but shallower community.[4] This, after all, would only further develop and formalise what Philippe de Schoutheete has called the existing 'sub-systems' within the EC: WEU (not formally linked to the EC, but increasingly strongly linked in the minds of its members), the developing Schengen Group, the multi-tier EMS.[5]

With Spain and Portugal, as well as Italy, determined to be 'in' on such inner groupings rather than left on the outside, the key country for such a development to grow is the UK—the primary target of the German Chancellery paper. As in 1949–50 and in 1957–8, British reluctance to accept the full commitment demanded by its French, German and Benelux partners provides the basis for an alternative outer group. When as in 1970–73 (and again in 1991–3?) British governments in their turn conclude that the advantages of full participation in the multilateral

---

[4] Published in the *Frankfurter Allgemeine Zeitung*, 19 July 1989.

[5] Philippe de Schoutheete, 'The European Community and its Sub-systems', chapter 6 in William Wallace (ed.), *The Dynamics of European Integration*, Pinter, London, 1990.

bargaining around which the West European system revolves outweigh the loss of national autonomy involved, the outer 'tier' becomes again a collection of small countries which exclude themselves for reasons of national identity and limited national interests: the three 'footnote countries' within the EC, the European neutrals outside—of which (apart from the fringe case of Turkey) only Sweden and Switzerland rank as economically significant.

The most important criterion for choosing between an inner core and an outer second tier is that the members of the outer tier should have voluntarily chosen to stay outside. It will be politically impossible, I wish to argue, for the structure of Europe in the 1990s to be built on the basis of an exclusive insiders' 'club', denying to countries such as Spain or Sweden—or, in time, Poland—the chance to accede. More than that: a system which is based upon assumptions of mutual reciprocity, which will impose increasingly heavy financial as well as political and regulatory burdens upon its participants in the next ten years (as I will argue below), depends upon the acceptance by all participants of the range of shared obligations in return for the shared benefits. Rising levels of Community expenditure, in particular as transfers to East European countries, will focus attention on 'free riders'; the question of Swiss participation in European integration, for example, is unlikely to be left entirely to the Swiss. *Delay* is acceptable in the full imposition of obligations and the full acquisition of privileges; delay will unavoidably be a factor in the approach of East European countries to full participation. But *denial* is not.

All the evidence we have so far, from the three east-central European potential applicants, from the Mediterranean experience, and from the distant hopes of others, is that the political symbolism of full membership has become too powerful for schemes of building a first- and second-class Europe to prove practical. How far *within* a developing Community new initiatives will develop on a differentiated basis is, however, an entirely different matter: the examples of Schengen and the EMS, in which sub-groups have set the pace (and defined the rules) for the rest of the Community, which these laggards will in time be expected to follow, will no doubt be followed in other areas—from environment to defence.

The policy agenda which this expanding Community will face is daunting in its complexity. To list some predictable items will give an indication of the tasks ahead:

1. *Reform (or collapse) of the Common Agricultural Policy.* Pomerania, Prussia, and Western Poland were the 'breadbasket' of imperial Germany; now crippled by socialised agriculture, but likely to witness an explosion of productivity as prices are raised and efficient methods of production introduced. Hungary, Romania and Bulgaria look to increased access to Western Europe food markets to help in financing their transition to a market economy. The incursion of additional agricultural production, most probably at highly competitive prices, into an

45

EC market already suffering a structural surplus will force further change. German agricultural ministers might conceivably attempt to block full access for produce from Poland and Hungary; but they are no longer in any position to block rising production from Brandenburg or Saxony.

2. *Environmental protection and improvement*. Scandinavian countries joining the EC are likely to make this area one of their priorities, defending their own high standards and seeking to extend them to others. 'Cleaning up Eastern Europe' will be a common European concern—and task, and financial burden; the scale of the task is only gradually becoming evident.

3. *Economic management*—with all that follows from closer formal and informal integration of the European economy, complicated further by the long-term re-integration of the former socialist countries into the European economy: substantial *regional transfers*, for infrastructural improvements, possibly even for budgetary support, adjustment policies for industries affected by more direct competition from Eastern Europe, the policing of investment flows and subsidies, etc.

4. *Border controls and migration policy*. Setting the boundaries of 'Europe' is only the preliminary to policing them and those who cross them: with a rising number of those left outside seeking to cross the 'European Rio Grande' which separates the rich world from the poor. We may anticipate—we can already see—demands from those countries most affected by migrants and asylum seekers for financial assistance from other European countries, for a recognition that they are holding the 'European front line' (I quote Austrian and Hungarian officials) on the common behalf. We may also anticipate hard negotiations about common rules and common rights in this immensely sensitive area.

5. *External relations, foreign policy and defence*. US enthusiasm for the EC Commission to take the lead in handling G24 assistance to Eastern Europe gave a clear signal that from now on the West Europeans themselves must accept the prime responsibility for economic development, political stability, and outbreaks of disorder to the East. Crises in Albania or Yugoslavia, another collapse of regime in—say—Romania, are for the West Europeans to take immediate responsibility. To the South the USA wishes to continue to take the lead; but, post-Gulf War, the terms and conditions of US–European partnership in maintaining order in the Mediterranean and Middle East will require much hard bargaining, both across the Atlantic and among the West Europeans themselves. The immense foreign policy implications of the emergence of an institutionalised Europe containing over twenty member states, accounting for a significant proportion of the global economy, without significant external military forces on its territory, will be discussed further below.

The financial implications for the Community Budget and other transfers among member states of the above are very substantial. This paper will not speculate on the scale or the duration of the transfers needed to assist East European states through the period of economic transition. But it should be noted that the *political* decision to accept a new member into the EC carries long-term *economic* consequences, in terms of expectations of 'equity' in Community transfers and demands for additional expenditure. Those left outside will also demand compensation: as concessions to East European agriculture and industry adversely affect the EC's Mediterranean associates, and as the republics of the old USSR struggle in their turn with economic reform. Any further moves towards common defence policy will also raise awkward issues of costs and benefits. It is not, for instance, self-evident that Britain should continue to spend twice as much on its contribution to the common defence as Italy, when potential future threats are likely to be far more directly to Italy than to the British Isles.

The institutional implications of the above are also extensive. Two rounds of enlargement have already shown that a wider Community requires more effective central institutions. An EC of twenty to twenty-four, with a larger central budget and a more extensive agenda, will require a much more developed capability for strategic planning, for developing policies and overseeing their implementation across the Community's extensive territories. Weaker member states—as we must assume the East European states will continue to be for many years—will demand continuing budgetary transfers, while their partners will demand in return closer monitoring of their economic policies and their administrative implementation of Community rules. The example of Greece is relevant here. Accepted into the EC for political reasons, with an administration unprepared to cope with the implications of membership and over-optimistic assumptions about the financial and economic benefits membership would bring, the Greek government found itself in 1990–91 suffering Community oversight of its monetary and fiscal policies, and targeted by those (like the British government) who saw an extension of Community competence over implementation as a necessary counter-weight to the shortcomings of the EC's politically-underdeveloped countries.

Indeed, one might argue—against much of the conventional wisdom— that enlargement to include East European states will necessarily tip the balance between the current loose confederal system and a tighter federal structure. The addition of Sweden, Austria, Finland and Norway to the current EC, in terms of size and numbers and of policy problems added to the current agenda, does not necessarily force significant further institutional change. But an increase towards and past twenty, with poor and poorly administered new entrants laying their needs at the Community's door, will force far more radical adaptation: tighter rules for decision-taking at the centre, extended central oversight of national implementation, substantially increased financial transfers, and more detailed conditionality on national political, economic and social behaviour in return for this scale of transfers.

Europe as a regional power

Civilian power EC, still within the Atlantic security framework, found itself playing—partly through its major members, partly as an entity in itself—an increasingly active role in global economic diplomacy and management in the course of the 1970s and 1980s. Post-cold-war Europe, with the wider European Economic Area progressively incorporated into the EC, will be forced to adopt a still more central role—and to recognise more explicitly the political and security implications of its international economic relations.

We are postulating that some sixteen to eighteen of the currently twenty-four members of the OECD will be within the EC by the year 2000. Incorporation of the EFTA economies into the EC will make more evident the regional character of the European economy. EFTA as a group—a slightly artificial construct—is the Community's largest trade partner, well ahead of the USA; combining the two groups will leave less than a third of national trade by EC and EFTA members going outside the area—a regional economy as self-contained as that of North America.[6]

Around this integrated economy will be grouped a wider periphery of dependent states, for all of which the EC will be the dominant trade partner, as well as a source of investment flows and public and private financial transfers—and the dominant objective of immigration by their rising populations. The reality that institutionalised Europe is becoming an economic 'power' will be unmistakable, with major regional and global implications: regional, in the impact of European policies on the poorer states around its edge, global in the need to bargain with the USA and Japan on the management of international financial markets, the rules of trade, technology transfer, environmental regulations, and policies towards the poorer countries. The weakening of the overriding shared security commitment will not make this bargaining easier.

The opening towards Eastern Europe has different implications for the EC. It brings added responsibilities, not added resources: needs to be met, not contributions to be used. Western Europe must now resume its historical concerns for instability in the Balkans, and develop policy instruments (political and diplomatic, economic—and also military?) for managing the region's international and domestic tensions. But it must also resume its historical links with Russia and the other 'states' of 'Eastern

---

[6] Per Magnus Wijkman, 'Patterns of Production and Trade', chapter 5 in *The Dynamics of European Integration*, *op. cit.*

East Europe', as these emerge from the Soviet empire.[7] How burdensome a responsibility that may become is not yet clear; nor is it clear how far that responsibility might stretch into the security sphere. But it is likely to prove primarily a *European* responsibility, with the United States concerned only with its global implications—and Japan perhaps taking some limited responsibility for economic assistance to republics whose borders reach its own.

The first meeting of 'European Foreign Ministers in the Framework of Political Cooperation', in 1971, discussed policy towards the Middle East—and found no basis for common positions in approaching an area so sensitive to their dominant alliance partner, the United States. Over the twenty years since then successive attempts to formulate European policies towards the oil-producing countries, the Arab and Islamic worlds, the parties to the Arab-Israel dispute, have foundered on awareness of American hesitations and consciousness that both in security terms and in the provision of economic assistance the USA calls the Western tune.

It is increasingly unlikely that this acceptance of subordination to the USA in Middle East policy can continue through the 1990s. US troops in Europe will be far fewer; those that remain will be more visibly present in support of American objectives outside Europe rather than of the common defence of Europe itself. Human links between Europe and the Arab and Islamic worlds will continue to grow, as second-generation immigrants become vocal citizens within the EC and other legal and illegal immigrants come in to join them; the dependence of North Africa, and to a lesser extent the Levant, on Europe will become more acute. The addition of Eastern and South-Eastern European countries to this institutionalised Europe will to some extent complicate the relationship, to some extent intensify it. Christian/Muslim relations are historically and politically sensitive in the former Ottoman countries, with surviving Islamic minorities; trade and migration between Western Europe and the Middle East flow overland across Hungary, Yugoslavia, Romania and Bulgaria. Trade with the Muslim world—in particular the wealthy oil-producing countries—is a natural outlet for the economies of South-Eastern Europe; Bulgaria and Romania were among the countries hard hit by the imposition of sanctions against Iraq. Increasing American dependence on imports of Middle East oil, as its own production declines and consumption continues to increase, together with continuing Israeli dependence on US financial transfers, will complicate transatlantic management of divergent interests towards Europe's immediate southern neighbours.

Western Europe has already overtaken North America as the first destination for the world's tired and poor, the huddled masses yearning

[7] These links were of course closest between Germany and Russia. Imperial Germany was pre-1914 Russia's most important trading partner and source of technology. But the importance of French and British capital, and of skilled workers and entrepreneurs from Britain, France and The Netherlands in the modernisation of Russia should not be forgotten.

to be free—and more prosperous. The pressures of migration from east and south will stretch European tolerance and preoccupy its policy-makers throughout the next twenty-five years. Historically, as Austrians now remind West Europeans, Europe's main waves of invading migrants have come from the east and the south-east, with smaller numbers attacking north across the Mediterranean. Hungary and Poland, in particular, fear being caught in between a European Community which is tightening controls on entry and a 'Soviet Union' which has lost the ability to prevent its people from leaving. But it is not just the Russian flow which is preoccupying. The immense diversity of those who are already picked up on the Austrian and Hungarian borders, collected at reception centres in Vienna and Berlin, sleep rough on railway stations in Warsaw, Prague and Budapest, provides a vivid impression of the scale of the problems European countries will face: Pakistanis and Nigerians coming across the land route, Turkomans and Mongolians coming out of the old USSR, Syrians and Iraqis fleeing instability and persecution, Kurds, Egyptians, Lebanese, Somalis. Stemming the tide and grappling with its consequences will involve institutionalised Western Europe in policies towards its dependent neighbours far more active than those of which its member states yet dream.

The reluctant superpower—or the crippled giant?

Ay, there's the rub: are Western Europe's policy-makers capable of raising their attention from the immediate preoccupations of the Community's current agenda to take on board the immensely ambitious agenda sketched out above? The prospects do not look encouraging. Further enlargement is now inevitable, within four to five years at most; yet the subject has by common consent been excluded from the agenda of the Intergovernmental Conferences of 1991. The demise of the CAP is now unavoidable; but every agricultural minister, including the British, appears dedicated to postponing it as long as possible. A fundamental shift in Europe's security context is underway, with major implications for the organisation of national and continental defence; but the debate has hardly moved beyond the rhetorical phase so far.

Pessimism suggests that overstretch and undercapacity will carry the inadequate structures of the EC down as the problems—and the piles of applications—mount. Optimism suggests that West European governments will muddle through as they have done for the past twenty years, being pushed into marginal steps forward by circumstances, recognising the inevitable without planning for it. The improvisation and reactive policy-making which have characterised Community responses since the East European revolutions began in 1989 have had their successes, in the provision of aid and the development of new programmes of technical assistance. But their failures have been more striking: the incoherence of the Community position in the negotiations for the East–Central European 'Mixed Agreements', unable to offer the concessions on agriculture, textiles and steel which are of most immediate value; the reluctance either to define a policy towards Yugoslavia or to use the Community's very considerable economic leverage until fighting had broken out between the Yugoslav federal army and Slovenian forces.

The burden of work on the Community's external affairs directorate-general increased much more rapidly than its staff in 1990–91; overload on the responsible Commissioners and officials has been evident in the conduct of the European Economic Area negotiations, which threatened to break down at several points in early 1991, and in Commission handling of the GATT Uruguay Round negotiations, as well as in its approach to Eastern Europe. The European Council and Councils of Ministers have swung from discussions of broad principles to immediate reactions to crises without addressing the details of the new agenda which the integration of Central and Eastern Europe into the West European system is now opening up. It may be that reactive policies, incremental adjustments of the Community *Acquis*, marginal increases in Community powers and modest strengthening of its institutional capabilities, will prove sufficient to meet the challenges posed. But it may well be not.

THE EUROPEAN COMMUNITY
IN THE NEW EUROPE

STEPHEN GEORGE*

PRECISELY what the position of the European Community (EC) will be in the new Europe that is now emerging is difficult to say, but it is bound to play an important role. That role will be determined partly by the overall shape of the new European architecture and partly by the future character of the EC itself. At the time of writing both these issues were under intensive discussion—the general shape of Europe in a variety of forums, the future character of the EC in an intergovernmental conference (IGC) on political union.

In this article an attempt is made to review the way in which the events in Eastern Europe at the end of the 1980s interacted with a debate that had already begun on the future nature of the EC and its relationship both to the member states and to other organisations such as the Western European Union (WEU), which were being spoken about as elements in the new European architecture.

Views on the organisation of Europe

There have always been different views about how Europe ought to be organised. Perhaps the two most influential and contrasting positions are those of the federalists and of the intergovernmentalists. Federalists have long argued that some form of federal European state is necessary to deal with the problems of interderpendence and to make Europe an effective actor in world affairs. The European Community has been seen by federalists as the basis of this future European super-state. Intergovernmentalists, on the other hand, have argued that the problems can be dealt with by co-operation between sovereign independent states, without the apparatus of a federal structure. They have tended to stress the dangers both for the national cultures of the states of Europe and for individual freedom of a super-state emerging.

In the past France has provided representatives of both voices in this debate. Jean Monnet, who devised the plans for both the European Coal and Steel Community and the European Atomic Energy Community, and who also promoted the idea of the European Economic Community, could be taken as representative of the federalist line of thinking, although it is probable that he would not have accepted the title of federalist himself.

---

* Stephen George is Senior Lecturer in Politics, University of Sheffield.

Charles de Gaulle was the clearest French representative of the inter-governmental approach to the problems of Europe, and the scourge of the federalist tendency within the EC in the 1960s.

More recently the French President François Mitterrand has adopted the rhetoric of federalism in his approach to the EC. Ironically, given de Gaulle's opposition to British membership of the EC, it is the British government that has generally carried the torch of intergovernmentalism since Britain became a member in 1973; and when she was prime minister Margaret Thatcher came to be seen as a second de Gaulle on European matters, especially following her strong restatement of the intergovern-mental position in her speech at the College of Europe in Bruges in September 1988.

That speech marked an important stage in an argument about the future of the EC which was already raging fiercely when the collapse of communism in Eastern Europe caused it to be extended into a debate about the position of the EC in the wider Europe.

The debate about the future of the EC

In 1985 the European Community embarked on a project to free the internal market of non-tariff barriers to trade by the end of 1992. This led to a rapid revival of economic activity, as companies engaged in invest-ment and mergers in anticipation of the new competitive climate to come. It also led to a dispute between the member states about the extent of the programme upon which they had embarked. The British government in particular seemed to want the '1992 project' to comprise no more than the freeing of the market. But for other actors the project had further aspects.

For the European Commission there seemed to be at least four other aspects to the programme. One was inauguration of a European pro-gramme of research in advanced technologies; a second was monetary union; a third was the so-called 'social dimension' to 1992; and a fourth was institutional reform to strengthen central decision-making in the EC. All but the first of these were challenged by Thatcher in her Bruges speech; but, in the weeks that followed, the leaders of the other member states almost all criticised the Bruges speech and defended the extended concept of 1992 as envisaged by the Commission.

Thatcher's critique of the extended concept of 1992 was based on the traditional tenets of intergovernmentalism: that 'willing and active co-operation between independent sovereign states is the best way to build a successful European Community'.[1] Other elements came into the critique: that minimal government is the best form of government; that social regulations simply 'raise the cost of *employment* and make Europe's

---

[1] Margaret Thatcher, *Britain and Europe*, text of the speech delivered at Bruges on 20 September 1988, Conservative Political Centre, London, 1988, p. 4.

53

labour market less flexible';[2] that Europe should not be protectionist. These were the fundamentals of Thatcherism as an economic and social programme, and the Bruges speech was an application of them to the European level. But the essential ground on which Thatcher took her stand was that of intergovernmentalism, and the other member states found themselves arguing the case for some degree of federalism in contrast.

There was thus disharmony in the EC about its future direction in the late 1980s. There was also a problem about the relationship of the post-1992 EC with its neighbours. In 1987 Turkey revived its application for membership; and in the course of 1989 and 1990 some members of the European Free Trade Association (EFTA) declared their intention to apply for full membership in order to be inside the single market. The Commission of the EC declared in its response to the Turkish application that there could be no question of a further enlargement until after 1992, and restated this position in response to an Austrian approach in July 1989. So the issue was held over, but remained a cause for concern.

Onto this scene swept the collapse of communism in East and Central Europe. The rapidity with which events unfolded in the course of 1989 caught everybody by surprise. The declaration by the new regimes in Czechoslovakia, Hungary, and Poland that they would be seeking eventual membership of the EC both brought the membership issue into sharper focus and fed into the disputes between the member states about the extent of the 1992 programme.

Nobody denied that the hope of membership had to be held out to these states in order to assist them in their transition to capitalism, and to help to stabilise democracy there. Thatcher was quick to claim that developments strengthened her arguments against the surrender of further sovereignty to the central institutions. She argued that these states had only just reclaimed their sovereignty from the Soviet Union, and would not be willing to see it handed over to supranational institutions in Brussels and Strasbourg. She also argued that the rate of progress towards monetary union and social harmonisation ought to be slowed because they would take the EC further away from any position that the Central European states could hope to attain in any reasonable period of time and so make it more difficult for them to join.

Against that, Jacques Delors, the President of the Commission, argued in a speech at the College of Europe in October 1989 that the developments in Eastern Europe actually made it necessary for the EC to move more rapidly towards political union, otherwise it would be pulled apart. A similar analysis was put to the European Parliament by François Mitterrand in speeches in October and November 1989.

What particularly worried Delors and Mitterrand in the latter months of 1989 was the progress towards the reunification of Germany following the

[2] Margaret Thatcher, *op. cit.*, p. 7.

collapse of the German Democratic Republic. The way in which the Federal German government dealt with this matter was surprisingly direct and effective, but it involved no consultation with either the Commission or Germany's supposedly closest ally, France. Up to that point the French and Germans had worked in tandem to push forward the closer integration of the EC, and had developed mechanisms for close bi-lateral collaboration on foreign policy and defence. The sight of the Federal German government going off on its own caused great concern in both Brussels and Paris.

In its defence the German government argued that it did not have the time to consult, so rapid was the pace of events, and in November 1989 Chancellor Kohl joined President Mitterrand in calling for the EC to strengthen its bonds so that it could act as a model of democracy and freedom for the East European states. Mitterrand summarised the new Franco–German line when he told the European Parliament that, 'The Community's role is to realise that it is the only attractive force on this continent. It must be a guiding light and a beacon across the horizon'.[3]

In April 1990 the German Chancellor joined with the French President in sending a letter to the Irish Taoiseach, Charles Haughey, whose government held the Presidency of the EC Council of Ministers during the first half of that year. The letter called for the acceleration of political unity within the EC in response to the developments in Eastern Europe, and for an IGC on political union. Predictably the British government rejected the logic of the argument that the Franco–German letter put forward. In a speech in Paris the British Foreign Secretary, Douglas Hurd, said of the initiative on political union, 'I do not find persuasive the argument that we must accelerate the pace of political integration in the Community precisely because of these dramatic events. The Community is not a vehicle that necessarily requires radical redesign when the landscape through which it is travelling changes'.[4] Nevertheless, he also added that if the other member states wished to convene an IGC, the British government would participate.

Intergovernmental conferences

It is a requirement of the founding treaties of the EC that any amendments to those treaties be preceded by an IGC, which then proposes amendments to a meeting of the heads of government. Any amendments agreed by the heads of government then have to be ratified by national parliaments. One IGC had been held in 1985–6, resulting in the Single European Act of 1987.

[3] Quoted in *The Independent*, 23 November 1989.
[4] *The Independent*, 25 April 1990.

One of the innovations in the Single European Act was that the European Monetary System (EMS) for the first time became part of a constitutional document, and it was therefore necessary to convene an IGC in order to implement the proposed move towards monetary union. This conference was agreed at the Strasbourg meeting of the European Council in December 1989, on a majority vote of eleven to one with Britain voting against. The IGC on political union which was proposed by the French and German governments was agreed on the basis of the same majority at the Dublin meeting of the European Council in June 1990. The two IGCs were to run in parallel, starting in December 1990. Agreement to this second IGC was conditioned by a number of factors. Perhaps first in importance was concern about the new Germany. Not only would the emerging state be an economic giant, there was also concern about the possibility of a revival of German nationalism following re-unification. Political union could tie down the new Germany, something that the Federal German government welcomed as much as did France and Germany's other neighbours.

A second consideration was the realisation that the demands for enlargement of the EC could not forever be resisted. There was a real prospect of a future EC of over 20 member states, and such a large organisation would not be able to operate effectively unless there was more recourse to majority voting in the Council of Ministers and some greater delegation of authority to the Commission. There was also a strong feeling among some member states, especially perhaps in Germany and Italy, that the EC risked looking hypocritical if it continued to preach the virtues of democratic government and to refuse membership to states that did not sustain democratic systems, while at the same time having a serious democratic deficit in its own decision-making procedures. There was a case to be made out therefore for increasing the powers of the European Parliament.

Another very important area for the IGC was that of security and defence. Proposals for an extension of Community competence to these areas had been around for some years, but had always been resisted by the Irish government because of what it saw as the conflict with its state's neutrality. There was also a neutrality problem for some of the prospective member states that were currently in EFTA.

The British government, too, had difficulties about seeing the EC acquire a defence dimension, both because of its attachment to the ideal of national sovereignty, for which an independent national defensive capability is crucial, and because of the importance that it attached to the Atlantic Alliance and to keeping the United States involved in the defence of western Europe. One of Thatcher's 'guiding principles' in the Bruges speech had been that, 'Europe must continue to maintain a sure defence through NATO'.[5]

[5] Margaret Thatcher, *op. cit.*, p. 8.

What brought security and defence to the top of the agenda was the risk of instability in the very backyard of the EC. The collapse of communism in Eastern Europe allowed the re-emergence of nationalist sentiments, and the revival of national rivalries that had been buried for decades under the blanket of communist rule. Also, the process of transition to capitalism was likely to be difficult even for the northern states of Eastern Europe, and even more so for the southern states such as Albania, Bulgaria and Romania. If regional conflicts did break out, it was unlikely that the EC would be able to sit back and not get involved. However, it was also unlikely that any one state would be happy to see another become involved in a policing operation within Europe in the way that French policing operations in francophone Africa had been tolerated in the past. Added to these considerations, and very influential, was the attitude of the Bush administration in the United States.

The attitude of the United States

US attitudes to the EC have always moved along a spectrum between the ideas of partnership and rivalry. The partnership pole represents the idea of burden-sharing; the United States has frequently looked for the West Europeans to help in the tasks of stabilising the capitalist system both economically and militarily. On the other hand, there has been frequent retreat from this position when the EC has begun to act independently. The ideal of successive US administrations seems to have been for an EC that would help the United States without challenging its authority.

After the arrival in office of the Bush administration the tenor of US policy towards the EC swung decidedly to the burden-sharing pole. A widely reported speech by Secretary of State James Baker in Berlin in December 1989 stressed the need for the Europeans to get their act together and make the EC into a useful partner in stabilising the new Europe that was emerging. This line ran directly counter to Thatcher's argument that there was no need for greater political unity or for monetary union. Her vision of an EC of independent nation states did not coincide with the desire of the US administration to have a clearly identifiable partner with which it could do business, and one with the capability to act decisively in a crisis.

The Sunday Times ran an article the weekend after Baker's speech in which it identified a number of important advisers in the State Department and White House as the originators of the policy: Robert Zoellick, Counsellor to the State Department and a man whom Baker had taken there with him from the Treasury, was seen as a leading figure in this move to encourage a more unified EC to relieve the burden on the United States. Dennis Ross, Director of Policy Planning in the State Department, was identified as an ally of Zoellick; and in the White House Condoleeza Rica, a Soviet specialist, and Robert Blackwill, a European specialist, were also seen as sharing the same analysis.[6]

Perhaps the difference from Thatcher in the US approach to future unity in the EC was most starkly pointed up in the statement that President Bush made to the European allies of the United States following his Malta summit with President Gorbachev in December 1989, when, in an echo of Mitterrand's words to the European Parliament the previous month, he said, 'The events of our times call both for a continued, perhaps even intensified effort of the twelve to integrate, and a role for the EC as a magnet that draws the forces of reform forward in Eastern Europe'.[7] Although Thatcher subsequently told the House of Commons that the President had telephoned her to say that his position remained one of full support for the open and liberal Europe that she also wanted to see, it looked as though her intergovernmental vision had been pushed aside by the US version of the new European architecture in favour of one that involved much more supranationalism.

The basis for this US attitude was largely economic, although it also recognised the realities of domestic politics in the United States. The hard economic fact that the Bush administration had to deal with was the twin deficits on the budget and the balance of payments, a legacy of the profligate Reagan years. This relative penury was instrumental in the decision to allow the West Europeans to take the lead in the reconstruction of the economies of Central and East Europe. The European Bank for Reconstruction and Development, which began work informally in September 1990 and was officially inaugurated in March 1991, drew half of its capital from Western Europe and only one quarter from the United States, a balance reflected in the nomination of a Frenchman, Jacques Attali, as its head.

To help to bring these domestic economic problems under control, the Bush administation was looking for a reduction in its external defence commitments, with the withdrawal of a larger number of US troops from Europe high on the list of possibilities. The problem here was that although the immediate military threat to Western Europe from the East appeared to have receded, the prospect of regional instability had increased. But leaving US troops in the region so that they could intervene if necessary in intra-European nationalist conflicts was not a viable option even if the United States could have persuaded others to pick up the bill. Avoiding entanglement in European wars is one of the oldest public prejudices in the United States. Much of the population is descended from people who emigrated to the United States precisely in order to get away from such conflicts. The thought of US lives being put at risk to sort out the old problems of the old continent was politically unacceptable.

Hence the pressure from the US administration for a greater degree of

[6] *The Sunday Times*, 17 December 1989.
[7] *The Independent*, 5 December 1989.

unity in the area of security in Europe. In particular, the administration was anxious that the EC should sort itself out on a supranational basis so that the United States could have a single identifiable interlocutor. US administrations have always had trouble in knowing with whom to deal in Europe. They would talk to the British on a particular issue, and then find that the decision on that issue was not influenced by the British. They would talk to the Germans, and then find that on the issue of most importance to them, the German view did not prevail. So to facilitate effective burden-sharing the administration was favourably disposed to the idea of some greater centralisation of decision-making.

Seeing the ground being eroded beneath her, Thatcher appears to have decided to counter-attack. In August 1990 she received the Statesman's Award of the Aspen Institute in Colorado, an international think-tank devoted to improving Western leadership. Her speech there looks as though it was intended to be an American Bruges speech.

The Bruges speech had taken the British intergovernmental view of the future EC onto the European continent. It may reasonably be assumed that it was intended as a direct intervention in the domestic political debate in other Community member states, because if it was intended for a purely British audience it would not have been necessary to go to Belgium to deliver it. On the other hand, the venue could not have been better chosen to generate the maximum publicity in other parts of the EC; and it achieved that, provoking groups and individuals in other member states to voice their doubts about the nature of the project that was being pushed forward by the Commission.

Aspen looks as though it could have been intended as a similar direct intervention in the domestic political debate in the United States about what the future of the new Europe ought to be. In the speech the then prime minister proposed a 'European Magna Carta' which she hoped to see agreed at the forthcoming summit meeting of the CSCE in Paris in November. It would entrench basic rights for all European citizens, including Soviet citizens, and would, amongst other things, enshrine the right to 'maintain nationhood' and for people to remain free from 'fear of an over-mighty state'. This idea seemed to have been aimed at the EC as much as at the Soviet Union, an impression strengthened by comments later in the speech when Thatcher insisted that the door must be left open for the East European states to join the EC, which meant that it must be a Community based on 'willing co-operation between independent sovereign states'. She repeated her assertion that the East European states, 'have not thrown off central command and control in their own countries only to find them reincarnated in the European Community'.[8]

Unfortunately for Thatcher this speech had very limited impact because

<hr />

[8] Transcript of speech supplied by Conservative Political Centre. Reported in *The Independent*, 6 August 1990.

it coincided with the Iraqi invasion of Kuwait and the beginning of an international crisis that fed into the debate on the future of the EC and the shape of the new Europe.

The Gulf crisis

Just as with the collapse of communism in Eastern Europe, the fragmented and slow reaction of the Community states to the crisis in the Gulf was claimed by both sides in the argument over the future of the EC as support for their case.

On 30 August 1990 Thatcher told a conference of the European Democratic Union in Helsinki that all the rhetoric about a common security policy contrasted with the hesitant reaction of some countries when practical measures were required, and repeated a favourite theme, that some other members of the EC were strong on words and weak on action. The clear implication was that the EC was not ready for closer political unity.

In September 1990 the Italian Foreign Minister and then current President of the Council of Ministers, Gianni de Michelis, told journalists that the Community's reaction to the crisis showed the need for the EC to take on a military capability, and that Italy would bring forward a proposal that the Western European Union (WEU) be incorporated into European Political Co-operation (EPC), the intergovernmental mechanism through which the member states of the EC try to co-ordinate their positions on questions of foreign policy. The aim of this incorporation of WEU would be to give the EC an effective defence and security dimension.

WEU is an organisation that was set up in the 1950s in the aftermath of the collapse of a proposal for a European Defence Community. Its importance has been overshadowed by NATO, but it was revived in the 1980s as a means of allowing those Community states that so wished to discuss defence-related issues without bringing defence into the forum of EPC where it would embarrass Ireland, and possibly also Denmark and Greece. These three Community members are not members of WEU.

When the Italian proposal was initially discussed by Foreign Ministers in early October 1990 there was no strong support from other states for the absorption of WEU into the EC, but there was support from both France and Germany for some aspects of the co-ordination of both foreign policy and security policy being decided by majority vote within the EPC framework, a position that the British government was unable to support. Douglas Hurd did, however, admit that the weak response to the Gulf crisis indicated that something must be done.

Eventually, after the change of British prime minister, the outcome of this line of thinking appeared in the form of the British paper to the IGC on political union. Hurd outlined these proposals in the 1991 Winston

Churchill Memorial Lecture.[9] He made it clear that the British government could neither accept the Italian proposal for WEU to be incorporated into EPC, nor the Franco-German proposal for majority voting to be extended to EPC. At the same time he dismissed the argument of more anti-European voices in the Conservative Party that the failure of the EC to respond effectively to the Gulf crisis meant that a common foreign policy was not feasible. On the contrary, he argued that greater unity was necessary to contribute to 'a more peaceful and orderly world'. To facilitate greater unity, the British paper to the IGC would endorse another idea that also had the support of the French, German, and Italian governments: that WEU should become part of some form of European union which would group the EC, EPC, and WEU as three related but distinct entities co-ordinated through the European Council.

Defence would thus be incorporated into an overall framework that would allow it to be handled on an intergovernmental basis alongside the supranational EC and the intergovernmental EPC. Such a multi-faceted entity would allow Britain to be a fully involved member of the new European union, whilst allowing states such as Ireland, which had doubts about the incorporation of the defence element, to play a full role in two of the three forums and absent themselves, or have only observer status, in the third. These ideas were eventually formulated by the Luxembourg presidency of the EC in April 1991 into a 95-page paper which was referred to as the 'non-paper'; this became the text around which the discussions in the IGC centred.

The nature and role of the EC in the new Europe

Already, before the two IGCs began work in December 1990, the debate on the future of the EC in the new Europe had come to centre around the two issues of the degree of supranationalism or of intergovernmentalism that should prevail in its internal arrangements, and the extent to which the EC would take on new functions, particularly with respect to external relations. There was no disagreement that certain economic, diplomatic, and possibly even security functions would have to be performed in the new Europe, and that they would not be performed willingly nor easily by the United States. The disagreement was over whether they should be performed by the EC acting as a sort of European super-state.

The strong intergovernmental line taken by Mrs Thatcher while she was the British prime minster made the debate appear polarised, Britain against the rest. In fact there were serious doubts in many quarters in the EC about the apparent ambition of Jacques Delors to increase the power and authority of the Commission; but it was difficult for the leaders of

[9] Transcript of speech provided by Foreign and Commonwealth Office. Reported in *The Independent*, 20 February 1991.

states where European integration remained a popular concept to appear to side with Thatcher, who had been consistently presented as an enemy of closer unity.

On the other hand, there was also considerable concern in Europe about the position of the newly united Germany, and a strong feeling even amongst those who had previously been allies of the British that it was necessary to constrain this new Germany by strengthening the European framework within which it had to operate, even if that meant some further surrender of their own national sovereignty. This applied particularly to Denmark, which changed its stance from support for the Thatcher line of a Europe of sovereign states to a more pragmatic and flexible position. Despite the apparent anti-German sentiments of some members of the Thatcher government, perhaps including the prime minister herself, the same conclusion was not drawn in London.

The removal of Thatcher from the leadership in November 1990 made it much easier to reach a consensus on both monetary union and political union. John Major's more pragmatic approach brought Britain into line with the position of those other EC states that were both suspicious of the ambitions of Delors and fearful of the potential for domination by the new Germany. Major's conciliatory and low-key style made it easier for other governments to express reservations about too large an increase in the power of the central institutions of the EC without appearing to side with an 'anti-Community' position. It may also have forced them to some extent to do so because the British government could no longer be relied upon to block unwelcome measures of centralisation.

On monetary union, the IGC began to move away from the precise timetable that had apparently been agreed at the Rome meeting of the European Council in October 1990, when Mrs Thatcher had isolated herself and pushed potential allies into the arms of the advocates of the Delors plan. There was increasing acceptance that economic convergence must precede any attempt to move to a monetary union, and discussion around how to achieve economic convergence without an unacceptable degree of direct intervention in the internal economic policy-making of member states made the evolutionary character of the British plan for a 'hard Ecu' as a parallel to national currencies seem increasingly attractive, especially in the context of a British government which was prepared to stress that this *was* an alternative route to monetary union and not a route devised to avoid that destination, as Thatcher had tended to imply.

On political union, the Luxembourg presidency's 'non-paper', while still containing elements over which there was less than total agreement, summarised the way in which thinking had been moving. It rested on the concept of a European Union, with the European Council at its summit, and incorporating within it the EC as one element, but also separate elements of a more intergovernmental nature to deal with external relations, including external security, and with internal aspects of security such as co-operation to control crime and terrorism.

The competences of the EC would be extended to give it a firmer role in social affairs, transport policy, technological research, and energy, and new competences in the areas of health, education, tourism, and cultural policy; but the risk of a creeping further extension of its role was to be removed by an explicit commitment to the principle of 'subsidiarity' (that the member states should continue to perform all functions that they had not agreed to cede to the EC because they could be better performed at that level). There was also a proposal to extend the powers of the European Parliament, which angered Jacques Delors because it implied a downgrading of the role of the Commission in the legislative process of the EC. The external policy and internal security aspects would not come under the EC institutional rules, and would continue to be governed by the principle of consensus. Defence would be handled through WEU, with the possibility that it might be incorporated as an extra element in the Union following the expiry of its existing treaty in 1996.

While a lot of issues remained to be decided, the shape could be seen here of an agreement that would take account of the concern not to create too powerful and centralised an EC, while at the same time tying Germany into a firmly restricting set of obligations, and making provision for the performance of the functions that would have to be performed by some European actor both in the new Europe and in the emerging new world order. Rather than a new superstate, what seemed to be emerging was an economic and social grouping that could continue to act as a magnet to the states of Central and Eastern Europe, combined with a new Congress of Europe.

WHAT ECONOMIC SCENARIO FOR EUROPE?

PATRIZIO BIANCHI*

THE current phase of the process of European integration cannot simply be considered as an extension of the previous model of economic integration. The Single European Act in fact pointed a new direction towards political and economic integration;[1] the removal of remaining non-tariff barriers with the purpose of achieving the completion of a single European market was coupled with a substantial revision of the Community's approach to institutional definition.[2]

In extreme summary this revision can be portrayed as the adoption of a neo-institutionalist and evolutionist approach, in which central authorities only assume the role of deciding general rules which favour a progressive normative readjustment, made by the most efficient agents, companies and local administrations.

On the other hand this very emphasis on efficiency raises the need to contend with the problems of equality and democracy once again, in as much as efficient market solutions do not necessarily translate into socially just and universally accepted solutions, as a wealth of economic literature has shown.[3]

In the past, problems of equality have been confronted in two ways in the European Community: first by giving the weakest countries the right of veto (recognised within a system of unanimous voting) with which they can block those initiatives which might have caused further economic imbalance between the member-countries, thus disturbing the political balance between them; second, by granting subsidies to areas and sectors in crisis, either from the national governments or from a central European bureaucracy which should compensate and regulate national imbalance.

During the economic crisis of the seventies, however, this mechanism jammed. There were signs of a political blockade within the same Community, in as much as the internal crisis in each country led the national governments to introduce policies to protect and safeguard their own

* Professor of Economics and Finance of European Communities at the University of Bologna, Italy. This chapter has been translated by Christopher Stevens.

[1] Commission of the European Community, *White Paper on Completing the Internal Market*, The Commission, Brussels, 1987; and 'The Single Act: a New Frontier for Europe', *Bulletin of the European Community*, Supplement, 1987.

[2] Commission of the European Community, 'The Economics of 1992', *European Economy*, no. 35, March 1988.

[3] T. Padoa Schioppa, *Efficiency, Stability and Equity: a Strategy for the Evolution of the Economic System of the EC*, European Commission, Brussels, 1987; K. Arrow, *Social Choice and Individual Value*, John Wiley, New York, 1963.

national industry. The different governments' vetoes were therefore rendered useless with regard to the Commission's active policy initiatives.

In the early eighties, however, an extensive group of companies and local administrations interested in overcoming this deadlock was consolidated. The rapid success of political initiatives in re-starting European economic integration can in fact be explained by the need for many strong nations to create an extension of their internal market suitable for their growth requirements, after years of intense internal re-organisation.[4]

Today, the new phase of European integration is characterised by the acceptance of a political vision focused on the efficiency of companies and of administrations, with emphasis on the positive effects of competition, not only between single units but also between productive and social systems. Indeed, the very model of institutional evolution inherent in the principle of 'reciprocal recognition' implies that local authorities and enterprises can converge in the definition of production standards and even social regulations so as to create positive local conditions for development. Thus, regions with strong structures in social and political terms, like the German *Länder*, can offer an environment which is in itself a positive externality for companies which are based there, thus anticipating and leading the whole normative evolution of the Community.

The adoption of the rule of majority voting for Community decisions strengthens this position by removing the powerful weapon of the veto and thus obliging the weakest countries to pursue rapid realignment measures. But there is simultaneously a need to require the strongest countries to offer the weakest the means to accelerate the development of less favoured regions. This perspective therefore gives rise to the concern that the new phase of European integration might accentuate regional differences, thus creating a substantial divergence beween strong regions and peripheral ones. The weak regions then appear so not only because their companies are less efficient but because their public administration and local social fabric are fragile, too.

The 'efficiency' approach, based on the recognition of the role played by the most efficient competitors, whether they are companies or governments, has been combined with far-reaching reform of the European Community's structural policies. This has been done with the aim of promoting and sustaining widespread entrepreneurial activity, especially in less developed regions, so as to reinforce the internal social fabric and the local economy.

This outline requires, however, that the favoured areas be well-delineated within a 'European system' and in a position to participate actively in this process of normative evolution, based on competition. Yet the seven transitional years between the declaration of the Single Act and its full implementation have been a period of complex structural

---

[4] For an analysis of the structural changes in European industries, see H. W. de Jong, *The Structure of European Industry*, second edition, Kluwer, Dordrecht, 1988.

65

transformation for Europe and have shown, among other things, that the less favoured areas are not a marginal but a relevant and decisive part of Europe as a whole. Moreover, the speed of events in Western Europe has swept away any possibility of prediction and, on the other hand, Western Europe has shown an economic vitality which was greatly undervalued in previous years.

Following a period of obvious crisis, which was so great that the annual growth rate of the gross domestic product (GDP) was significantly reduced and unemployment rose (especially because of the increase in the UK, Ireland and Greece), there has recently been an evident upturn.

This upturn comes at a time of world economic expansion, which the very act of completing the single market tends to consolidate, favouring the development of techical investment (as seen in Table 1) and of financial investment activities. The growth of industrial concentration operations in fact dates back to 1987 as proof of a rapid structural change within European industry.[5] Unemployment also declined (see Table 2).

TABLE 1   GROWTH OF INVESTMENT AND EMPLOYMENT IN THE EC (annual percentage or variation)

	1960–73	1973–81	1981–84	1984–87	1987–90
GDP	4.8	1.9	1.6	2.6	3.4
Employment	0.3	−0.1	−0.5	0.8	1.4
Investment	5.6	−0.4	−0.1	3.6	6.7

Source: EC, *XXII General Report on Economic Activity in the European Community*, The Commission, Brussels, 1989, p. 34.

TABLE 2   LEVEL OF UNEMPLOYMENT IN THE EUROPEAN COMMUNITY, AS PERCENTAGE OF TOTAL ACTIVE POPULATION

1973	1981	1984	1987	1990
2.8	8.1	10.8	10.4	8.7

Source: EC, *XXII General Report on Economic Activity in the European Community*, The Commission, Brussels, 1989, p. 35.

A moment of drastic change, however, occurred in 1989: the political events in the East quickly changed the European political reference framework. The slowing down of the economy, which hit every country, with the exception of Federal Germany in 1990, illuminated very clearly the many internal problems in marginal European regions. Meanwhile,

[5] The number of operations in Europe has increased constantly between 1985 and 1989; the EC registered 480 operations in 1984–5, 562 in 1985–6 (an increase of 17.1 per cent), 708 in 1986–7 (26 per cent) (European Commission, *XVIII Report on Competition Policy*, The Commission, Brussels, 1989).

immigration from countries in the Mediterranean Basin also increased pressure on Europe.

Such diverse structural problems must evidently influence the future development of the Community, and they probably cannot be confronted and resolved merely by structural policies directed at less favoured regions.

Differences and homogeneity in the EC

The good performance of the European economy in the eighties was the result of national and regional situations which were still very different. Many regional disparities show, both in terms of per capita gross production, and in unemployment and the categories affected by it (women and under twenty-fives). It is not just a matter of considerable differences noticeable between regions belonging to different countries but also between different regions within a single country (see Table 3).

Through a consideration of the gross internal product by region, expressed in terms of purchasing power standard (PPS), substantial gaps appear between European regions: given a European average of 100, figures vary from the 182 of Hamburg and the 54 of Greece and Portugal. These differences are much greater than those between national figures.[6]

The differences have partially narrowed with time due to replacements of investment in peripheral regions and migration toward stronger areas; nonetheless major disparities remain. These see a group of northern regions perpetually in a position of strength and a group of southern regions permanently on the lowest revenue level. The only significant changes are the more rapid growth of the German regions and the relative decline of the regions of Great Britain and Belgium.

From this early evidence it is clear that a centre and a periphery exist: given a standard purchasing power of 100 per inhabitant, the following all rate over 120: Hamburg, Ile de France, the Aosta Valley, Brussels, the Northern Netherlands, Bremen, Liguria, Lombardy and Emilia-Romagna, Hessen, West Berlin, Luxembourg, Piedmont, Baden-Württemberg. Below 80 are the whole of Greece, Portugal and Ireland, Southern Italy and large areas of Spain. Vast areas of France and Great Britain are, however, little above these modest figures.

Therefore a Europe can be identified which is characterised by a central

---

[6] Per capita income for 1988 (in PPS) the richest region (Hamburg, 28.841 ECU) is 3.78 times higher than the per capita PIL of the poorest region (Nisia, 7429); the relation between per capita income in PPS of the richest country (Federal Germany) and the poorest country (Portugal) falls however to 2. The PPS is a unit of measurement which expresses the price of an identical volume of goods and services for each country and which allows a comparison of states based on the real purchasing power of citizens, taking different price levels into account; accounting in per capita income without PPS adjustment shows much greater differences.

TABLE 3   REGIONAL DISPARITIES IN THE EC, 1988

	Population (000s)	GDP (millions ecus)	Per capital GDP (purchasing power equivalents)*	Index**
TOTAL EC	324116	4031571	15828	100
BELGIUM	9883	127031	15971	101
Flanders	5693	73598	16063	101
Wallonia	3213	34194	13225	84
Brussels	977	19239	24466	155
DENMARK	5130	90997	17184	109
GERMANY***	61418	1017432	17907	113
Schleswig-Holstein	2625	36190	14906	94
Hamburg	1578	42112	28841	182
Lower Saxony	7229	103148	15425	97
Bremen	657	14093	23183	146
North Rhine Wesphalia	16752	266612	17204	109
Hessen	5569	104107	20208	128
Rhineland Palatinate	3628	53518	15947	101
Baden-Württemberg	9369	163781	18897	119
Bavaria	11077	183482	17906	113
Saar	1047	15993	16514	104
W. Berlin	1888	34397	19697	124
GREECE	9992	44435	8819	54
North	3227	13766	8268	52
Central-South	2291	10183	8614	54
Attica	3526	16755	9209	58
Nisia	948	3732	7629	48
SPAIN	38996	287922	11821	75
North-West	4525	31041	10982	89
North-East	4196	36450	13907	88
Madrid	4914	41764	13606	86
Centre	5425	34441	10165	64
East	10550	87251	13242	84
South	7939	46511	9380	59
Canary Islands	1449	10464	11561	73
FRANCE	55750	804189	17168	108
Ile de France	10312	225272	26001	164
Paris Basin	10201	134816	15729	99
North Pas de Calais	3937	45695	13815	87
East	5032	66069	15626	99
West	7428	89103	14277	90
South-West	5850	72179	14686	93
Central-East	6533	90689	16523	104
Mediterranean Area	6458	80367	14812	94
IRELAND	3538	27494	10304	65

TABLE 3   (*continued*)

	Population (000s)	GDP (millions ecus)	Per capital GDP (purchasing power equivalents)*	Index**
ITALY	57450	701777	16422	104
North-West	6293	88473	18900	119
Lombardy	8911	144331	21775	138
North-East	6491	89489	18534	117
Emilia-Romagna	3949	59499	20255	128
Central	5838	76606	17639	111
Lazio	5127	71327	18703	118
Campania	5691	44881	10602	67
Abruzzi-Molise	1592	16268	13740	67
South	6795	54054	10695	66
Sicily	5116	42307	11117	70
Sardinia	1647	14544	11873	75
LUXEMBOURG	373	5555	19131	121
NETHERLANDS	14760	193264	16244	103
North	1611	25032	19273	122
East	2987	32513	13502	65
West	6896	96740	17403	110
PORTUGAL (Continental)	9761	35298	8583	54
UNITED KINGDOM	57065	696177	15994	107
North	3084	32457	14659	93
Yorkshire and Humberside	4912	53851	15271	96
East Midlands	3952	44968	15848	100
East Anglia	2018	24021	16578	105
South East	17359	257309	20648	130
South West	4599	53426	16181	102
West Midlands	5210	57048	15263	96
North West	6385	72016	15710	99
Wales	2843	28634	14030	89
Scotland	5124	58113	15797	100
Northern Ireland	1579	14344	12654	80

*Purchasing power equivalents express for each country the price of an identical volume of goods and services.
**Data in previous column expressed in terms of EC average = 100.
***Borders of former West Germany.
Source: Eurostat.

axis, with high revenue, and a progressively more depressed periphery. This image of polarisation is further demonstrated by analyses which take account of territorial infrastructure, quality of life and other indicators, of all those elements which can be considered positive external factors for companies and citizens.[7] Through a consideration of international relations, communications, economic capacity, research and technology and cultural organisation it becomes even more obvious that on top of an old centre given as the area of early industrialisation in Belgium, Holland, Eastern France and North-West Germany, there is now a long line which unites London with Milan.

DATAR[8] defines this as a *Mégapole* to show that it is a single conurbation which divides Europe vertically into two increasingly diverse halves. This megalopolis, in fact, masses around Frankfurt, having to its north the old line of development towards Bonn and Cologne and therefore Amsterdam and Brussels, and to the south moving towards the Munich, Stuttgart and Zürich triangle before reaching Milan. By this rather forced but useful geography, attention is drawn to the role of London, Paris and Hamburg. Madrid, Rome and Vienna follow a long way behind; and Barcelona, Marseilles and Lyons through to the Po Valley look promising.

As for the rest, there are the different peripheries: the entire Iberian peninsula with few, already noted, exceptions; the whole of Central and Southern Italy; and again the whole of Greece, Ireland and Great Britain (apart from the South-East), Denmark, northernmost Germany, and finally the Atlantic area of France itself.

Pirelli's analysis offers a seemingly different geometry which nevertheless results in the unambiguous establishment of a 'European heartland'. The crucial element in this analysis is the consideration of the line of development which coincides with the Rhine Valley, stretching as far as the sea in the north and London by extension, and to Milan in the south. Its internal nature is in fact quite different, as it is necessary to talk of an old heart arranged around the Paris, London, Cologne triangle and a new heart around the more southerly triangle which has Frankfurt, Stuttgart and Munich in the north, reaches Emilia and Florence in the south and gathers in Lyons, Marseilles, Barcelona and Valencia in the west.

Using synthetic indicators of centrality, which combine all these facts (which are in truth not entirely homogenous), a clear-cut European core takes shape. It consists of the three central German *Länder* (Nordrhein-Westfalen, Rheinland-Pfalz, Baden-Württemberg), the regions around the

---

[7] Different studies have recently confronted these aspects. As well as the *Regional Statistics Yearbook*, Eurostat, Luxembourg, 1987, see I. Begg, 'European Integration and Regional Policy', *Oxford Review of Economic Policy*, vol. 5, no. 2, 1989, which reflects on these facts, and also works of remarkable analytical depth, such as Pirelli, Ufficio Studi, *Le Regione Europee in Prospettiva*', Quaderni di Formazione, no. 71, 1989, and DATAR, 'Les Villes Européennes', La Documentation Française, 1989; Pirelli considers roads, motorways, railways, ports, airports, telephone subscriptions, electricity consumption, hospital beds; DATAR adds light infrastructuralisation: fairs, congresses, cultural offerings, press circulation and the so-called *activités technopolitaines*; both studies then consider research activities, universities and centres of advanced education, and the role of financial and banking institutions in production activities.

[8] *Ibid.*

major North Sea ports and the metropolitan areas of London and Paris. Around this there is an area of expansion consisting of the Parisian Basin and Eastern France, the English Midlands, North Italy and the remaining German regions. There is a further minor development area and finally a periphery of Portugal, the Spanish South, Southern Italy and Greece.

On the other hand, the relevance of major urban centres re-emerges clearly, be they those of the German megalopolis or Paris and London. The power of attraction of large metropolitan areas is also confirmed by recent studies on Europe, for example those on Vienna. The development of tertiary activities linked to the financial management of the economy, or to service activities, requires an urban continuum, which on the one hand changes the social structure of the city, but on the other increases the localised advantages of the activities, and underlines the convenience of urbanisation.

European cities, and capitals in particular, also have different levels of importance: the major communications infrastructures, the power of attraction for banking, insurance and management enterprises dependent on the existence of effective financial markets, and the wealth of promotional and cultural initiatives put the different cities in very different positions in relation to each other. A large conurbation with inferior services, poor transport infrastructures, demographic pressure and a high crime rate becomes thoroughly unattractive and its negative aura then expands over all the vast subnational, or even national, area that is connected with it.

Certainly minor urban centres can develop important roles in attracting development, but this only seems possible if they are well connected to each other and form an urban continuum of the type exemplified by the Rhine Valley. In this case, for the centres of the Po Valley, for the area between Valencia, Barcelona and Saragossa and for the Southern French area between Lyons, Marseilles and Nice, the main element in development will be the creation of infrastructures linked to airports, motorways and underground systems, but also development of universities and research centres, trade fairs, coordinated development of production services, and cultural and educational activities on an international level. In this sense the effort of the French government to develop the southern triangle undoubtedly seems to be fruitful, leading to the growth of an already well-developed area. The transfer of major research and university activities to the south (for example the transfer of the *École Centrale* to Lyons, and the transfer of many laboratories to Sophia Antipolis) has been a precise indication, which has also been sustained by important infrastructural investments. On the other hand, the vast area outside the line which connects Paris and Lyons—Nice—Marseilles still seems destined for a much slower development; for the regions of western France it is a matter of areas with a meagre population density, and a meagre demographic dynamism and poor drawing power. Moreover, in the north, regions such as the Pas de Calais and the nearby areas of

71

Belgium exist, which still have problems of decline linked to a lengthy restructuring of old industrial organisations.

German centrality

It is time to consider the reasons for Germany's confirmed central position. What emerges clearly is that along the Rhine Valley the urban fabric has become substantially denser, and this has led to the definition of a continuous and extensive urban structure which nevertheless has no centre of attraction as in Paris or London. All the efforts of one country have been concentrated on this conglomeration, which, while in some respects disadvantaged by Germany's quite exceptional political situation before 1990, has also benefited. First there is the concentration forced by all the activities in this relatively highly-favoured area, due to its long-standing settlement and the extraordinary external economy at its disposal, which means that the Rhine axis directs and therefore orders all commerce. Then it must be remembered that Germany, like Japan, was able to concentrate all its efforts on reconstruction after the war without having to invest in defence. Best of all, for many years Federal Germany was fated to live off the advantages of the industrial and military system which sustained the American economy, without having to pay for the effects in terms of public deficit and ensuing inflation.

Using a dualistic scheme of analysis of regional development (a scheme, that is, by which the country is divided in two regions, wherein growth is progressively differentiated due to the more dynamic region draining the resources of the slower one) the separation of the Eastern *Länder* led to the paradox that the expanding areas first drained the human resources—above all qualified technicians—of the less-developed area (the Eastern *Länder*), but did not then have to absorb the cost of balancing this, precisely because these backward regions were incorporated into another completely separate state.

The expansion phase was finally completed with the use of a very strong supply of unskilled labour, which, unlike in Italy, was foreign and therefore quite separate from the national workforce; it could for that reason easily be kept in disdainful association. The same recent immigration has different characteristics to those seen in France, Great Britain, Holland and Belgium, where the immigrants came from previously colonised countries and therefore countries which had a sort of referential obligation for their respective colonisers.

Moreover, these elements coincide with the definition of an institutional order which had a firm grasp of how to link the diverse representative parts of the system, from the organisation of banks to local governments and unions: the very ownership of German companies was entrusted to administrative boards based around a large bank, on which all these parties sat. Thus a social and political continuum was created which allowed the management of rapid changes without substantial damage to the interior of the country. It is this solid ownership web within German industry which guarantees the success of the restructuring of the companies gained with the unification of 3 October 1990.

Indeed, reunification of Germany has possibilities for economic success, despite the obvious tensions connected with transition, precisely because the dense net of economic and social ties which links the structure of the federal economy can be extended into the territories of the East. The weight of necessary adjustment is considerable but manageable for the federal authorities, even if they remain very uncertain about the cost and the timescale of an effective economic integration of the two areas.

TABLE 4   THE GDR AND THE FRG: KEY STATISTICS

	GDR[1]		FRG[1]	
	1970	1988	1970	1988
Area (000 km²)	—	108.3	—	248.6
Population (millions)	17.1	16.4	61.7	61.5
Age structure				
−15 years	23.3	19.3	23.2	14.6
15–65 years	61.1	67.4	63.6	70.1
65 years and over	15.6	13.3	13.2	15.3
Working population[2]	45.5	51.5	44.0	48.1
Nominal income/GNP[3]				
Current prices				
Total (billion)	n.a.	356.0	675.7	2 121.7
Per capita ('000)	n.a.	21.7	11.1	34.5
Constant prices				
Total (billion)	121.6	268.4	1 135.0	1 701.8
Per capita ('000)	7.1	16.4	18.7	27.7
Public-sector spending[4]				
Total (billion)	70.6	269.7	265.5	945.6
Per capita ('000)	4.1	16.4	4.3	15.3

1. Including East and West Berlin respectively.
2. In per cent of total population.
3. In East German marks and Deutschemarks respectively.
4. Net national income in constant 1985 prices for the GDR, gross value added in constant 1980 prices for the FRG.
Source: Sachverständigenrat, Sondergutachten 20/1 1990, Anhang 1; OECD, Economic Outlook, OECD, Paris, 1990.

The German Democratic Republic (GDR) was, however, a country of small to average dimensions with approximately a quarter of the population of the FRG and a GNP 10 to 15 per cent of the FRG's; its production machinery, although more efficient than the other socialist economies, showed such low productivity characteristics that drastic restructuring operations were nevertheless required (see Table 4).

The path of rapid unification (opening of borders on 9 November 1989, monetary and economic union on 1 July 1990, unification on 3 October 1990) in fact generated many internal problems, particularly in connection with the 1:1 conversion of the DM (Western Mark) and OM (Eastern Mark) and therefore with the readjustment of the expenditure flow. If the exchange rate between OM and DM is considered equal, the 1988 average gross monthly wage income of the GDR was DM1300 compared with the FRG's DM3300, therefore about 40 per cent; the productivity of the GDR was approximately a half of that of the FRG; moreover, employment was concentrated in manufacturing, defined in a state-planned economic scheme, which had no international market nor any competition in the internal market. The structure of prices in the GDR was also quite different to that of the FRG, with the prices of basic commodities much lower and the prices of durable goods much higher than those of the FRG.[9]

The restructuring of East German industry led to a drastic reduction in employment which caused widespread unemployment and great social tension in the East. In the space of four months, between July and October 1990, unemployment in East Germany reached 550,000 and there were approximately 1,750,000 part-time workers. By June 1991, however, half of West German companies had either invested directly in the East or had bought companies from the trustee company which was set up for the sale of companies which were already the state possession of the GDR. Unification in fact led to the establishment of extraordinary privatisation and industrial reorganisation bodies, which, however, in due course had to manage the social problems connected with unemployment. It has further been estimated that the productivity of companies in the East might rise by about 15 per cent a year, thus reaching the levels of the West in about three years.

A significant example of effective economic transition taking place is given by the reunification of the two Carl Zeiss companies created after the war. The Jena (Thuringia) Carl Zeiss is the oldest and most prestigious German optical company; after the war the head office was nationalised by the GDR. At the same time a new Carl Zeiss was created in Baden-Württemberg. On 13 June 1991 the *Treuhandanstalt* announced the reunification of the two companies; the western company had originally stated that it was not interested in the direct acquisition of the eastern company as it considered the plant obsolete and the local market undesirable. Then, however, it proceeded to a level of unification which foresaw that the two proprietor-regions of the two companies (Baden-

---

[9] For example, 5 kg. of potatoes cost OM0.85 in GDR in 1988, and DM4.94 in FRG; 1 kg. of meat OM9.80 and DM17.19; childrens' shoes OM18.50 and DM60.60; monthly rent OM75 and DM411; tramway tickets OM0.20 and DM2.07. On the other hand, a washing machine costs OM2300 and DM981 respectively; a refrigerator OM1425 and DM559; a colour television set OM4900 and DM1539 (OECD, *German Economic Survey*, OECD, Paris, 1990, p. 60).

Württemberg and Thuringia) would found a Foundation in which the profitable western and eastern activities would converge, whilst the unprofitable activities of the eastern company would remain separate in a company which would have to be helped by the *Treuhand*; the latter then projected subsidies of 3.6 billion marks for this single company, essentially aimed at meeting the social cost of restructuring: in fact only 10,000 of the current 27,000 employees could be re-employed. Thus, only the potentially profitable parts of the previous activities would be separated and re-incorporated with western companies, without the social costs of restructuring which would remain the responsibility of the *Treuhand*.

The reunification of the five Eastern *Länder* is a great opportunity for investment, which could keep internal demand high for coming years. This demand would have to be sustained either by growth in the demand for durable goods, buoyed up by the revalued savings made by a level exchange rate, or by demand for investment from private companies, which are needed to restructure the eastern companies, or by federal and local public demand. West German businessmen have estimated that investment in the East will be about six billion dollars a year.[10]

The major infrastructural investments to be completed in the next few years, like the reconstruction of railways, motorways and telecommunications, for example, and the cost of moving the capital from Bonn to Berlin that was decided at the end of June 1991, therefore project volumes of investment which will provide opportunities for the economy of new Federal Germany notwithstanding the obvious social and political problems connected with the management of the transition.

Despite the serious problems connected with the reconversion of a state-planned economy to a market economy, and despite the recession coinciding with the Gulf Crisis, all indications are favourable. Indeed, in the period 1989–91 the German economy was the only one in Europe to show growth.

With unification the 'central' role of the new united Germany in the European economy is therefore strengthened. Indeed, the distance between Germany and the other major countries of the EC becomes even clearer. Thus, if a clear French supremacy can be identified in the origins of the European Community, and a progressive balancing between France and the FRG, Italy and the UK in the seventies, German supremacy has become increasingly obvious since the eighties. It is now being consolidated in even clearer terms with the reunification of the Eastern *Länder* and the opening up of the countries of the East.

North and South Europe

An analysis of South Europe is well delineated by the identification of areas which show growth and those which are in decline. As described

[10] UNIDO, *Industry and Development: Global Report 1990–91*, UNIDO, Vienna, 1990.

above, there is an arc of Mediterranean regions between Valencia and North Italy which showed sustained rhythms of growth in the eighties. This 'North of the South' can effectively become a new pole of attraction for European development; however, it has to pay for many infrastructural limitations, such as, for example, the European lines of communication which were all conceived in a vertical direction.

Thus, as with German unification and the opening of the countries of the East, the construction of horizontal lines of communication will become important. It will also be necessary to construct fast communications networks in the Mediterranean arc. If these do not come about in a short space of time, traditional lines of development between these areas and the respective political and economic capitals will prevail.

In the years 1988 to 1990 we have, however, witnessed a potential reduction in the disparity in incomes in real terms within the Community; the positions of Spain, Portugal and Ireland have improved and moved closer to the European average: on the other hand the position of Greece has most recently deteriorated, as has that of some Southern Italian regions (see Table 5).

What level of investment attraction do these areas have? (See Table 6.) In the present framework it seems that the level of attraction inside areas which are apparently similar varies greatly. In Spain, for example, the triangle between Seville, Jerez de la Frontera/Cadiz and Huelva seems to be far superior to other southern areas. Andalusian growth is, however, taking place within a growing Spanish economy, in an area of long-standing industrialisation (dockyards) and with large public investment.

In this context Southern Italy seems to lose much of its attraction, precisely because of the massing of problems linked to the poverty of urban structures, the deterioration of the environment and insufficient infrastructure. The consequence is a well-noted disaffection, for example in the flow of international investment which seems systematically at this point to have deserted Southern Italy and to be directed exclusively towards Spain.[11] (See Table 7.)

Therefore if there emerges a significant problem for Southern Italy linked to the communications infrastructures and even more to a general problem of urban restructuring, it should be pointed out that the huge Italian public deficit will scarcely permit future filling of this gap in infrastructural endowment of the southern territory with public funds.

The analysis of the southern area of the EC would not, however, be adequate if the countries of the southern shores of the Mediterranean were not taken into account. An analysis of these countries in fact suggests a very worrying situation. An element which will necessarily characterise the immediate future of Europe will indeed be migrations from outside the community, in particular from the Mediterranean Basin.

In demographic terms Europe appears clearly divided into areas with

---

[11] ISMERI EUROPA, *Il Sudeuropa: una analisi strutturale*, Rome, mimeo, 1990.

TABLE 5   PER CAPITA GDP, SOUTHERN EUROPE

	1980	1985	1989	1980–89
Italy	102.5	103.6	104.8	2.3
Mezzogiorno	69.9	70.9	72.3	2.4
Centre-North	119.0	121.8	123.3	4.3
Spain	73.4	71.8	75.7	2.3
Portugal	54.2	52.1	54.5	0.2
Greece	58.2	56.0	54.0	4.2
W. Germany	113.8	114.4	113.3	0.5
France	111.9	110.7	108.5	1.2
EC North*	107.6	108.0	107.8	0.2
All EC	100.0	100.0	100.0	

*All EC countries except Italy, Greece, Portugal, Spain.
Source: Eurostat and ISMERI-Europa.

TABLE 6   GROSS FIXED CAPITAL FORMATION, CURRENT PRICES, AS PERCENTAGE OF GDP

	1961–70	1971–80	1981–89
Italy	26.2	24.6	21.1
Centre-North	24.8	22.7	19.8
Mezzogiorno	30.8	28.0	22.3
Spain	24.0	24.5	21.0
Portugal	23.4	26.5	26.4
Greece	21.4	24.2	19.2
All EC	23.2	22.7	19.7

Source: Eurostat.

TABLE 7   DIRECT EXTERNAL INVESTMENT, 1980–87

	1980–83		1984–87	
	inwards	outwards	inwards	outwards
Italy	3098	4668	5321	7825
Spain	5470	1158	10111	1392
Portugal	533		888	39
Greece	1765		1841	

Source: IMF Statistics of Balance of Payments, various years.

different demographic dynamics, from areas which are plainly negative to
areas of strong growth, from areas which attract population to stagnant
ones. A high-density central European area, but one with ever-declining
rates of local birth, can immediately be identified, and a periphery which
appears less dense with the exception of conurbations around capitals.
Peripheral areas certainly have higher birth rates but generally lower population densities and little capacity to attract immigrants. The situation is
different, for example, in Naples which shows high density, high birth rates
and a high-level attraction for immigration.

TABLE 8   PROJECTED DEMOGRAPHIC DEVELOPMENT, EUROPEAN
COMMUNITY AND MEDITERRANEAN BASIN, 1985–2000

	Population 1985 (millions)	Population 2000 (millions)	Growth (per cent)	Percentage aged under 25
W. Germany*	61.00	58.40	−4.00	17.00
France	55.00	56.80	3.30	22.00
Denmark	5.10	5.10	0.00	18.00
Netherlands	14.50	15.20	5.00	19.00
Belgium	9.90	9.80	−1.90	19.00
Luxembourg	0.37	0.37	1.90	17.00
United Kingdom	56.40	57.00	1.00	20.00
Ireland	3.50	4.10	16.50	29.60
Spain	38.50	41.70	18.00	26.00
Portugal	10.30	11.10	8.00	26.00
Italy	57.40	57.80	1.00	21.00
Greece	10.10	10.90	8.00	22.00
All EC	322.00	330.00	3.00	19.00
Morocco	24.30	37.50	59.00	46.00
Algeria	22.20	35.50	60.00	46.00
Tunisia	7.20	9.70	35.00	40.00
Libya	4.00	6.70	60.00	46.00
Egypt	48.30	67.30	39.00	40.00
Israel	4.20	5.20	29.00	33.00
Syria	10.60	18.10	70.00	47.00
Turkey	52.10	71.30	37.00	39.00
Yugoslavia	23.10	24.60	6.50	24.00

*NB 2000 projection is for boundaries of former West Germany.
Source: Ufficio Studi, Pirelli, 'Le regioni europee in prospettiva', Quaderni di formazione,
no. 71, 1990.

This situation can be contrasted with the much more considerable
pressure of North African countries. Table 8 shows, for example, the
demographic structure of the countries of the Mediterranean Basin as it
appeared in the years 1985 to 1990. North Africa shows some 40 to

45 per cent of its population to be under 15 and a fair estimate foresees possible employment for no more than one in ten of them.[12]

The economic situation of these countries has moreover greatly deteriorated in the eighties; the growth rhythm, which had remained high in the fifteen-year period up to 1980, slowed down abruptly in the first half of the eighties and then made a modest recovery between 1986 and 1988; the food dependence of these countries has greatly increased in the eighties and the loss shown in current accounts has risen in consequence.

In the next twenty years, therefore, the Mediterranean Basin will become a crucial point for the Community: the countries of Southern Europe will increase their demographic weight within the Community, increasing the burden on less-favoured areas of the Community; demographic pressure coming from the south will also be very heavy; indeed the Mediterranean European regions will have approximately 130 million inhabitants in 2015, but at the same time North African and Middle Eastern countries overlooking the Mediterranean will have approximately 370 million inhabitants (of which 270 million are in Turkey, Egypt, Algeria and Morocco).

The EC, moreover, has held an ambiguous attitude to these countries, offering itself as an economic and political referent but in reality maintaining a very limited commercial and co-operative policy which is certainly inadequate for the size of the problems. Agreements of association or co-operation drawn up in the second half of the seventies have not been able to achieve the agreed objectives. In the commercial sector the main limitation has been the protectionist measures taken against food products in the early eighties. The extension of the EC to the North Mediterranean countries has recently eroded market quotas for the agricultural produce of these countries and the additional co-operation agreements (1987–8) were limited to the guarantee of existing import levels until 1995.

The countries of Eastern Europe

The problems of the Eastern countries of Europe are now added to these still considerable imbalances between the countries of West Europe. The democratic transition, brought about with the changes of 1989 culminating in the German reunification of 3 October 1990, is taking shape through profound changes in the internal management and ownership structures, which nevertheless translated into a substantial slowing-down, if not total halt, of industrial production activity.

Considering, for example, the variation in GDP (gross domestic product), MVA (manufacturing value added) and manufacturing employment, the fall in production of the last four years becomes apparent (see Table 9). Obviously this need to complete major structural transformations

[12] UNIDO, *op. cit.*

during a period of internal standstill aggravates the causes of social tension and makes political control of democratic transition difficult.

Which areas seem to be in a position to link into the strong development area, and what problems arise for this reconnection? In the East European sphere it is necessary to distinguish the problems of areas that have previously been industrialised (essentially Hungary, Czechoslovakia and Poland) from areas which were marginalised even before the assertion of central governments and economies (the Balkan area).

TABLE 9 ANNUAL PERCENTAGE GROWTH IN GDP AND MVA, WORLD REGIONS

	Gross domestic product (GDP)			Manufacturing value added (MVA)		
	1989	1990	1991	1989	1990	1991
North America	3.10	2.50	3.20	3.60	1.70	3.60
W. Europe	3.40	3.30	3.80	4.50	3.60	4.60
E. Europe	2.10	0.40	0.60	2.20	0.90	−0.30
Japan	4.90	5.00	6.10	6.10	6.80	8.40

Source: UNIDO, *Industrial and Development, Global Report 1990–91*, UNIDO, Vienna, 1990.

Table 10 shows how there are important internal differences within Eastern countries, but above all how the economic and social structure in 1988 was far from the OECD average.[13] Per capita income of the GDR was twice that of Romania. It is also clear that the growth of per capita income in all countries was greatly slowed down in the eighties, bearing out the economic crisis which was then irreversible. Romania was itself a borderline case which after sustaining growth well above the OECD average in the seventies collapsed in the early eighties.

The same table shows how the socialist economies were opened to international commerce, above all in the sphere of the CMEA (Council for Mutual Economic Assistance), but also how the same countries had an important flow of manufacturing goods towards the countries of the OECD. It must, however, be noted that a clear structural difficulty for these economies is shown in the fall in the size of their export quotas in the OECD area, in particular in the cases of Czechoslovakia and Poland as well as Romania. In the last three years, however, only Czechoslovakia and Hungary have shown a reversal of this trend.

The economic evolution of recent months, marked by the very important internal political events in Eastern countries and in the old Soviet Union especially, and the dramatic events connected with the Gulf crisis, nevertheless show the existence of different attitudes to a full renewal of relations with the countries of the European Community. These changes must be compared with the complex problems of structural

[13] OECD, *Economic Outlook*, OECD, Paris, 1990, p. 49.

and institutional order which will be involved in the transition from state-planned to market economies.[14]

Czechoslovakia, Poland and Hungary bear witness, although with different attitudes, to the immediate effect of reintegration. These attitudes are clearly shown by the political events of recent months and simultaneously by the state of relative deterioration in which the economies of these countries are now found.

Czechoslovakia performed considerably better than the other Eastern countries in 1990. With a fall of only 1 per cent in GNP in the first half of 1990 Czechoslovakia reacted much better than other countries to the first phase of the restructuring of its own economy by a system of centralisation and closure leading into a new phase signalled by the presence of important market elements.

The choice of the Czechoslovakian leaders therefore seems to be for a slow readjustment which avoids massive employment problems and strong inflationary tension with obvious relapses in terms of social destabilisation. In the first half of 1990 the government in fact succeeded in containing the rise in retail prices to under 1 per cent and the rise in consumer prices to under 4 per cent. In the second half of the year substantial rises in the prices of foodstuffs were fixed, which nevertheless appear to remain within the limits of control thanks to a careful fiscal and monetary policy carried out by the central authorities.

Even if industrial production declined in 1990 and energy and mining production also contracted, generating negative effects in terms of foreign dependence in sectors crucial to development, the rise in investments in fixed capital and especially in machinery must be noted. According to reliable opinion, seen in the light of other sources, it is fair to estimate that investments rose by 3 per cent during 1990, approximately 40 per cent of which was concentrated in industrial activity and particularly in the modernisation of machinery, rather than in the construction of installations. This is evidence of a strategy of small but safe steps in the quest for a recovery of productivity in the sectors already in existence, such as machine construction.[15]

---

[14] In structural terms the whole order of relative specialisation needs redefining, still being strongly orientated towards the production of basic goods such as metal products, non-electrical machinery and plastic products (UNIDO, *op. cit.*, p. 57); it should be pointed out that services, too, either for individuals or companies (government purpose and market service) remain underdeveloped in Eastern countries (OECD, *Services in Central and Eastern European Countries*, OECD, Paris, 1991). In institutional terms, moreover, it should be remembered that this transition implies a complex redefinition of rights of ownership. This redefinition becomes essential to any further economic and political stabilisation (OECD, *Transformation of Planned Economy, Property Rights Reform and Macroeconomic Stability*, OECD, Paris, 1991).

[15] A decisive reorientation of exports toward western countries, a good increase in the number of local private companies (from 86,000 in December 1989 to 224,000 in June 1990), a not too disastrous infrastructure in the Bohemian area, accompanied by a cautiously positive judgement of the activities of the Czechoslovakian economic authorities, all suggest

TABLE 10   BASIC INDICATORS FOR CENTRAL AND EASTERN EUROPEAN COUNTRIES

	Soviet Union	Bulgaria	Czecho-slovakia	German Democratic Republic	Hungary	Poland	Romania	OECD
General indicators								
Population (m, 1988)[a]	286.4	9.0	15.6	16.6	10.6	38.0	23.0	824.8
GDR ($bn, 1988)[b]	1 590.0	50.7	118.6	155.4	68.8	207.2	94.7	12 073.0
GDP per capita, $[a]	5 552.0	5 633.0	7 603.0	9 361.0	6 491.0	5 453.0	4 117.0	14 637.0
Growth of GDP[a]								
1971–80	3.1	2.8	2.8	2.8	2.6	3.6	5.3	3.3
1981–85	1.7	0.8	1.2	1.9	0.7	0.6	−0.1	2.5
1986–88	2.3	1.9	1.5	1.7	1.5	1.0	0.1	3.5
Living standards (1987)[c]								
Cars per 1 000 inhabitants	50.0	127.0	182.0	206.0	153.0	74.0	11.0	385.0
Telephones per 1 000 inhabitants	124.0	248.0	246.0	233.0	152.0	122.0	111.0	542.0
Structural indicators								
Share of labour force in agriculture[a]	21.7	19.5	12.1	10.2	18.4	28.2	28.5	8.0
Gross domestic investment/GDP[d]	33.2	32.7	24.7	29.2	28.5	36.5	37.1	20.6
Share of private enterprise in NMP/GDP[e]	2.5	8.9	3.1	3.5	14.6	14.7	2.5	70–80
Relative energy intensity (OECD = 1)[f]	2.6	2.2	1.9	1.6	1.5	1.9	2.7	1.0
Percent of workforce with secondary or higher education[g]	27.3	n.a.	29.4	n.a.	33.8	28.9	n.a.	61.0

Trade indicators

Total exports of goods as percent of GDP (1988)[h]	6.8	23.0	19.7	13.7	14.7	6.4	11.2	14.4
Manufactured goods exports as share of exports to non-socialist countries[i]	63.1	59.3	72.4	77.3	79.6	63.4	50.6	81.8
Percentage change of share of OECD markets[j]								
1978–89	−26.7	−18.5	−44.0	−25.2	−7.8	−32.3	−46.3	—
1986–89	−13.0	−19.9	0.9	−9.1	1.5	−23.5	−27.8	—

(a) CIA, *Handbook of Economic Statistics*, 1989.
(b) PlanEcon data.
(c) CIA, *Handbook of Economic Statistics*, 1989; OECD data are approximate.
(d) Economic Commission for Europe, Economic Survey of Europe 1988–89, and OECD estimates. Data for Bulgaria and East Germany are for 1987.
(e) PlanEcon; OECD data refer to four countries and are intended to give an approximate range only.
(f) Calculated on the basis of total energy consumption in TOE in 1987 from the OECD, World Energy Statistics and Balances, 1989, and PlanEcon estimates for GDP; all data are for 1987.
(g) National source data reported in PlanEcon; OECD data average for 16 countries, percent of total population.
(h) OECD Series A data and ECE; East German data include intra-German trade.
(i) OECD Series C and PlanEcon; manufactures is defined as SITC 5–9. OECD ratio is for 1987.
(j) OECD Series A; data for German Democratic Republic exclude intra-German trade.
Sources: OECD.

83

The judgement is more cautious in the case of Hungary, which now suffers from the fall of its exports in roubles and must therefore confront a massive reorientation, but nevertheless is asserting itself positively.[16] This result was achieved by a rapid deregulation of exports which caused the number of companies with export licences to rise from 350 in 1987 to 2,000 in 1988 and more than 10 thousand by mid-1990. These positive facts are, however, accompanied by great pressure on internal prices, massive problems of industrial restructuration and serious problems of energy provision, which was previously almost entirely dependent on the Soviet Union. It is widely felt that the Gulf crisis will have greatly damaged the Hungarian economy and introduced inflationary stimuli and strong destabilising elements.

Poland has shown a remarkable ability to adapt, so much so that exports to Western countries, which were almost stagnant in 1989, literally exploded in the early months of 1990. Given that imports, especially from the 'zone of the rouble' have fallen by around 40 per cent in turn, contrary to expectation, 1990 showed a remarkable trading surplus, estimated at 2.5 billion dollars in currency and 2.7 billions of transferable dollars.[17]

The export of machinery has been particularly important and bears witness to an upturn in production and competition in this field which has traditionally been considered important for Polish economic integration in international commerce. Even in this case, however, uncertainties remain, closely linked to the development of the internal and international political situation: strong pressure on prices; the difficult reorganisation of large industrial complexes; great vulnerability, notwithstanding the important coal reserves, to a new oil shock linked to the Gulf crisis; and above all a general backwardness which shows especially in per capita income. These all bear out difficulties which cannot be overlooked in the process of integrating Poland into the European sphere.

The serious nature of the internal ex-Soviet Union situation is, however, the crucial element of this phase. The fall of GNP accelerated during 1990 and eventually went over 4 to 5 per cent according to reliable estimates.[18] Inflation continues to accelerate; investment fell in 1990, according to various estimates by around 9 to 10 per cent; the public deficit grew; the balance of payments showed a heavy deficit (in the early months of 1990 it reached 9 billion roubles, an increase of 210 per cent compared to the same months of 1989); while the national debt rose to the point when

---

optimistic development and integration possibilities for Czechoslovakia. This leads many agents to consider investment possibilities as an alternative to Southern Italy and Spain, and in many cases to East Germany.

[16] In the first eight months of 1990, currency exports rose in value by 13.7, with increased figures of 43 per cent for exports to Germany. Given that currency imports have remained almost stationary, there is now a currency surplus of $623m (*PlanEcon Report*, 9 November 1990).

[17] *PlanEcon Report*, 26 October 1990.

[18] *PlanEcon Report*, 23 November 1990.

Western lending banks cut their exposure until the government was induced considerably to reduce its currency reserves.

The complexity of the ex-Soviet Union economic situation is such that it is certainly not possible to redraw it here, even in an extremely abridged form; on the other hand the importance of the political to the development of the economic situation is so clear that it is not possible to make forecasts, which would certainly prove inadequate with respect to the serious nature of the problem. It is reasonable, however, to wonder in a European perspective to what extent the internal ex-Soviet Union crisis might determine the block of European integration.

From the few facts already presented and from the wealth of existing literature, a reality for Eastern countries which is now very different and quite distinct from the ex-Soviet Union situation seems to emerge. Among the countries in the East the areas in most direct contact with Germany seem in a position to follow a rapid, though not smooth, path of integration. Commercial facts confirm that these countries turn principally to Germany rather than to Europe in general. Their exports are directed at Germany and the enabling flow of investment comes from Germany. Other countries, such as Italy, certainly are important partners, but Germany remains the obvious reference point.

In this frame, however, a painful note must be reserved for the countries of the Balkans. These were the most backward countries of the Council for Mutual Economic Assistance (CMEA) and their relative decline has, moreover, been even sharper in recent years. Yugoslavia itself has suffered inflationary movements in the recent past which have undermined the promise of development which seemed assured only ten years ago.

The deficit of the Yugoslavian balance of trade was two billion dollars in 1990, according to the figures of the federal government, production dropped by 10 per cent and not the 2 per cent forecast in January, and approximately a third of companies had to close, having accumulated irredeemable debts. In Yugoslavia's case, however, the regional differences between the North (Slovenia and Croatia) and the South (Serbia, Macedonia, Kosovo, Bosnia and Montenegro) have grown in a very significant way in recent years, in a manner which has aggravated the conflicts between the northern republics and the federal government and led to the declaration of the independence of the two northern republics and the conflict beginning in June 1991.[19]

Reform of the structural funds and the role of the regions

In the early period of its operation, the policy-making approach of the European Economic Community was more sectoral than territorial, with

---

[19] A detailed analysis of the Balkan situation can be found in S. Bianchini, 'The Adriatic Southeast European Area: the Balkans', *The International Spectator*, XXV, 4, 1990.

an increasing disparity in economic development seen in many areas of the member states. The overcoming of this disparity was considered to be a problem that should be resolved through the initiative of individual states, while at that level it was considered necessary to confront them by initiatives set in motion by central government. The establishment of the fund to finance development projects of less favoured regions was not foreseen by the Treaty of Rome, but in the mid-seventies the importance of not postponing its conception any further emerged.

In 1975, The European Regional Development Fund was based on the premise that regional policies would have to be considered a responsibility of the national government rather than Community or regional authorities. The destination of funds was based on fixed quotas agreed directly by the national governments. The first reform of the fund in 1979 was brought in with the aim of introducing the principle of co-ordination between the Commission and the national authorities. A new phase of the reform began in 1984, when the system of fixed national quotas was abandoned and a mixed system was introduced, based on an established minimum quota plus a supplement to be negotiated with the Community. 'In 1984 the Community abandoned the fixed quota system in favour of a mixed system which was partially fixed and partially negotiated.'[20]

Substantial reform goes back to the approval of the Single European Act. This amended the Treaty of Rome in the introduction of article 130 A–E. The reform of structural funds, which came into power on 1 January 1988, must be considered one of the most significant changes to the Community's policy-making approach. The new model is distinguished by the planned distribution of allocations based on national plans presented to the Commission for approval. Since regional governments have to be involved in the drawing up of these plans, the major result of the reform was an explicit recognition of the role which must be played by such governments.

The reform of structural funds is therefore based on the territorial concentration of integrated measures, directed by different political leaders. The new strategy for European integration established by the Commission means to surpass the previously dominant role of national government, thus bringing the regions into play as the main elements in the policy-making process. In the initial phase the destination of structural funds was decided by national governments; in the second phase the destination was decided bilaterally by the Commission and the national governments within a rigid framework of national balances; in its third phase the Community is moving towards a multilateral decision-making process based on rather complex inter-government understanding which involves the Commission, the national governments and the regional ones. An ample quota of Community funds, which has rapidly been increased

[20] R. Leonardi, 'The Regional Revolution in Europe', European University Institute, Florence, mimeo, 1990.

in recent years, has been transferred to companies and local authorities, but the most important element of the new phase is that Community transfers have been directed to national incentives; this was made possible by the reinforcement of articles 92–94 (as shown by the Commission), but also by the fact that the financial resources of the structural funds have to be granted jointly by the national and regional authorities, though on a basis established by the Community itself.

The new approach overturns the former practice of national government, which consisted in the distribution of financial resources to individual companies to compensate for structural imbalance. The aim is to move towards a progressive structural rearrangement by reinforcing the local network of production and service relations in order to stimulate the endogenous market forces.

There are, however, many limitations to this approach. The first of these is due to the very structure of the Community budget which continues to devote most of its funds to the protection of agricultural producers, keeping limited quotas, although they have increased significantly in recent years, for structural and innovatory measures (see Table 11).

The concept of 'regions' and the extension of regional powers vary from country to country. The regionalisation process in Europe is the result of different trends; some countries accepted decentralisation in reply to the political pressure of ethnic groups and to the pressure to recognise the multiplicity of national communities within a single state (Belgium and Spain); in other cases, regionalisation has been the consequence of a division of political power, but has not involved any ethnic dispute (France and Italy); other countries are still very centralised (Greece and Portugal); Great Britain is internally divided into large areas which can certainly not be reduced to regions, and Germany is constitutionally a federal state.

It should also be emphasised that regional governments are not active in equal measure even within individual countries. In all European states the most active are those which administer the most developed areas (like Catalonia, Lombardy and Emilia-Romagna, Baden-Württemberg, and Rhone-Alpe); they claim autonomy on a national level aiming at transnational alliances with other strong regions and a direct and explicit relationship with the Commission. These regional governments are used to managing their administrative organisation efficiently and managing the local conditions which stimulate widespread entrepreneurial activity.

On the other hand, the economic crisis of less favoured areas is generally accompanied by weak local administrations which are traditionally dependent on the central authorities and are used to dealing with local problems requiring direct support from their national government, rather than autonomously implementing new development projects. The new approach risks failure since, among the new elements, those which are effectively capable of taking part in the decision-making process are already at the helm of the strongest areas of the Community; and national

TABLE 11 EC BUDGET (reclassified according to 1990 budget scheme)

	1983	1984	1985	1986	1987	1988	1989	1990
1. Agricultural funds	13124	18333	19995	22112	22961	29740	26761	26522
2. Structural actions	3171	3476	4085	5771	5995	6802	9488	11532
3. Innovation support	421	719	706	759	657	1136	1695	2071
4. Other interventions	2998	2363	2376	3228	5770	3597	2415	3005
5. Reimbursements and reserves	4280	2357	1271	3304	2785	2539	6065	5715
6. Total	23994	27248	29139	35174	38168	44950	46424	48845

Source: Annual Report, various years.

governments could further consolidate their position, upholding the role of defending less favoured areas through the relaunching of central measures.[21]

This seems to be the case in Southern Italy. After numerous years of measures directed by central government, the current situation is very complex; some areas have tried out the model of widespread industrial development (above all the coastal regions of the Adriatic), other regions have islands of industrialisation based on the attraction of foreign and public investment, or on the stimulation of endogenous forces. Moreover, the regional governments, after a long period of centralisation of development policy, do not seem capable of interacting on a European level as necessitated by the Community's new approach.

This also becomes the limit for the extension of this territorial approach to the countries of Eastern Europe, where the problem of starting a process of endogenous growth again is linked to a crucial problem of reconstruction of local institutions.

The new structural policy approach requires a systematic and balanced application of the Single Act and of the New Union Treaty in the different member states, with harsh penalties for those countries which, like Italy, show substantial delays in the enactment of the Community's instructions.

Conclusions

The aspect of Europe today is very different from that outlined in the mid eighties; the European Community has definitely been strengthened by the phase of economic and political reorganisation which followed the Single Act. Nonetheless, this has come to pass in a substantially deteriorated international situation; the Soviet crisis, the internal American crisis, the very serious Gulf crisis and the difficult position of underdeveloped countries make future economic forecasts uncertain. In this context the European Community nevertheless remains a strongly developed area which has recently shown growth.

Differences stand out within Europe, however, which this recent development has failed to eliminate and has partially exaggerated. Indeed a polarisation has become even more evident around very well-defined central areas and around large urban conglomerations which seem to give a new role to peripheral economies which have only grown rapidly in the last two decades. Southern Europe only seems partially to have made up its arrears and the new economies of the East are turning to Europe, and bringing fragile internal situations with them.

Undoubtedly we can identify an essential German centrality which

[21] I have developed this theme in 'La réorientation des politiques structurelles de la CEE', *Revue du Marché Commun*, n.350, September 1991, pp. 599–603, and in P. Bianchi and N. Bellini, 'Public Policies for Local Network of Innovators', *Research Policy*, n.20, December 1991, pp. 487–497.

unification has increased, but which the opening up and restructuring of the Eastern countries has made even more apparent. Federal Germany, moreover, has internal requirements for growth. It can be estimated that merely by maintaining an effective growth rate of at least 4 per cent per annum the unemployment created in what was the GDR could be absorbed in a reasonable period of time (three to five years). This need to maintain such a high growth rate is also an element which will pull the European economy along.

Obviously this European development will become a great attraction for migratory flows from underdeveloped countries, and especially from North Africa, but also from the countries of East Europe.

The current phase of European integration is nevertheless a period of very complex transition towards economic integration, and also towards political unification. A crucial element in the process is the overturning of the Community's approach to policy-making. The Single European Act defined the transition from a centralised state model, expanded in the fifties from national states into the Community, to a model based on inter-governmental negotiation, founded on three levels of government (community, state and region). The new Union Treaty, signed at Maastricht, confirms this approach by establishing a new Council of Regions.

The new approach requires different relationships between institutions and market forces; the principle of 'reciprocal recognition' requires a strong relationship between national and entrepreneurial authorities, with the purpose of applying rules, defined for specific interests but compatible with and capable of directing the general policy-making process; the reform of structural funds generalises an approach based on partnership, extending this method to local development projects. Nonetheless, this course will oblige the Community to confront the problem of the organisation of its budget, half of which is still dedicated to the protection of agriculture; moreover agricultural protection still appears to be the element which blocks commercial exchange with the countries of the Mediterranean Basin which put pressure on Europe.

In conclusion, the economic scenario for the coming years sees a Community in which the still significant disparities and the growing external pressures definitely require further development of production efficiency through a vigorous assertion of competition; however, the values of efficiency do not seem enough to confront the problems of equality and stability which are connected to them.

EX ORIENTE LUX?
POST-CELEBRATORY
SPECULATIONS ON THE
'LESSONS' OF '89

TONY JUDT*

WE are all 'Europeans' now. In Western Europe, during the nineteen-eighties, this notion entailed little more than an acceptance, more or less enthusiastic, of the European Community's drive for political unity and economic uniformity. It was reflected in a reduction of the more superficial barriers to human and material commerce and in a distinctive style, common to political speeches, automobile design and the more conspicuous forms of cultural consumption. 'Euro-chic', in short. It also spoke to a curiously restrained, even provincial vision of the possible meaning of supra-national undertakings, confined geographically to the accidentally-established contours of the post-war settlement and with little attention to any larger vision of politics. Its most enthusiastic proponents, predictably, were publicists and politicians in countries like Spain or Greece, recent additions to the Community for whom 'Europe' meant an opportunity to modernise their economies under the protective umbrella of Brussels and to dispense with unhappy memories of social stagnation and authoritarian rule.

Since the overthrow of Communism in Eastern Europe, the significance of the terms 'Europe' and 'European' has shifted considerably. Hungary (in November 1990) and Czechoslovakia (in February 1991) have joined the Council of Europe, now twenty-five strong, and have aspirations to membership of the Community itself. The 'Alpe-Adria' group, discussed in Perulli's contribution to this volume, founded in 1978 as a quadrilateral association of central European states (Italy, Hungary, Austria and Yugoslavia) with shared regional concerns, has been expanded into the Pentagonal Group with the inclusion of Czechoslovakia in May 1990. Europe, for many, now stretches from the Atlantic to the Carpathians.

This transformation is neither unproblematic nor uncontentious. Does 'Europe' include Slovenia and Croatia, and if so why not the rest of the disintegrating multinational state of Yugoslovia? Why was Poland excluded from the Pentagonal group?[1] If Lithuania looks to Europe and

* Tony Judt is Professor of History at New York University. His forthcoming book, *Passé Imparfait: les intellectuels en France, 1944–1956*, will be published later this year.

[1] With the result that some Polish intellectuals and politicians, feeling aggrieved, have threatened to abandon 'central' Europe and look east once again . . .

receives welcoming signals, why would not the same hospitality be extended to the Western Ukraine? What do the erstwhile citizens of Communist states mean when they talk, as many now do, of 'rejoining Europe', and what does their audience in the West understand them to be saying?

Behind this apparently minor question, a sort of speculative parlour game (where is Europe? Who's in, who's out?) which has so captured the attention of Continental intellectuals in recent years, there lie deeper issues. The meaning attached to the category of 'European' by political writers in the East today has much to do with their understanding of the reasons for the collapse of Communism and the options facing its successor regimes. It informs the very language in which political and moral thought has been re-cast in the speculation of dissident thinkers before and after the fall. In what follows I shall propose some reflections on the state of post-Communist thought in Central Europe, its echoes (accurate and distorted) in the West, and its future prospects.

In the usage I am describing, 'European' is parasitic upon the notion of 'Central Europe'. Ever since their absorption into the Soviet sphere, intellectuals in Europe's other half were at pains to insist upon the distinctive identity of their part of the continent, its vital role in the creation of modern culture and the historical inappropriateness (as well as the political costs) of its relegation to adjunct status in an 'Asiatic' empire. This insistence was initially addressed primarily to western audiences, in the form of an appeal: please don't forget us! It was revived, following the brief illusions of the post-Stalinist thaw, by the new opposition circles of the nineteen-seventies in Poland, Czechoslovakia and Hungary and finally achieved a wider and sympathetic hearing thanks to the popularity of the writings of Milan Kundera and the growing international reputation of persecuted writers like Václav Havel and Adam Michnik.[2]

Under Communism the significance of the vision of 'Central Europe' lay in the distinction it drew between Russian political traditions, in which state and society were conflated into a single repressive unity, where intermediate institutions could not exist and where all initiative and authority lay with the party-state, and those of the West, where the powers and claims of the state were firmly delimited and in which 'civil society' knew an autonomous and variegated existence. Beyond a problematic nostalgia for some hypothetical golden era of Central European culture and liberty, the advocates of 'Europe' were pressing the case against totalitarianism. Its originality, in the writings of people like Havel, Michnik, George Konrad and many others, lay in the tactical lesson drawn from the experience of life under Leninism; rather than fight the system on its own terms, with alternative political programmes and fruitless efforts to replace the Communist state with one of their own imagining, the object

---

[2] On this, see the discussion in Tony Judt, 'The Rediscovery of Central Europe', *Daedalus*, Winter 1990, pp. 23–54.

should be the creation of civil society within the very walls of the prison. By living 'as if' in freedom, the victims of repression, as individuals and as a community, would re-create, *de facto*, the conditions for a civil society, the moral and intellectual space in which future liberation would be born of daily practice.[3]

Implicit in this approach, and rendered explicit in the writings of theorists like the Hungarian Mihaly Vajda, was the view that Communism was not simply a distortion and abuse of socialism's European sources, but something quite different. The Leninist revolution had been a peculiarly *Russian* (and thus non-European) device for the modernisation of the Russian Empire, a way for it to catch up with the West and maintain its imperial claims without conceding to Western (capitalist, democratic) forms of modernity. It shared with the Western socialist traditions only a deep suspicion of the individual and a common unease at the idea of an unregulated maximisation of goods and competition of interests. Whether this was an appropriate vehicle for the development of the territories over which it ruled was not an open question. Few eastern Europeans would have gone so far as to claim for Leninism, much less Stalinism, that it was in any sense what the Russians *deserved*, but quite a number were inclined to believe that it was well in keeping with their traditions, notably the Byzantine inheritance in which the spiritual and secular authorities were so closely intertwined. What was almost universally asserted, however, is that socialism in this guise was neither deserved nor appropriate in the countries seized after 1945.

With the disappearance of the Communist regimes, the former dissidents have adapted the significance of 'Europe' to slightly different ends. The choice now is not between totalitarianism and liberty, but between competing political families claiming the abandoned territory. In every former Communist nation, this choice can be reduced, in large measure, to the conflict between 'populists' and 'Europeans'. The former are heirs to the language and programmes of an earlier era, echoing the concerns and the prejudices of Poland's National Democrats, Slovakia's nationalists or the various ethnically-based movements for autonomy of Yugoslavia's national republics. Their electoral programmes and their popular appeal make subtle but emphatic play with the need, for example, to preserve Hungary for the Hungarians, to reduce the role of 'outsiders' in the local economy, or to restore the pride (and on occasion the former frontiers) of nations and peoples frustrated by the memory of slights and defeats dating to 1920, 1848 or beyond.

In this context, the Europeanists, who are often the same men and women known to the West a decade earlier as dissidents, speak instead of catching the European train, joining the European family, returning to

---

[3] I have analysed these writings at some length in Judt, 'The Dilemmas of Dissidence: the Politics of Opposition in East-Central Europe', in *Eastern European Politics and Societies*, 2, ii, 1988, pp. 185–240.

Europe, etc. By this they mean that excessive reference to the 'nation', or the attempt to divide, for example, post-Communist Czechoslovakia or Bulgaria along ethnic lines, is both harmful in the short term and liable to be self-defeating over time, forcing these countries back into the ghetto of squabbling stagnation which was their common condition before the Second World War. Politicians like the Hungarian Free Democrat leader Janos Kis, or Czechoslovakia's President Havel, are quite open about this. The fading away of Communist power is an opportunity for Europe's eastern half to adopt the political and economic forms of the West, certainly, but it is something more important; a chance for the region to escape the *moral* underdevelopment which has been the bane of politics in these lands ever since the emergence of nationalist aspirations in the last century. To be European, for Kis or Havel as for Adam Michnik in Poland, is to think beyond their frontiers, to transcend the provincial and destructive terms of traditional debates.

Here, as in the earlier use of 'Europe' as a counterpoint to Russia, the European idea is of interest not so much for what it contains as for what it opposes. In the Hungarian and the Polish elections of 1990 there was an acrid flavour of ugly pasts. Charges and counter-charges of cosmopolitanism, anti-semitism, populism, an insufficiency of national feeling and so forth were hurled back and forth, quite burying what few efforts were made to debate serious problems of an economic, ecological or constitutional nature. In Croatia and Serbia, mutual suspicions, fuelled by repeated reminders of past cruelties and injustices, pollute any rational discussion of Yugoslavia's future. Those who plaintively point to 'Europe' are certainly making a point about the need to draw closer to the prosperous West and benefit from its institutions and its wealth, but mostly they are just protesting in despair at the intolerance and the apparent anachronism of the political discourse which has sprung up from the ruins of Soviet 'fraternity'.

The themes of Eastern European debate

In these circumstances, does anything remain of what only yesterday seemed like the fertile shoots of a new political vision? The political theorists of the erstwhile opposition have been forced into the public sphere, becoming politicians, editors, even presidents. Constrained to address themselves to mundane issues and urgent choices, they have understandably had little occasion on which to reflect upon the application of their earlier speculations to their present condition. The very 'anti-politics' which so seduced Western readers makes no sense in present circumstances, just as the charmingly abstract vision of a once-and-future 'Central Europe' of the spirit seems somehow etiolated and shrivelled when reduced to a struggle against Slovak nationalists or the bigoted electoral propaganda of Polish demagogues.

The theoretical issues around which the 'European' debate has swirled in this region are many, but in the realm of political ideas they can be reduced to four themes: the recreation of civil society, the appeal of 'liberalism', the obsolescence of the categories of 'left' and 'right' and the prospect of a 'third way'. These are topics which have also engaged the attention of Western thinkers in recent years, as we shall see, though in subtly different terms. Of these, the interest in 'civil society' has been the most obsessive, and perhaps the most confused.

For critics of Communism, civil society seemed an unproblematic category. It stood for everything that Communism was not: a vision of public affairs in which the place of the state and authority was distinct and delimited, in which citizens exercised autonomy and occupied a social arena whose various attributes—culture, politics, the market in goods— were the outcome of private or collective preferences, decided upon by free choice and the balance of competing needs and wants. Little attention was paid to the distinction between 'civil society' and 'political society', with the result that in a curious way the political thought of dissidents reversed but did not rethink the very categories and experience of Communism itself: just as the Soviet-imposed regimes forbade politics but thereby politicised every aspect of daily life, so their opponents imagined a counter-society in which politics, in the classical sense, would be effectively absent. They would doubtless have blenched at the thought, but there was something almost Hegelian about their writings, where civil society was largely confined to contractual relationships (whether moral or economic), in which individual interests would regulate themselves.

This may have been a necessary condition for the radical rejection of traditional political aspirations and their replacement by Havel's power of the powerless, the invocation of the importance of 'living in truth'. But in the vacuum left by the implosion of the regime *political* society inevitably re-emerged. The imagined realm of free moral persons turned out in practice to be peopled by all sorts of actual and very political interests and individuals, who played with some success upon the prejudices and fears of society itself. The easy identification of binary categories—private/ public, individual/collective, non-governmental/governmental—proved radically insufficient to capture the complexity of a situation in which it became quickly clear that Communism had indeed atomised and degraded society but not destroyed it. The newly coagulating social forces cannot be defined or led according to the simple distinctions which worked so well in opposition. Civil society in contemporary Poland or Hungary, not to speak of Yugoslavia, is composed of many antagonistic groups with distinctive and often incompatible goals, some of whom also aspire to control of the state.

The curious confidence placed in the phrase 'civil society', which became almost a ritual incantation during the nineteen-eighties, a way of blaming 'the state' for everything that had happened, was perhaps the last ironic echo of a powerful tradition of Marxist thought in Central Europe, a tradition which long pre-dates the arrival of the Red Army. The critics of Communism, in other words, were still confining themselves to the categories first articulated by the founders of the ideology under which they lived; all they had done, and here too they followed a well-established cliché of the official doctrine, was 'invert' the epistemological priorities of the official language. Just as Marxists came to place an absurd ontological faith in the capacities and rationality of the state, so Marxism's courageous critics of recent years ascribed similar powers to the civil society which that state had so efficiently reduced.

In this light, it is easier to understand the paradoxical status of 'liberalism' in recent pronouncements. Political thinkers in Central Europe are perfectly well aware that liberalism is a problematic term, a category whose meaning is indistinct even in countries where it is an established part of the political landscape. Some of them also know that in its usage within the continental tradition it is utterly different from the liberalism associated with J. S. Mill or the democratic traditions of North America. And no-one growing up under Communism could miss the historical association between political liberalism and the material inequalities of capitalism. But the virtues attaching to liberalism, in all its forms and with all its limitations, are simply these: that liberalism is in principle incompatible with any strong view of the state, and the political *forms* of liberalism are those which most closely approximate to the idealised account of civil society as offered by Communism's opponents, and by those who now oppose the nationalist, populist and often authoritarian heirs to Communism.

The paradox is that in the post-Communist lands liberalism cannot be expected to emerge naturally and gracefully from the circumstances and traditions of civil society. It has no roots in the political culture of the region, and this is a defect for which Communism is only partly responsible. Accordingly liberalism in Poland, Czechoslovakia or Hungary today is a *project*. It has to be invented or, worse, imported (hence the orientation towards 'Europe'). But there are three problems with this. In the first place, liberalism, where it does exist in the civic and constitutional traditions of countries like Britain, the Netherlands or Italy, is an accident, the imperfect product of long and very particular histories. In those rare instances where it has been grafted onto some previously illiberal roots, the circumstances have been special indeed: a major domestic revolution and/or a cataclysmic defeat in war, often followed by sustained foreign occupation. These conditions do not apply in Europe today. Even those ex-Communist states best placed to adopt the forms of liberal life (Czechoslovakia, perhaps Hungary) have far to go before their new constitutions will reflect anything very real about the society itself; the relative failure of would-be liberal parties to establish themselves as contenders for power is only the most obvious symptom of this problem.

Secondly, to make of 'liberalism' a political project is doubly contradictory. Political projects, goal-oriented programmes of an ideological nature, are precisely what the new politicians of Central Europe have so fervently forsworn. But even were this not the case, liberalism is a poor candidate for such an undertaking. What, after all, can it mean to say that one seeks to make a society liberal? Is liberalism an indivisible package, ranging from the maximisation of legal rights to the unfettered play of private economic interests? Beyond the obvious concerns with the policing of private conflicts, of what do the liberal state's legitimate prerogatives consist, and on what grounds deriving from within liberal theory itself? These are hardly original questions—they are the starting point for much of modern Western political thought. But that is the point; in the West these are essentially contested issues within a given institutional and cultural framework. In the East, it is the very terms of that framework itself which have yet to be constructed, and for all its long tradition of speculation on the matter, liberalism 'as such', precisely because it does not exist and has never had to think itself into existence as a working system, offers little guidance.

The third problem is that even among those in Central Europe today who call themselves liberals and seek to reconstruct their societies in keeping with a liberal vision, the content of that vision varies enormously. Many people who now call themselves liberals would not hesitate to adopt the label 'social democrat' were it not that it is still polluted by its association with 'socialism' and thus by extension with the old regime. Social democracy depends on a view of the state as a necessary and beneficial partner in the construction of a harmonious and just world based on some regulation from above of the distribution of resources and goods. It is thus at a heavy discount just now. No intellectual wants to be caught saying that state intervention in private affairs, or restrictions on private property, are necessary, much less good in themselves, even though this is what some of them still privately believe, and it is certainly what many voters, especially the poor and the unskilled want to hear. Similarly, true conservatives (of whom there are many all over the region, especially among Catholic activists and ex-Communist legislators) would welcome strict regulation of private morals,[4] censorship of the more aggressive elements of a free press and a firm central hand in economic matters, especially when it comes to keeping national resources out of the hands of foreign entrepreneurs. But while these too are things that many people might like to hear, they smack of authority and control, and politicians and writers thus feel somewhat embarrassed about expressing such opinions too bluntly (except in Romania, where none of these considerations apply). So everyone is 'liberal'.

---

[4] A distinction is in order here. Ex-Communists are liberal on abortion but regard the pornography now publicly available in Budapest and elsewhere as evidence of the decline of public morals since their departure. Catholic politicians agree on pornography, but would also ban abortion and other areas of free choice, threatening to introduce legislation along such lines in Poland and Slovakia in particular.

Thus the aspiration to a liberal future is complicated by the uncertain status of political labels. If everyone is a liberal (former Communists included), the shape of a liberal post-Communist society becomes even cloudier than would otherwise be the case. Just how problematic this is can be seen when one considers the new usage of the terms 'left' and 'right'. On the one hand the very vocabulary of 'left' and 'right' has been jettisoned as redundant, speaking as it does to political and ideological categories which Communism both exemplified and rendered meaningless. On the other hand, this is the only vocabulary available for purposes of collective identification in electoral politics. But its content is mysterious. Broadly speaking, the 'right' in Central and Eastern Europe today comprises those who believe in a strong state, intervention in various spheres of civil and economic activity, strict regulation of public behaviour. Thus ex-Communists, Catholic politicians and nationalist demagogues are on the 'right'. On the 'left', reasonably enough, are those who oppose such views. But among the things they oppose is the continuing stranglehold of the bureaucratic state upon economic initiative and innovation. It is thus the self-described 'left' in Central Europe which favours a rapid shift towards a free market, with all the entailed risks of foreign ownership and extremes of wealth and poverty, as well as the predictable costs in unemployment and social dislocation.

The irony of these alignments is not lost on the protagonists. But the ex-Marxist, ex-dissident 'left', liberal in its attitude towards the market but instinctively social-democratic in its desire to see preserved (or created) a degree of social justice and public welfare, could point to Western analogies. In Spain, it is the Socialist Party of Felipe Gonzales which has striven to divest the state of its privileges and to unleash market forces for the creation of wealth, while conservatives in Madrid bemoan the decline of a long Hispanic tradition of protection and intervention by a paternalist state. What is peculiar about Central and Eastern Europe is not the 'mix and match' character of new political coalitions, but the inability of local practitioners to describe accurately—or honestly—what it is they are doing. This is partly the consequence of the understandable desire of political theorists to claim some continuity in their thinking over recent years; hence their assertion that the terms 'left' and 'right' have lost their significance and should be replaced by non-traditional categories. This would be more convincing were there any sign that these were forthcoming, or that anyone knew what they might look like. 'Liberal', after all, is neither very new nor very enlightening as categories go.

More than this, though, the current ambivalence about political labels in post-Communist societies arises from a half-articulated desire on the part of many intellectuals to identify a 'third way', a set of social and political arrangements which could sustain an optimistic and positive vision of the good society without retreating into discredited or irrelevant labels and projects. This 'third way' would probably be of little interest if we confined our attention to the realistic prospects for the region's future; real-world constraints of resource and capital shortage, ethnic conflicts and political divisions mean that almost everyone would be happy to settle for the minimum of political stability and material security.[5] It is true that long-standing habits of dependence mean that much of the population would instinctively feel more secure looking to Sweden as a model rather than to the minimalist state fondly supposed to have nurtured the success of the United States, which is why social-democratic parties, whatever they call themselves, will probably come to occupy an important role. But for intellectuals at least, the 'third way' means something else, and it points to something about Central European political culture which Western observers occasionally miss.

There is, within the writings of the former dissidents, a distinct and reiterated suspicion of the West. In the earlier writings of Havel and some others it occasionally shaded into anti-modernism. This in turn was closely bound up with the rejection of Marxism which so shaped the thinking of the generation now taking over. The hyper-rationalism of modern life and thought, the belief that ours is a world that can be understood, controlled and transformed, was for many critics of Communism the original sin of the modern world. Both the epistemological errors of Marxism and the banal evils of Communism were thus treated as but the logical, absurd outcome of a moral error whose roots could be traced to the hubris of the Enlightenment. If Communism were ever defeated, care should be taken not to allow its place to be taken by the very (Western) obsession with production, technology, accumulation and consumption of which the Soviet experiment was but the distorted, unsuccessful echo. Havel and others are today much too busy to pursue this line of reasoning in detail, but his presidential speeches still carry traces of this concern, and it should come as no surprise that there has for some time been a cult of Heidegger among political theorists and philosophers in Budapest and Prague.

At the heart of this moral, almost aesthetic distaste for the crude, crass consumer culture of the West, can be found a continuity with the theme of 'Central Europe' noted earlier, the dream of a different path for Europe, neither totalitarian nor anarchic, carrying the torch for a cultural vision which would return the Continent to common aspirations congruent with its heritage and not dependent on materialist goals at once overweening and ignoble. It is this sentiment which makes the 'liberal' project of Central European intellectuals so opaque. It is, after all, the characteristic of the wealthy liberal West that it has paid for its freedom not only in inequality of economic opportunity but also in the steady expansion and encouragement of a popular culture whose forms and content are far from pleasing

---

[5] Thus Vaclav Klaus, the leader of Civic Forum's 'free market' faction (now a separate party) regards a rapid and uncompromising dismantling of the 'planned economy' as the necessary condition of future progress. For him the 'third way' is impracticable and incoherent, a nostalgic confusion of means and ends. But there are many who dissent from this view, and they probably have behind them the majority of the Czech electorate.

to many. It may not be that democracy and liberty in a mass society necessarily entail such costs, but necessary or not they are a fact, and there is something curiously illiberal, as well as obscurantist, about the desire to shape and constrain liberty so as to assure a different outcome. The snobbery of Central European intellectuals when faced with the reality of the West is perhaps explained by deeper feelings of insecurity and an understandable accumulation of resentment ('You may be wealthy, but we have preserved Culture.'). It is none the less a widespread sentiment, and should be acknowledged as central to any account of contemporary thought in this area.

One important source of this cultural critique of modernity and the West is the special place of intellectuals themselves in Central European culture and politics. Of Western societies, only France can claim an intelligentsia with a comparable sense of its own centrality and significance, a similar self-identification with the nature and purposes of the nation. But in France (or rather in Paris) the claims of intellectuals are modified in practice by the distinct and centuries-old presence of a state, with its own apparatus, projects and means. In Central Europe, until 1918 and since 1948, the identity of Czechs, Poles, Slovaks, Serbs and many others has been largely the work of intellectuals. The latter, playwrights, poets, musicians, novelists and philosophers, not only can claim responsibility for imagining their nations into existence and furnishing them with a language, a literature, a cultural map of their place in the continent, but have also been the agents of continuity and survival in times of hardship, oppression and even collective dispersal or destruction. There is thus a natural and understandable tendency among intellectuals in Prague, Warsaw, Budapest or Bucharest to treat their social visions as something more than mere idle speculation in the manner of scribblers in Milan or Oxford.

Hence the confusion surrounding 'civil society', which proved sadly inadequate to the tasks imagined in its name by imprisoned dissidents. Hence the hypostasised category of 'liberalism', which Central European philosphers invest with the same protean powers once ascribed to the term 'proletariat' by three generations of Bolsheviks. And hence, in the end, the suspicion of the West. To be sure there is a genuine dislike for the world of 'Dallas' and Coca Cola. But what makes many such thinkers insecure and uneasy is the essentially inductive character of the very liberal philosophy whose contingent virtues they otherwise admire. It is the fact that culture in general and intellectuals in particular have so small a role in Western public life, that rather than define and mould Western society they seem often to be reduced to describing and commenting upon it, which so disturbs observers from the East. Communism may have persecuted free-thinkers without mercy, but no-one could ignore the compliment it paid them in so doing. Every dissident dragged off to prison was further evidence of the *continuing* importance of intellectuals, and thus of culture, under totalitarianism. Communism, in this special sense, represented continuity with the Central European past, if only despite itself. Western liberalism, some fear, may strike the region a truly mortal blow.

Lessons for the West

The irony of this situation is that one of the things about Central European thinkers which has most alarmed Western commentators of the Left in recent years has been the very extent of their admiration for the West, their desire to emulate much of what Western society takes for granted! In the sixties and seventies this alarm could be written off as the result of an acute case of false political consciousness; Western revolutionaries in 1968 did not see, could not know that it was they who represented the last gasp of a discredited utopia, and that the despised aspirants to 'bourgeois liberty' in Prague and Warsaw were the radicals of the future. Today things are different. Few cling to what nearly everyone regards as the wreckage of the great visions of the nineteenth century; but commentators like Paul Thibaud, the former editor of the Paris monthy *Esprit*, express disquiet at the apparent failure of Central European thinkers to reconcile the legitimate objectives of individual achievement and social 'modernisation' with the no-less-pressing claims of community or nation.

Thibaud, like so many Western observers, is finding in Prague or Budapest dilemmas and contradictions whose true interest, for him, lies in their curious resemblance to debates and problems nearer home. Don't be so quick to emulate us, he warns them—look at how unsuccessful *we* have been in addressing the sorts of dilemmas you now face! There are those, in East and West alike, who hear in such admonitions disturbing echoes of earlier times: don't look at us, ours is an awful society, you are lucky to be where you are. This could be Sartre, lecturing Czechs or Russians on the evils of liberal capitalism. But the comparison is a trifle unfair. In France today, as in Italy, Germany and elsewhere, there is more interest in and sympathy for the unfolding developments to the East than has ever been the case. This is because the collapse of Communism, and the accompanying debates and dilemmas, coincide with similar doubts and upheavals in Western political culture itself.

In the West as in the East, the categories 'left' and 'right' have undergone considerable cosmetic surgery in the recent past. It is true that in the West today most of the attention is paid to the left half of the body politic, but in the longer view this only serves to restore the balance—during the first half of our century it was the political Right which was undergoing profound and traumatic transformations, ushering in its present adaptations to the ground rules of liberal democracy and some measure of social protection. But the modern Left, by contrast, is a mess, in Britain, France, Germany and most notoriously in Italy, where the largest Communist Party in the free world spent a year haggling over the new name with which it sought to symbolise and affirm its adjustment to a new political order. Who, now, has confident and firmly-grounded views about the case for state ownership or restrictions upon the free market? If being on the Left means, as used to be said, believing in the Desirable, while those on the Right confined their attentions to the Possible, what do we now believe to be either desirable or possible, and in the name of which transcendent political projects and social goals?

Central Europeans thus have no monopoly on confusion in this sphere; nor are their hopeful elucubrations on the theme of liberalism so very different from some recent contributions to Western political debate. If Central Europeans are a little more aggressively realist in their adoption of rights-talk this makes good historical sense, but the problems in constructing a rights-based system of public ethics or social legislation are fundamentally the same in Hungary as they are in France, where the local traditions have also been weak in such matters. Just as the Hungarians and others now translate and comment upon the works of Robert Nozick or John Rawls, so the French are eagerly devouring Karl Popper and Isaiah Berlin, aggressively importing the sort of categories and arguments which their own political culture short-circuited after 1830.[6] The results are broadly comparable: a confusion of languages and concepts and a loss of equilibrium. Thibaud's sense of the need to sort out the boundaries between private claims and public duties reflects a wider French anxiety which he is merely transposing on to others. In Paris today there is little consensus about what sort of a liberal compromise should replace the old ideological divisions, and even less sense of how you would know whether that compromise was correct or workable. It is notorious that Mitterrand and Rocard, no less than Kohl (or Kinnock), make political decisions by the seat of their psephological pants, reading polls and adjusting the thermometer of state and party policy to the apparent temperature of civil society. More troubling is the suggestion that no-one has a better idea.

It does thus seem as though what unites Europe today is the common uncertainty of its political life, a shared sense that we have lost our ideological bearings. Even liberals, who might be expected to luxuriate in the defeat of political extremism, are gnawed by self-doubt. In order to see why this is so we have to ask what, precisely, are the lessons now being learned from the experience of post-Communism. Until very recently, the pedagogical message seemed limited but clear: the West demonstrates the virtues of freedom and the East articulates them, the difference being that the former has the good fortune to do so by experience, the latter through counter-example. Since 1989, however, the message has changed.

The first lesson from the East now concerns the limits of theory. Despite their protestations to the contrary, this is as much of a shock to Central

---

[6] They have also begun to evince a taste for the work of Ronald Dworkin, though it is difficult to see how his peculiarly juridical conception of rights could ever be grafted onto French Republican and parliamentary roots.

European intellectuals as to their Western admirers. Almost nothing about the events of 1989 and thereafter conformed to expectation. The good news and the bad have taken people equally by surprise. Everyone knew that Marxism no longer mapped with any accuracy the contours of experienced life, and was incapable of moulding them to its designs. But that the abandonment of Marxism should signal the collapse of *any* attempt to speculate accurately on the nature of politics was a point of view confined to a few moralists, and not held very firmly even by them. Yet beyond the most technical constitutional tasks, previous writings on the themes of civil society, the desirable forms of politics, the contours of the state have had no impact on the shaping of post-Communist society.

One reason for this is the unexpected weight of the past. Like Marxists, today's liberals, whether in East or West, have no idea how to accommodate or explain ethnic violence, racial prejudice or the enthusiastic revival of past national grievances. History, the study of which was encouraged by dissidents as an antidote to Communist-induced amnesia, is now a problem in its own right; where once Central Europe was a desolate land of forgetting, it is now burdened by an excess of memories, some of them accurate, none of them good. This, too, is a lesson whose reception in the West should be all the easier in that the last two decades have shown liberal societies to be not much better equipped to handle similar tensions. No-one who has watched the French grapple helplessly and belatedly with the dilemma of racism and the needs of a huge and growing community of Arab, black and foreign-born residents will feel inclined to patronise Havel as he and his colleagues cope inadequately with Slovak nationalism and daily attacks on gypsy families. Croats and Serbs have no monopoly on mutual antipathy; Flemings and Walloons are no better. The difference is that history and geography have dealt them a better hand and mollified ancient wounds.

This is a major reason why 'liberalism' doesn't seem a very satisfactory solution, even to liberals. The free-market in ideas, the unrestricted circulation of privately-produced goods and a state with limited interventionary powers mean very little in such circumstances. At best they provide a context in which hitherto suppressed political languages and collective grievances can be displayed. Events in Eastern Europe today are a salutary reminder to Western Europeans that we have for too long failed to think very seriously about such problems. And yet they are the ones which matter. As Czechs close their border to Poles, Poles panic at the prospect of an influx of Lithuanians and Ukrainians, Slovenes and Croats flee the impoverished southern Yugoslav masses of Macedonia, Montenegro and Bosnia, Slovak nationalists publish hate literature about Hungarians and Czechs and populist politicians in Hungary hint grimly at the Jewish 'control' of Budapest, cheery advocates of 1992 should take careful stock. We may be on the very edge of a generation of massive out-migration all across the continent. Soviet Jews may emigrate (reluctantly) to Israel, but others can only go West. If the erstwhile European

Community closes its doors to the countries east of Vienna it will not only betray its ideals but will anyway already have to handle huge underclasses of immigrants and ethnic minorities in Paris, Berlin, Milan, Marseille and elsewhere. If it allows limited access for its eastern neighbours, it will face problems of unemployment, ethnic conflict and political polarisation on a massive scale, as the pull of economic opportunity and the push of inter-communal tensions drive tens of thousands of Slavs and others into Germany, Italy and elsewhere.

Between the limited capacity of political theory to capture the new realities of public life, and the uncomfortable realisation that the urgent political issues are an ugly and unexpected combination of real demographic problems and revived communal antagonisms, post-Communist Central Europe turns out not to have much to offer the West by way of models or lessons. We are a long way from *fin-de-siècle* Vienna.[7] Yet at the same time the news from 'over there' really is rather salutory, a sort of Mirror for Modern Princes. Who now remembers the smug prognostications for 1992, those glowing images of a wealthy united Europe sailing past the US and Japan in the peaceful struggle for economic hegemony? Europe now is a troubled place, divided along every conceivable fault-line. Uncomfortably investigating its own troubled past (in Germany, France or Italy no less than in Poland or Hungary), a laudable activity but hardly calculated to induce confidence, it has already recovered from the euphoric 'victories' of 1989. No-one, from Liverpool to Lodz, knows exactly what to ask of the state, what to expect from the 'free market'. From Sarajevo to Strasbourg bureaucrats make troubling estimates of immigrant numbers with all their consequences for politics, education, housing and employment. Arbiters of high culture in Paris and Prague share a common sense of anxiety, more or less that articulated a decade ago by Pierre Bourdieu when he pronounced the major issue facing intellectuals today to be their own imminent disappearance. Ours would seem to be an age of reduced expectations in every sphere except one. For the first time since the High Middle Ages, a traveller will find fundamentally similar concerns, articulated in largely similar vein, throughout the continent. The essential non-communicability of political projects, social expectations or cultural norms which for so long divided East from West, North from South, has been overcome, for the time being. For good or ill, we are indeed all Europeans now.

---

[7] At least as imagined . . . In reality, there was much about life in the capital of the declining Habsburg Empire which anticipated present dilemmas, beginning with the volatile ethnic intermix and politicisation of racial and national resentments.

GERMANY IN THE NEW EUROPE

ROGER MORGAN*

In early autumn 1991 Germany's Foreign Minister Hans-Dietrich Genscher held a series of three widely-publicised meetings which, considered together, indicate the breadth of Germany's interests in the contours of an emerging new Europe, and the potential extent of the influence which Germany can exert in bringing it about. First, in a meeting between Genscher and his French counterpart Roland Dumas (the latest in a series of literally hundreds of Franco-German ministerial encounters in the seventeen years since Genscher assumed his present office in 1974), the Bonn-Paris 'tandem' laid down its joint ideas on the steps which December's EC summit should take to make more concrete the goals of economic and monetary union and European political union. These included: significant progress towards a common currency managed by a European Central Bank (in Genscher's eyes, a bank to be modelled on the German Bundesbank); parallel progress on the political-institutional front, including increased powers for the European Parliament (again an idea which appeals in detail more to Bonn than to Paris); and steps towards European military cooperation, in a form designed to make the Western European Union, under Franco-German leadership, something more like a defence agency of the Community than a European pillar of NATO. The outcome of this Franco-German meeting also reflected Genscher's strong insistence that the European Community, while proceeding with its proposed 'deepening' at Maastricht, should simultaneously pursue 'widening' in the sense of guiding not only Austria and other EFTA countries, but also and above all the new democracies of East Central Europe, towards eventual or even early membership.

In Genscher's second meeting, with his American counterpart James Baker, the emphasis was naturally on the prospects for the NATO summit to be held in Rome in mid-November, a month before Maastricht. Genscher insisted here again that a Western organisation should redefine its objectives, in the light of the revolution in East-West relations, so as to develop cooperative structures for European security to replace the old confrontation, and that the whole Atlantic alliance should commit itself to establishing formal consultative links with the Soviet Union's former satellites, and to providing concrete support for the Eastern reform movement. The joint declaration by Genscher and Baker duly endorsed these

* Professor of Political Science, European University Institute, Florence, and author of several books on European and German affairs; currently engaged in a study of the effects of German unification on German policy towards Europe.

aims, but, as a member of Genscher's staff put it, the Germans had found that it had 'not gone without saying' that the statement should speak of a 'common responsibility to help the reform movements to succeed'.[1] By placing this emphasis on the need for NATO's understanding and support for Germany's Eastern neighbours, Genscher was responding in his own way to President Bush's invitation to Bonn to join Washington in a 'partnership in leadership', issued early in 1989 in the distant era when Germany's division, and Europe's, looked as if they would be eternal.[2]

The third of Genscher's bilateral appearances was made with Boris Pankin, at that time the Foreign Minister of the Soviet Union. At a Moscow session of the 38 member-states of the Conference on Security and Cooperation in Europe, it was they who led a joint move to give the organisation more effective powers to intervene in international and potentially even in domestic problems, in the interests of European security and order. While the CSCE as an institution obviously does not have the same significance as the EC or NATO, German policy has favoured its upgrading as a pan-European forum, in which the Soviet Union could play an increasing part in resolving common problems.

Each of these three little vignettes of Mr Genscher with an influential foreign partner reflects an essential dimension of the structure of Germany's foreign relations in the new Europe. The Paris connection has been the basis of a Franco-German leadership in the European Community (discontinuous and at times faltering, to be sure, but on balance consistent and effective); the link with Washington has made Bonn a highly valued (partly because potentially a somewhat disquieting) member of the Atlantic alliance; and Bonn's direct line to Moscow (cleared tentatively by Adenauer in 1955 and definitively by Brandt in the early 1970s) has provided the basis for German-Soviet cooperation not only in the CSCE framework but in other European contexts as well.[3]

Paris, Washington and Moscow are by no means the only targets for German diplomatic efforts relating to Europe. London has appeared intermittently as a relevant partner (though the preferences of most British prime ministers have inevitably projected the UK mainly as a minor ally of America in the NATO context, rather than a potentially significant player in the EC game with France);[4] and many other capitals throughout Europe are of obvious importance to Germany. However, the geo-political position of the country has almost inevitably meant that the *lignes de force* of German interests have linked Bonn with Paris, Washington

[1] Quoted in *Die Zeit*, 11 October 1991, p. 13.

[2] For a contemporary impression, see the author's contribution 'The Elephant and the Chickens? German Dilemmas', in *Encounter*, November 1989.

[3] A detailed survey of German-Soviet relations is given by Michael J. Sodaro, *Moscow, Germany and the West from Kruschev to Gorbachov*, I. B. Taurus, London, 1991.

[4] See William Wallace, 'Foreign Policy: the Management of Distinctive Interests' in Roger Morgan and Caroline Bray (eds), *Partners and Rivals in Western Europe: Britain, France and Germany*, Gower for Policy Studies Institute, Aldershot, 1986.

and Moscow. The corresponding 'three circles' of Bonn's foreign policy—those of West European integration, North Atlantic security commitments, and pan-European cooperation—have all been essential for Germany's interests since at least the 1960s: the first two, indeed, for much longer. Bonn's practice of operating within the framework of three overlapping circles may, for British observers, recall London's ambition in the years after 1945 to function as a leading actor in the three circles of Western European cooperation, the Anglo-American 'special relationship', and what was then still 'the British Commonwealth'. It remains to be seen whether Bonn's attempt to reconcile its three circles (sometimes the need appears to be for squaring them) will be more successful in the long run than London's has been; in any case, each of Bonn's three relationships is buzzing with activity as the 'new Europe' takes shape, and it is worth considering what Germany is trying to put into, and get out of, each one of them.

As noted already, Bonn's relations with Paris and with Washington (the EC and NATO circles) are very long-established—in many respects they pre-date the very founding of the Federal Republic in 1949—and what is going on in these two relationships is in a sense the continuation of an established pattern. While it is clear, of course, that the current arguments about the future both of the EC and of NATO contain some radically new features (the special urgency of doing something drastic both about West European integration and about North Atlantic solidarity has been underlined by the revolutionary events in Europe since 1989), there is still a certain element of *déjà vu* about both endeavours.

The attempts of the Maastricht summit to consolidate the EC and Germany's anchorage in it, at the same time as developing new relations with the East, carry echoes of an earlier European summit (by an ironic coincidence, also under Dutch chairmanship, in 1969 at the Hague), when Kohl's predecessor Willy Brandt worked to secure the Community's 'completion, deepening and enlargement' (enlargement to the UK, Ireland and Scandinavia at this stage) partly in order to provide a solid Western base for his new *Ostpolitik* of cooperation with Germany's Eastern neighbours.[5]

Again, the current agonising reappraisal of the *raison d'être* of NATO, while it is in essential respects unique because of the apparently total evaporation of the 'Soviet threat', inevitably carries echoes of the great debates leading to NATO's Harmel Report of 1967. Then, the Alliance formally acknowledged that its purpose was to be a dual one: the deterrence of aggression on the one hand, and the pursuit of détente on the other. NATO's present process of redefinition is, to be sure, vastly more complex—the 'Old West' has to give itself a radically new purpose—but there is still a faint sense that on this great issue, as in the EC dimension,

---

[5] See Roger Morgan, *West European Politics since 1945: the Shaping of the European Community*, Batsford, London, 1972, pp. 222ff.

Germany and the rest of us are treading at least a dimly familiar path: if we have not exactly 'been here before', we have at least been on a path leading towards something like 'here'.[6]

By contrast, the third circle—the Moscow connection and the CSCE framework which faintly prefigures a new pan-European order—really does contain some dramatically new ingredients. Whatever habits of East-West consultation Bonn may have developed with Moscow (and with other Eastern capitals) in the twenty years between Brandt's visit to the Kremlin in 1970 and the Kohl-Gorbachev meeting of 1990 in the Caucasus, they were nothing like Bonn's links with Paris or Washington; and in any case the landscape to the east of the Elbe has been transformed by the unification of Germany, the disintegration of the Soviet Union, and the *Drang nach Westen* of a mass of ex-satellites all clamouring to be let into the Community, or NATO, or both. In this dimension of European affairs, surely—the dimension which represents the really unprecedented aspect of the 'new Europe'—there is a new role for the united Germany? (A Germany whose very creation was a vital part of the transformation, and which now, as a single state, has significant frontiers with Poland and Czechoslovakia, and thus a direct link with the whole area of the former Soviet empire.) Surely, after Hitler's demolition of the old foundations of Germany's economic and cultural influence in the East (not least through the near-extermination of the East European Jewry which was a principal guardian of German *Kultur*), there is a historical void in Germany's relations with *Ostmitteleuropa* and Eastern Europe (Russia included), where German policy has no established foundations to build on?

On the face of it, we could certainly expect this to be the case. And yet, on further reflection, one way of starting to assess the role of Germany in the new Europe would be to suggest that, new though this Europe may be in many ways, it also shows signs of reverting to an older one: a Europe in which the German role was ambiguous, sometimes even contradictory, but always highly influential. At the time of Willy Brandt's *Ostpolitik* of German-Soviet reconciliation in the early seventies, a Christian Democrat politician, in Moscow for an informal conference between German and Soviet research institutes, was buttonholed by a Moscow researcher who told him:

> Although our government is now working with Brandt and the German Left, we have never forgotten our friendly relations with your Centre-Right, for instance our Rapallo Treaty of 1922 or the Berlin Treaty signed by your Minister Stresemann with our Commissar Chicherin in 1926. The time for such cooperation will surely come again.

Twenty years later, when this very cooperation, between Kohl and Gorbachev, had significantly eased the unification of Germany, another German participant in a similar German-Soviet round table was asked by

[6] See Roger Morgan, *The United States and West Germany, 1945–1973: a Study in Alliance Politics*, OUP for Royal Institute of International Affairs 1974, pp. 179–181.

his Russian hosts: 'As you Germans have so much influence with the Ukrainians, could you not persuade them to remain inside our reformed Soviet Union?'[7] (The background to this odd request, it seems, was that the leaders of the Ukraine, on a visit to Munich, had been assured of Bavaria's sympathy for their wish for more independence from Moscow—a story which illustrates the ambiguous nature of the messages emanating towards the East from a Germany which may or may not be influential enough for these messages to be effective.) There are many similar stories of old German links with the East being picked up and revived. For instance, the senior official who prepared the ground for Bonn's establishment of diplomatic relations with the Baltic states (Berndt von Staden, a retired Permanent Secretary of the Foreign Ministry) is descended from one of the famous Baltic German families; he had last been in the area as a young officer in the Estonian army before the Soviet take-over in 1940!

Limits to German ambitions

But how much substance can there be in this exciting but in a way predictable revival of ghostly links between Germany and an *Ost- und Mitteleuropa* that is radically different from the area where German influence was once so strong? Will the revival of Germany's economic and political links here lead to a re-balancing or re-evaluation? What will follow the intriguing re-establishment of the old connections (here as in Czecho-Slovakia, where a whiff of Habsburg revival is in the air as a Prince Schwarzenberg advises President Havel in Prague's Hradcany Palace, and a Count Kinski addresses the Diet of Slovakia in Bratislava—urging them to go for European federalism rather than Slovak separatism)?

At the level of nostalgic cultural tourism for Germans through a once-familiar landscape which the war and the Iron Curtain brutally cut off—the area from 'Königsberg' (Kaliningrad) in the north to 'Laibach' (Ljubljana) in the south—'the Germans' will show an increasing curiosity and interest. At the level of hard politics and economics, however, any serious reorientation will take time.[8]

Germany and her leaders, not surprisingly, are really not in a mood to develop any grand designs for a pan-European structure based on German power and influence, despite all the rhetoric from Mr Genscher about a new construction rising from the present network of Eastern connections. We have to remember, after all, that in the two years since 1989 the somnolent and self-satisfied Federal Republic—the country

[7] The German protagonists in these encounters were respectively Karl-Heinz Narjes and Lothar Rühl.

[8] For a useful collection of assessments and documents covering the years 1989 and 1990, see Adam Daniel Rotfeld and Walter Stutzle (eds), *Germany and Europe in Transition*, OUP for Stockholm International Peace Research Institute, 1991.

whose citizens regularly answered opinion polls by saying that the country they most aspired to resemble was Switzerland—has been through some profoundly unsettling experiences, which are not yet over. If Bonn's political establishment, and the banking fraternity in Frankfurt, show signs of policy overload, it has to be remembered that the rush of public events in Germany since 1989 has left them with hardly a calm moment, let alone a dull one.

Even leaving aside the murder of two leading financiers (Herrhausen and Rohwedder) and the failed attempts on the lives of two leading politicians (Schäuble and Lafontaine), there has been an air of latent and sometimes overt drama in Germany, occasionaly verging on hysteria. Election results have veered erratically one way and the other: the euphoric votes of confidence in 'Kohl, the Chancellor of unity' which brought his Christian Democrats great gains in the *Land* elections of the GDR area in March 1990, and in the first all-German elections in December, gave way to a swing to the Social Democrats in early 1991, which cost Kohl his home state of Rheinland-Pfalz, and then in turn to a swing against both big parties at the Bremen election in September, which brought ominous gains for the extreme-right Republican Party.

Simultaneously with this electoral volatility, and no doubt one of its causes, Germany has been experiencing the strains and stresses of coming to terms with the fact of unification. The inspiring slogan of 1989 'Wir sind ein Volk', certainly expressed a reality which was powerful enough to bring the German people into a single state within a year—with the agreement of the four 'allied powers', who quite quickly realised that this process was unstoppable. But the problems of bringing the two parts of Germany into a single national community have proved to be immensely difficult, and will continue to be so. Forty years of division have implanted differing attitudes to politics, to work, to social relationships and expectations, in ways which now produce serious frictions between *Ossis* and *Wessis*, as Easterners and Westerners feel their way towards a single national identity. The first impact of the transition to a market economy in the East is large-scale unemployment, as the hopelessly uneconomic industrial plants are closed down; the first impact of unification on the West—an identity. The first impact of the transition to a market economy in the East as the Western part of the country transfers unprecedently large amounts of its wealth to rebuild the economy in the East. While *Ossis* complain of the arrogant and dominating behaviour of the *Wessis*, these in turn often protest at being taxed for the benefit of Easterners who, as the Westerners see it, expect to become rich without doing an honest day's work. At every level of society, as a torrent of media discussion continues to show, the problems of progressing from *Einheit* (formal uniting of two states) to *Einigung* (the bringing-together of two very different societies) entail very considerable stresses and strains. The enormous gulf between the ex-GDR area and the West will of course narrow over the next few years (some experts maintain that the State of Saxony has the resources and skills to overtake even Baden-Württemberg by the late 1990s), but the whole complex problem of adjustment will continue to preoccupy the Germans for many years to come.[9]

Superimposed on the social and economic strains of unification came the crucial decision about whether Germany's future seat of government should be Bonn, the provincial capital of the last forty years, or Berlin. The controversy in early 1991 which led up to the German parliament's narrow vote in favour of Berlin was marked by a passionate confrontation between viewpoints which raised the fundamental question of the new Germany's internal structure, and its orientation towards the new Europe. Supporters of a move to Berlin, from President Richard von Weizsäcker downwards, argued that the re-establishment of a united Germany should be completed by the re-establishment of Berlin as capital, partly because this would give encouragement to the deprived regions of the former GDR and partly because it would signal the new Germany's friendly interest in the neighbouring states to the East, whose potential relations with the European Community would depend heavily on German support and encouragement. Those who supported the continuation of Bonn as capital argued that the Rhineland city symbolised the forty-year success story of the Federal Republic—by far the most democratic and stable regime in Germany's history—whereas a move to Berlin would hark back to the traditions of Prussian authoritarianism and Nazi militarism, not to mention the dictatorship of the GDR. There were of course countless further arguments on each side; after months of bitter polemic, the arguments which won the day for Berlin were at least in part those reflecting the need for West Germans to recognise the brave achievements of East Germans in fighting successfully to bring national unity about. After decades in which West Berlin had been maintained by the West as the declared capital of a future reunited German nation, it would have been dishonourable to expect the East Germans simply to accept rule from far-away Bonn. Moreover, the economic plight of the ex-GDR area, and its continuing need for material support from the West, could be more clearly kept in the minds of cabinet ministers and top officials if their place of work was in Berlin, in the centre of the affected area.[10]

Even though detailed examination showed that the actual move of the governmental machine to Berlin might well be delayed for up to a decade, for want of financial and other resources, the controversy on this issue, like the problems of party-political fluctuations and the reconciliation of Eastern and Western societies, contributed greatly to distracting the

[9] For a comprehensive analysis, see Klaus von Dohnanyi, *Das Deutsche Wagnis*, Droemer Knaur, Munich, 1990.

[10] President von Weizsäcker's memorandum of February 1991, arguing the case for Berlin, is reprinted in his book *Von Deutschland nach Europa*, Siedler, Berlin, 1991, pp. 221–227. A more detailed discussion, again ending in favour of Berlin, is in Klaus von Beyme, *Hauptstadtsuche. Hauptstadtfunktionen im Interessenkonflikt zwischen Bonn und Berlin*, Suhrkamp, Frankfurt a.M., 1991.

Germans from any ambition to extend German power and influence in the new Europe. A further development which contributed to the same effect was—perhaps paradoxically—the rise of extreme right-wing agitation and xenophobia during 1991. Whereas right-wing extremism had usually been associated with expansionist policies towards the outside world— particularly in Germany—the widespread outbreaks of brutal aggression against foreigners which marked the summer and autumn of 1991 seemed to concentrate essentially on forcing unwanted immigrants to leave the country. A main cause of the atrocities—which began in the former GDR but quickly spread westward—was a violent reaction against the compulsory 'international socialist solidarity' which the East German state had forced its citizens to observe in relation to immigrant workers from Cuba, Vietnam or Mozambique. The pent-up frustration at this policy—which seemed to many East Germans to have deprived them of housing or employment—was then aggravated by a dimension of extreme nationalism stimulated by the achievement of national unity.

In the euphoria of rediscovering and redefining an all-German identity, it was hardly surprising that a few extremists were carried away into nationalist excesses, at the expense of vulnerable groups of non-Germans. The wave of violent racist attacks did, in fact, help to focus public and political attention on the very real problems resulting from Germany's extremely liberal policies concerning the welcome given to political asylum-seekers (a deliberate reaction, like so much else in the Federal Republic, against the barbarism of the Third Reich), and from the open door policy which allowed immigrants of German origin to come in hundreds of thousands.

The disturbances arising from this range of problems certainly played their part in dissuading the Germans from thinking of any grandiose plans for extending Germany's influence over their European surroundings. Insofar as the problems of asylum-seekers and would-be immigrants impinged on thinking about Germany's place in Europe, they resulted in a widespread view that, in order to restrain further mass immigration into an already over-full Germany, inducements should be given to potential immigrants—Poles, Volga Germans and others—to stay in the East rather than move. This might be achieved, it was widely agreed, by economic aid to promote the development of the Russian and other East European economies, and by bringing Germany's Eastern neighbours into stable and structured relationships with the European Community.

Thinking in Germany about the role the country should play in the 'new Europe' was thus conditioned, or hampered, by Germany's quite understandable preoccupation with a number of issues concerning the country's internal processes and internal arrangements. What lines of European policy could be seen to emerge, in this confused and many-faceted situation?

Limits to German influence

It is of course too early to tell exactly how the vast internal changes in Germany will influence German policy towards a Europe which has also, at least in the East, undergone changes of an equally radical kind. A few years from now, when the traumas of unification have been overcome, and Germany can focus more clearly on its external objectives, it may well be that German designs for Europe will still have the basic shape they have today: commitment to a deeper union of the Western European Community, flanked by a continuing security partnership with the United States and an increasingly close relationship with the Eastern neighbours, tending towards their actual membership of the Community. There are at least strong indications that German policy in the early nineties will continue to try to hold the balance between these three essential dimensions of policy, though the scope they respectively offer for German initiatives may well change: in particular, Germany's ability to influence Washington is likely to decrease considerably, and her influence in the European Community may also diminish (though to a lesser degree), while Germany's voice in the shaping of a really new 'pan-Europe' is likely to become more powerful.

The reason why Bonn's influence on Washington may be expected to decline is essentially that the United States, in the period following the end of the Cold War, is probably heading for a distinct disengagement from the affairs of Europe. One indication of this is the substantial withdrawal of American ground forces from Western Europe, and another is the re-orientation of Washington's diplomatic priorities to the Middle East (following the military victory over Iraq) and other non-European areas. Even though American interest in the stability of Europe as a whole will obviously remain strong, and Washington will naturally want to co-ordinate the general lines of its policy with Bonn (as in the Genscher-Baker discussion sketched above), the period when Bonn was able to exert decisive influence on American policy appears to be over.

As far as the European Community is concerned (this means in the first place, though not exclusively, Bonn's relations with Paris), it would be more accurate to suggest that Bonn's capacity to influence the EC in the direction of change is likely to be less in the future than it was in the past. This may be partly a matter of deliberate choice on Bonn's part: the perspectives of German influence on the broader Europe—pan-Europe—are more open, in terms both of challenges and of opportunities; and if Bonn's EC partners are going to resist the reforms which the Bonn government proposes (for instance, substantial increases in the powers of the European Parliament), why should Germany continue to expend resources and energy on the struggle? Another reason for a slackening in German efforts for closer integration of the EC is the degree to which Germany's economic resources have been pre-empted by the costs of reunification: this must underlie the slowing-down of the EC timetable in which Chancellor Kohl, in February 1991, approved a revised German draft treaty on Economic and Monetary Union which provided for the establishment of a European Central Bank to be reached only with Stage III in 1997, not in 1994 as earlier envisaged with France.[11] More generally, however, Bonn's capacity and/or inclination to press its EC partners into comprehensive deepening of the Community may well decline as the costs of doing so become greater. If London and Paris are adamant that Community institutions should not obtain significant increases of power (or if Paris wishes for substantial monetary integration without the corresponding institutional development on which Chancellor Kohl has so far insisted), will Bonn not be inclined to let the Community remain at roughly its present level of integration (which suits German interests very well in many ways), rather than to continue to press for change? A further reason why Bonn may prefer to wait for a new consensus to mature, rather than pressing for it now, is that the EC's conferences of 1991 have hardly scratched the surface of the problems posed by the probable enlargment of the Community beyond its present membership of twelve, and this prospect requires a great deal of hard thinking.

This brings us back to Germany's view of the prospects to the East. Some of the elements of a German role in this new area for Western initiatives—indeed in some ways an area of chaos, positively crying out for Western initiatives—have already been mentioned. They include the gigantic economic and psychological effort of reintegrating the former GDR area with the national fatherland, including the symbolic move of the capital back to the East. They also include the initiatives to extend the scope of NATO's interest to Central Europe, and to give new powers and new life to the CSCE; and further, the manifest German commitment to develop the European Community's relations with its Eastern neighbours to the point of welcoming them into membership as early as this is feasible.

One might add other indications of Bonn's active interest in the Eastern part of the continent: German haste to recognise the independence of the Baltic states (and to look after the economic interests of Kaliningrad/ Königsberg); a corresponding demand by Bonn for early granting of self-determination to Croatia and Slovenia (a demand urgently pressed in summer 1991, then modified to comply with the EC consensus, then strongly revived later in the year, as EC mediation appeared to fail and the plight of Croatia worsened); the commitment of substantial German aid to the disintegrating Soviet Union, combined with the active cultivation of the Russian President Boris Yeltsin (whose visit to Germany in November 1991 was his first to a West European country); and Germany's demands in NATO, as a contribution to East-West confidence-building, for an early ban on short-range nuclear missiles.

[11] *Agence Europe*, 27 February 1991.

It should be noted in passing that Germany's fairly strong assertion of her views on these matters—and on others, such as the establishment of full national control over the German armed forces, and the request that the German language should be more widely used in the institutions of the EC—reflects a new self-confidence, which is probably a natural consequence of Germany's achievement of national unification. It should also be recalled that any aspirations Germans may cherish to play a greater international role certainly do not extend any distance beyond Europe. Germany's reluctance to consider even the possibility of an active military role in the Gulf War in 1990–91 was the subject of strong criticism in the United States, Britain, and elsewhere; and the assurances given by Chancellor Kohl and other Christian Democrat leaders that the constitution would be amended, to ensure the constitutionality of German participation in any future UN military actions of this kind, appear to have evaporated in the face of strong reservations on the part not only of the opposition, but also of Mr Genscher's Free Democrats. Later in 1991, it was noticeable that an appeal by the new American Ambassador in Bonn for Germany to become a more active partner of the US in relation, for instance, to China, to Korea, to Cambodia, or to various parts of Africa, was greeted with no enthusiasm whatsoever.[12]

The new Germany's international rôle, at least as far as political objectives are concerned, will thus be essentially focused, for quite understandable reasons, on Europe. What is more, the kind of policies which Germany will pursue towards European problems will be shaped by the factors—external and internal—outlined above. The biggest change could perhaps be summarised by saying that whereas for forty years the term *Europapolitik*—'policy on Europe'—has essentially meant policy towards and within the European Community, the new Europe will bring a redefinition. This does not mean that German policy will swing away from the West to concentrate on new opportunities in the East: the view that the EC was a device of foreign powers for constraining Germany's independence, and that a united Germany can now break free and play a national role in co-operation with the East, is that of an insignificant minority.[13] It does not mean, either, that Germany can be expected to take the line sometimes associated with British policy, namely that the Community should be extended to embrace all the new democracies of Central and Eastern Europe as rapidly as possible, precisely on the calculation that 'broader will be shallower', and that the aim of supranational integration will be, mercifully, diluted in a loose and large free trade area.

The mainstream of German thinking about Europe, and the main thrust of German *Europapolitik*—taking account of the new fact that we are now

[12] *International Herald Tribune*, 19 September 1991.

[13] For instance Herbert Kremp of *Die Welt*, quoted extensively in Peter Glotz, 'Neue Deutsche Ideologie' in *Der Spiegel*, 30 September 1990. See also Glotz's book *Der Irrweg des Nationalstaats. Europäische Reden an ein Deutsches Publikum*, Deutsche Verlags-Anstalt, Stuttgart, 1990.

in a Europe where events not only in the old EC area but in the East as well can be shaped by German policy—is likely to show much less dramatic changes than those just sketched. The balance of German economic interests, cultural affinities, and political preferences will remain over-whelmingly with the West (including the continuing security link with Washington), and the new ingredient of purposeful interaction with the East will be added only cautiously and sparingly. It is true that some people in Germany speak as if a further deepening of Germany's Western ties must be made conditional on a parallel development of those with the East. For instance Hans Arnold, a retired ambassador, writes:

> Just as it is impossible for the EC to build a wall on Oder and Neisse, it is impossible to prevent a stronger orientation of German foreign policy towards Eastern Europe, determined by the central situation of Germany. It will be possible to consolidate Germany's ties in the West, in the transformed Europe of tomorrow, to the extent that the European states to the East of Germany can be linked in with the West.[14]

It must be said that this specific statement of conditionality—which appears to mean that Germany can take no steps towards the further integration of Western Europe unless her Eastern neighbours can some-how be brought along too—is very far from the official thinking of the Bonn government, and very far from the policy steps actually being under-taken. In most material ways, the mainstream of German activity in Europe still flows strongly westward: symbolically, the Bundesbank and Finance Ministry are busy working out the details of the projected (West) European Central Bank at the very moment when the Deutsche Bank (long active in the East) has gone to the lengths of actually closing down its Moscow branch because of lack of business and lack of prospects.

German finance and German diplomacy will of course be increasingly involved in the East, but only within severely circumscribed limits. It is a fairly safe bet that the seventieth anniversary of the Treaty of Rapallo (16 April 1992) will not see any signs of a German Eastern involvement remotely comparable with the accord signed in 1922, and its wide-reaching implications.[15] For the Germans, as for the rest of us, 1992 is likely to be mainly a year of continued preoccupation with the shape (and only to a lesser extent with the size) of the European Community we have established in Europe's Western part. The objectives of Germany's *Europapolitik*, defined realistically, are likely to be: in Western Europe, modest advances in the further integration of the Community; in the Atlantic dimension, a continued attempt to consolidate NATO, at the same time as developing its new role in enhancing pan-European security; and in the Eastern direction, a cautious but purposeful exploration of the

[14] Hans Arnold, 'Die EG zwischen Vertiefung und Erweiterung', in *Europa-Archiv*, 1991, No. 10, p. 326.
[15] See Roger Morgan, 'The Political Significance of German-Soviet Trade Negotiations, 1922–25' in *The Historical Journal*, VI, 2 (1963), pp. 253–271.

possibilities—which may prove to be either quite wide or very narrow—of promoting economic development and political stability in the backward part of a newly-defined European continent.

FINLAND IN THE WAKE OF EUROPEAN CHANGE

DAG ANCKAR AND VOITTO HELANDER*

BEFORE becoming a sovereign state, Finland was subjected to Swedish and Russian rule for a long time. In the late Middle Ages, she was incorporated into Sweden, and for the next seven hundred years, up to the early nineteenth century, remained a Swedish county. In 1809, Finland was ceded to Russia as a consequence of the so-called Finnish War of 1808–1809 and incorporated into Russia as a Grand Duchy, with relatively wide autonomy in her domestic affairs. Finland thus had a central government of her own, as well as her own banking, customs, and postal systems. During the whole period of Russian rule (1809–1917), the 1772 Form of Government Act of Sweden remained in force in Finland, and the country preserved its legal and social affinity with the Nordic community.

Finland gained independence in 1917, taking advantage of the revolutionary situation in Russia to break free from the Russian Empire. During the inter-war era, the relations between Finland and the Soviet Union remained unstable and even hostile. The contacts between the countries were narrow and formal, and one interpretation of Finland's position between East and West which was rather popular at the time emphasised the role of Finland as the last outpost of Western civilisation and values against those of the East. In this interpretation, Finland lay on the borderline between West-European culture and Byzantine—or Eastern—culture. During the Second World War, Finland fought against the Soviet Union, and as a result of the war had to cede Karelia to her eastern neighbour. Finland was also forced to pay heavy reparations to the Soviet Union. In comparison with several other European countries that fought on the losing side Finland was, however, fortunate. Finland was never occupied, and the political system of the country remained more or less intact.[1]

The Second World War marked a turning point in Finnish–Soviet relations. The establishment of functional, friendly, and trustful relations with the Soviet Union, whose super-power position became indisputable after the war, was now an essential task for Finnish foreign policy. At the same time, however, Finland wanted to maintain good relations with the

* Dag Anckar is Professor of Political Science at the Åbo Academy University, Finland, and Voitto Helander is Associate Professor of Political Science at the University of Turku, Finland.

[1] There are several good expositions of Finland's post-war foreign policy. See, for instance, George Maude, *The Finnish Dilemma: Neutrality in the Shadow of Power*, Oxford University Press, 1976.

Western countries, especially her Nordic neighbours, and she chose to pursue a policy of neutrality as a means of keeping the country out of conflicts and of developing good relations with all major powers. The change in Finland's foreign policy soon brought about radical improvements in Finnish–Soviet relations. However, these relations have not been unproblematic. They were tested during the 'Nightfrost crisis' of 1958–1959 and the 'Note crisis' of 1961–1962, two events which carry evidence of lingering Soviet suspicions against developments in Finnish domestic politics.[2] Finnish and Soviet views of the extent to which Finland may really function as a neutral country have also at times been in conflict, and it was only in 1989 that Finland's neutrality was acknowledged in un-ambiguous terms by the Soviet leadership. Finland's position has not always found understanding in Western circles. The concept of 'Finland-isation', which was introduced to the international political debate during the days of the Cold War to illustrate the position of a country that is subordinate to Soviet interests, is an example of one-sided Western inter-pretations of Finnish aspirations. On the whole, however, Finnish policy has received recognition in the international community, and in 1975 Finland hosted the Conference on Security and Cooperation in Europe.

The profound system changes in Eastern Europe and the Soviet Union, as well as the détente between East and West, will of course affect Finland's position in a variety of ways. Although the emergence of a New Europe certainly implies more than a transformation of the Soviet position and of Soviet society, the specific weight attached to the Soviet Union in Finland's foreign policy makes the Soviet changes especially important from a Finnish point of view. The following discussion will dwell on three topics in that area. We shall first comment on some aspects of Finnish foreign policy and security, and then turn to the economic relations, which have been damaged, rather than promoted, by the recent events. Thirdly, the developments have had and will have consequences for the political culture in Finland, especially in the field of foreign policy, and these consequences merit attention.

Towards flexible neutrality

Like most foreign policy signals and instruments, post-war Finnish foreign policy doctrine has been context-bound. It has departed from two convic-tions and lessons. The first is that the geopolitical situation of Finland is determined once and for all and that Finland can never again act against the vital security interests of her eastern superpower neighbour. This lesson was learned during the wars against the Soviet Union between 1939

---

[2] These crises are described and analysed at length in Raimo Väyrynen, *Conflicts in Finnish-Soviet Relations: Three Comparative Case Studies*, Acta Universitatis Tamperensis, Ser. A Vol. 47, 1972.

and 1944. The other conviction is that the division of Europe into two parts, each dominated by a superpower, is a permanent political arrangement, which constitutes a frame of reference for the behaviour of Finland. The general foreign policy line that Finland has pursued, as well as the concrete undertakings of the country in the area of security policy and foreign policy, are deductions from this framework, and they are rooted in two corner-stones.

One is neutrality; the other is the Soviet–Finnish Friendship, Cooperation and Mutual Assistance Treaty, signed in 1948 and cancelled in 1992 as a consequence of the disappearance of the Soviet Union from the political scene. In terms of history, culture, and her economic and political system, Finland is a part of the Western world; because, for geopolitical reasons, this affiliation cannot have foreign policy manifestations, neutrality has been the only conceivable foreign policy solution for Finland. The treaty, on the other hand, assured the security of the Soviet Union, as it forbad the use of Finnish territory for attacks against the Soviet Union. However, the two corner-stones have been to some extent incompatible, one consequence of which is that foreign observers often found the Finnish doctrine confusing and not fully convincing. Finnish attempts to explain and clarify the relation between these two central components of the country's foreign policy doctrine have not always been successful, and have often added to, rather than curtailed, the confusion and the misperceptions. The incompatibility resulted from some central stipulations in the text of the treaty.

The signatories to the treaty agree that Finland must deter any attack from Germany, or an ally of Germany, against Finnish territory, or through it against the Soviet Union. This stipulation was certainly in full conformity with the obligations of a neutral country. However, a further stipulation which provides that Finland must rely on Soviet military aid, if necessary, conflicts with the principles of neutrality. Finnish interpretations of the treaty assumed that aid from the Soviet Union can be given only if both parties recognised the necessity of aid; however, this was not explicitly stated in the treaty. Furthermore, the parties agree to confer if a threat of an attack exists, which obviously means that both parties have the right to initiate consultations whenever they find that the geopolitical situation calls for such initiatives. Other stipulations in the treaty, such as those concerning mutual participation in the maintenance of international peace and the development of economic and cultural relations between the parties, were unproblematic with regard to the principles of neutrality. However, the stipulations concerning aid and consultations have clearly been burdens for Finland's neutrality.

A superpower confrontation in Europe would have been a touchstone for Finnish neutrality, and it is conceivable that the treaty increased, rather than decreased, the difficulties Finland faced. In short, the treaty made Finland an ally of the Soviet Union in the eyes of both NATO and the Soviet Union, and an ally which claims neutrality is not accorded credibility by non-allies, nor acceptability by alliance partners. Therefore, attempts to contribute to the maintenance of peace in Europe and the rest of the world have been natural, and even necessary, features of the Finnish foreign policy. These attempts have also aimed at solving the role ambiguities that the treaty creates.[3] Finland faced the simultaneous requirements of fulfilling the military obligations of the treaty and directing the country's foreign policy so that the military obligations will not become actual and cause damage to the credibility of Finnish neutrality. The way to solve this role ambiguity was to minimise the influence of political and military factors that may destabilise the situation in the Nordic region and in adjacent areas; hence, the Finnish need to pursue an 'active and peaceful policy of neutrality', to quote one basic expression of the Finnish foreign policy liturgy.

The dramatic changes in the European scene came as a surprise to the Finnish political and scientific establishments. When the present Finnish Minister of Foreign Affairs, Paavo Väyrynen, defended his doctoral thesis in the field of international relations at Åbo Academy University in 1988, he developed one of his main themes, an attempt to predict the future applications of the Finnish foreign policy doctrine, by arguing that the developments in the Soviet Union would hardly affect the ideological and political antagonism between Eastern Europe and Western Europe.[4] In the same vein, one of the leading Finnish scholars in the field of international politics argued in a book published in 1988 that 'the international context of contemporary neutrality ... will in all likelihood remain broadly the same for at least the next fifteen or twenty years'.[5] Today, a high extent of confusion and uncertainty marks the Finnish intellectual climate. This is, of course, only natural. The whole frame of reference for defining and defending the national interest of the country has disappeared. The corner-stones are suddenly no longer there. An internal transformation is going on in the former Soviet Union, and the region no longer presents a threat to the Western world. The Warsaw Pact has ceased to exist; Germany has reunified; the countries of Eastern Europe have experienced political revolutions; the political and ideological divide between East and West has passed away. For what purpose, then, is Finnish neutrality now needed? In relation to what and whom should neutrality now be pursued?

The current international situation has two main implications for Finnish foreign policy. One is the need to adapt to the changes on the level of theory and doctrine, and to develop new guidelines, and a new intellectual basis, for the conduct of foreign policy. This is a very difficult task,

[3] Raimo Väyrynen, 'Neutrality and Non-Alignment: The Case of Finland', *The Non-Aligned World*, Vol. 1, 1983, p. 355.
[4] Paavo Väyrynen, *Finlands utrikespolitik—den nationella doktrinen och framtidens mänsklighetspolitik*, Söderström, Förlags Ab, 1988, p. 208.
[5] Harto Hakovirta, *East-West Conflict and European Neutrality*, Clarendon Press, 1988, p. 56.

and it is understandable that the official Finnish interpretation of the transformation is cautious and stresses continuity rather than change. There are several objective reasons for this. It is unclear, to say the least, how the changes will affect the military geography of the high North, and it may be a wise policy to adhere to established and tested patterns as long as the future constellations are hazy and difficult to analyse. An emphasis on the need for stability and continuity in the nation's foreign policy is also imperative from the point of view of the organisational interests of the foreign ministry: one likely consequence of a change in the intellectual foundation of Finnish foreign policy would be a rapid transformation of the administrative process in this field towards management procedures less centred on the foreign minister than is the case now.[6] However, the changes in the international environment of Finnish foreign policy are definite and irreversible, and sooner or later they must have an impact on the Finnish way of looking at European politics and on Finland's role in the European security setting. Cautiousness may be a virtue today; tomorrow it will become a burden.

The second implication is of a more immediate nature. The changes in Europe have lessened the importance of neutrality and offered neutral states more scope in terms of interpretations of neutrality. Neutrality is no longer as great a restraint on a country's freedom of action as it used to be; neutral countries may adapt to changes, and alter their behaviour, without abandoning neutrality as a guiding principle for action. This is important for Finland, as it directly affects the country's possibilities to negotiate with the European community and to participate in European economic integration.

The restraints on the participation of neutral countries in West European integration have to do with the connections of the integration with the Western bloc and with the potential limitations on the sovereignty of participants that follow from integration. The first of these restraints is no longer concern for Finland. In earlier instances of integration, Finland has been careful to extend to the former Soviet Union the same trade privileges she has received through Western integration and to treat the Soviet Union in the same manner as her Western trade partners. For instance, the concessions to the EC countries through the agreement between Finland and the EEC signed in 1973 were also granted to the Soviet Union. Now that the former Soviet Union and the East European countries themselves seek to improve their economic relations with Western Europe and to share the benefits of integration, the integration of neutral countries with the EC economies does not give cause to political objections in Eastern Europe.[7] Although the implications of closer relations with EC for neutrality policy may seem unclear, neutrality is no longer a definite

    [6] Lauri Karvonen and Bengt Sundelius, 'Surviving the New Europe: Nordic Neutrality Between International Change and Domestic Institutionalisation' (forthcoming).
    [7] Pauli Järvenpää, 'Finland: An Image of Continuity in Turbulent Europe', *The Annals of the American Academy of Political and Social Science*, Vol. 512, 1990, pp. 136–137.

obstacle to the development of such relations. As to the consequences of integration on Finnish sovereignty, this restraint is clearly still valid, not least in terms of attitudes and dispositions in Finnish domestic politics, which are not ready to accept qualifications to Finland's right to decide her own affairs. Curiously enough, such attitudes are especially strong in those political quarters that were previously the most eager spokesmen for political and economic concessions towards the Soviet Union.

Economic policy

Economic policy has constituted one of the most important instruments for stabilising Finnish–Soviet relations during the post-WWII era. Starting from a zero-situation, Finnish–Soviet economic relations extended rapidly. It may be noted that the massive reparations that Finland had to pay to the Soviet Union after the war were one important reason for the rapid increase in Finnish–Soviet trade. The fulfilment of the war indemnity requirement presupposed vast investments in the metal and engineering industries. When the indemnity had been paid off, deliveries continued on a commercial basis.[8]

With certain exceptions, Finnish–Soviet trade developed favourably until the mid-eighties. In the fifties, Finland became the most important Western trade partner of the Soviet Union. She retained this position until the seventies, when Germany overtook her. In 1988, Finland still remained in second place in the Soviet Union's Western trade, even if her relative share had declined somewhat from the early eighties.

From the mid-fifties to the late eighties, the Soviet share of Finnish foreign trade was very high, about one fifth of the total. With the exception of the early seventies, the Soviet share kept rising until the mid-eighties. In the early years of the 1980s, the Soviet Union clearly topped the list of Finland's trade partners. In 1983, the Soviet share of the total volume of Finnish imports was as high as 25.7 per cent, and in 1982 the corresponding share of the aggregate volume of Finnish exports rose to 26.7 per cent.

Even if the formidable Russian share declined during the eighties, the Soviet Union maintained her priority position in Finnish foreign trade until the turn of the decade. The Soviet share remained much higher than that of the other East European countries.

Soviet trade has been advantageous to Finland for several reasons. The most important reason has been the opportunity to secure Finland's energy needs through vast imports from the Soviet Union. By far the most important imports have been oil and natural gas. They have constituted as much as about 85 per cent of all imports. Finnish exports to the Soviet

---

[8] Concerning Finland's trade with the Soviet Union, see e.g. Heikki Karkkolainen, 'Perestroika Opens New Trade Opportunities', in *Business Finland 1989*, Sanomaprint Business Publications, 1989; and Olle Anckar, 'Finlands utrikeshandel', in Ulf Lindström and Lauri Karvonen (eds), *Finland. En politisk loggbok*, Almqvist & Wiksell International, 1987.

Union, on the other hand, have mostly been highly refined products, such as special ships—icebreakers, for instance—engines, and clothes. Soviet trade has also effectively levelled fluctuations in the demand for Finnish products. This was important, for instance, during the period following the 1973 oil crisis.

It may be noted that Finnish–Soviet economic relations have not been restricted to the exchange of goods alone. An agreement covering cooperation in science and technology was signed in 1955, and these activities have been coordinated by a joint committee. In the eighties, capital investment has grown in importance. In establishing joint ventures with a Soviet partner, Finland has trailed Germany as the second Western country, with a share of ten per cent.

The success and stability in the economic sector may, to a great extent, be attributed to certain special arrangements in Finnish–Soviet trade relations. Finland is, in fact, the only Western state that has conducted her trade with the Soviet Union within a bilateral framework. Barter arrangements have characterised Finnish–Soviet trade. This kind of barter trade has presupposed the implementation of a relatively complicated mechanism in which the role of the state has been of a greater importance than it would have been if convertible currency had been used.

The economic agreements between the countries constituted the basis of the system, which was composed of three levels. The long-term programmes set out the broad outlines for a decade and a half. The five-year frame agreements have been based on the long-term programmes. In the annual trade protocols based on the five-year general agreements on bartering and payments, the volume and quality of the commodities has been determined more accurately. The payment system has adapted to the Soviet planned economy. With a clearing arrangement in place, there has been no need for convertible currencies.

It may also be mentioned that Finland granted most-favoured-nation status to the Soviet Union in bilateral trade in 1947. When Finland became an associate member of EFTA in 1961 and made an agreement with the EEC in 1973, the same tariff privileges which were granted to her partners in these organisations were also granted to the Soviet Union.

The implementation of the agreements has been conducted by joint commissions. The Finnish side of these commissions has been based on a corporatist arrangement. Representatives of the government under the leadership of the prime minister have constituted one segment of the delegation. Leaders of the industries, together with delegates of the trade union movement, have constituted the other segments. This kind of composition has made it possible to take different societal and economic interests into consideration. Such an arrangement has also given certain continuance and stability to the system.

It may also be stressed that the trade policy measures have been in the interest of the highest political leadership of Finland. The president of the republic has followed the developments in economic policy very closely.

Especially in crisis situations, the presidents have not hesitated to intervene in the difficulties of trade policy. One example is the intervention of President Kekkonen to solve the difficulties with the Soviet leader Khrushchev after the crisis period of the early sixties. It may also be stressed that several large construction projects have first been given a push in discussions of the highest political level before being incorporated into the official agenda of the trade policy organisations.

Recently, Finnish–Soviet economic relations suffered badly for several reasons. The collapse of the Soviet economy, together with certain developments in the world economy, had profound consequences for the content, volume, and institutional arrangements of Finnish–Soviet trade. It is true that the bilateral trade system experienced its first troubles already in 1982 when the price of oil declined. As a result of the decline of the oil price in 1986, the trade became more and more imbalanced, as Soviet imports were unable to match Finnish exports. During the last years of the eighties and the first years of the nineties, the level of trade rapidly decreased. It is true that Soviet trade with Western countries in general decreased in recent years. However, her trade with Finland dropped more than that with the other Western countries.

During the last half decade, different kinds of attempts to repair the imbalance of Finnish–Soviet trade were made. Despite these efforts at restructuring the system of clearing payments, the deadlock was not resolved. In early 1991, the system of bilateralism on the basis of barter was dissolved at the request of the Soviet Union. However, the system change was not able to correct the imbalance. On the contrary, by mid-1991, Russian debt to Finland had increased to a point of 1 500 Finnish marks per capita, six times the Soviet Union's average debt to the Western countries. It may be stated that this time the efforts to solve the problem at the highest political level failed.

As a result of the dissolution of the clearing system, the agreements based on planning periods, as well as the trade commissions which implemented the agreements, have lost significance greatly. In short, this means that in the future Finland has to adapt to the market system with convertible currencies. This kind of competitive system will make Finland's position in the Russian market more unstable and more difficult to forecast.

The profound changes in Finnish–Soviet trade relations have had certain direct consequences for the Finnish economy. Especially those industries that were very dependent on the Soviet market—such as shipbuilding, textiles, clothing, and footwear—have suffered badly from the stagnation of Soviet trade. It has proved very difficult to shift from the Soviet market to the Western market. This is caused partly by the high level of labour costs in Finland. Another reason lies in the difficulty of utilising highly specialised Finnish technological know-how in the Western market; it is, for instance, impossible to sell icebreakers to most Western countries.

During the eighties, the Finnish economy performed consistently better than the OECD average. The annual rate of growth was high; inflation and unemployment were under control; foreign debt remained relatively low; national income per capita grew to be one of the highest in the world. In 1991, a deep recession struck the Finnish economy. The recession was mainly of a domestic origin. But the rapid decline in Soviet trade has undoubtedly deepened it. In mid-1991, the future prospects for the Finnish economy were not very bright. And this time Soviet trade cannot be expected to remedy the situation either.

Towards a 'definlandised' political culture

During the time of Russian rule in Finland, the political culture of the country was devoid of any genuine civic spirit. The recognised Russian ruler legitimised the whole governmental system, and an independent national sense of community was only slowly developing. Large segments of the population were not political subjects at all, and the Russian regime, assisted by the domestic bureaucracy, was efficient in suppressing reforming ambitions. The system was steered from above, and it promoted attitudes of submission. Changes ensued slowly; the impact of the period of Russian rule weakened only gradually.

In a paper dealing with the development of the political culture of Finland, Jaakko Nousiainen makes reference to a Christian-patriarchal bureaucratic community culture which was maintained by a relatively united élite and accepted by the common people long after the masses in many other Western countries had been mobilised to perceive their position and to act on behalf of their privileges and ideas.[9] This culture retained some of its characteristics even after the mobilisation of political groups that took place in Finland during the first two decades of this century. Paternalistic traits remained on the mass level for a long time. Even in the 1950s, the average citizen of Finland was still a class-bound political actor, who responded to demands expressed by ideologies and political leaders and followed—rather than challenged—authority. The Finnish voter was no floating voter; he took his political cues from party identification and political tradition and was attached to the political system through fixed and immobile mechanisms. He was, in Nousiainen's words, 'a class voter who received his party affiliation when he was born, whose behaviour in a segmented society was supervised by a homogeneous social environment, whose attitudes of dissatisfaction were primarily ideological reactions, and who followed his leaders, sometimes with enthusiasm, sometimes muttering, but without revolting, and without changing camp'.[10]

All this has changed now. In the 1950s, Finland was still a politicised society, with rather deep cleavages and only a limited potential for a

[9] Jaakko Nousiainen, 'Suomen poliittinen kulttuuri', *Politiikka*, Vol. 25, 1983, p. 12.
[10] *Ibid.*

politics of compromise. However, during the second half of the 1960s, Finland took a definite step to a new political élite culture, one in which all relevant interests were accommodated in the decision-making processes, and all important interests were supposed to leave their marks on the final decisions. Gradually, Finland became a consensus polity. Finnish politics also look different on the mass level. Voters are no longer linked to politics in terms of social class and political tradition: the floating voter has appeared in Finnish politics, and issue-voting is a rule rather than an exception. The authority of the political leaders is much contested, and the general importance of the party system is declining. To a large extent, the changes are dependent on each other and on factors unrelated to the upheavals in Europe and the Soviet Union; they are consequences of, for instance, the rapid industrialisation of the country in the 1960s, a marked growth of the public sector, a rapid equalisation of the social class basis of society, and an increase of the political resources of the citizens in terms of information and education.[11] However, recent developments in the environment of the Finnish political system are not without importance for an understanding of Finnish political culture today and tomorrow. The developments have directly affected the foreign policy segment of the culture, which has recovered from an earlier stage of degradation.

During the late 1950s and the early 1960s, Finnish foreign policy became more active, and the foreign policy debate in Finland at that time was quite animated, displaying marked differences of opinion among the political parties.[12] However, since the 1962 re-election of President Kekkonen, who was ostentatiously supported by the Soviet Union, the situation changed. During his first term as president, Dr Kekkonen had been a rather controversial political actor, who did not enjoy the complete confidence of the public and the political élites. However, in the aftermath of the crises of Finnish–Soviet relations in 1958 and 1961, in which he, by means and methods that are still to be clarified, was able to come out as a forceful and able national leader, his position was strengthened. His strong constitutional prerogatives and unveiled ambition in domestic politics soon turned the political field into a conglomerate of yes-men. In fact, Finland experienced in the 1970s a sort of internal Finlandisation, which had many elements: the persecution of individuals and groups who dared to speak against the president and his foreign policy, the persecution also of anti-communist and anti-marxist attitudes which were regarded as damaging for Finland's relations with her eastern neighbour, spill-over effects from this attitudinal pattern to the areas of culture, art, science and mass media, and the emergence of various informal networks acting as guardians of the foreign policy orthodoxy. The authoritarian past of the Finnish political culture reappeared in new manifestations; the political

[11] See Dag Anckar, 'Liberalism, Democracy and Political Culture in Finland', *Acta Academiae Aboensis, Humaniora*, Vol. 62 nr 5, Åbo Akademi, 1983.
[12] Dag Anckar, 'Party Strategies and Foreign Policy: The Case of Finland, 1955–63', *Cooperation and Conflict*, Vol. 8, 1973.

climate became petrified and unintellectual. The situation is aptly described in a recent paper by a Finnish scholar:

> In the Finnish political game the Soviet Union became an important actor. After the oil crisis of 1973 and because of the growing trade with the Soviet Union, the 'Soviet Card', as it was called, became still more important. The situation was complicated by the existence of a strong, but internally split, Communist Party which had to be made to accept the economic policy of the government. The major political parties in Finland, even the Conservatives after 1974, began to compete with each other for the best relations with the Soviet Union and criticism of the Soviet Union would have led to political suicide in Finland, not necessarily because of Soviet influence but because of the attitude of Finnish politicians. A serious problem was that internal Finlandization moulded the whole Finnish political culture.[13]

When Mauno Koivisto succeeded Urho Kekkonen as president of the Republic in 1982, he was expected to be somewhat more positively disposed towards a revitalisation of the foreign policy debate. In an early speech as president, he recognised the need for continuous foreign policy analysis and maintained that a foreign policy discussion which was inspired by the national interest was of vital importance for Finnish democracy. However, it soon became evident that there was a limit to the understanding the new president was willing to show for deviant contributions to the debate,[14] and the fact that the debate has recovered today cannot be attributed to any dramatic change in leadership style and leadership policy. The change has come about as a consequence of the Soviet and East European developments, which have eliminated earlier constraints on the formation and expression of opinions. The degree to which a change in the climate of debate has occurred may be illustrated by one incident.

When, in 1982, the first author of this essay suggested in a paper[15] that the treaty between Finland and the Soviet Union invites, rather than deters, attacks against or through Finnish territory and therefore cannot be regarded as an efficient instrument of security policy, the reaction of the Finnish establishment was vehement. The Ministry of Foreign Affairs announced that the views of the author were completely wrong, and the party press was flooded with editorials and statements repudiating the views of the author. The leading Social Democratic paper much regretted that it was impossible to discharge the author from his professorial chair; representatives of the Swedish press in Finland, which is usually regarded as liberal in tone, forgot about liberalism and cried out for self-censorship; the communist press interpreted the paper as an attempt, backed by unspecified imperialist and military quarters, to send up a trial balloon. Pertinent arguments were seldom introduced in this public execution; in

---

[13] Erkki Berndtson, 'Finlandization', *Government and Opposition*, Vol. 26, 1991, p. 31.

[14] Krister Ståhlberg, 'Public Opinion in Finnish Foreign Policy', *Yearbook of Finnish Foreign Policy 1987*, Finnish Institute of International Affairs, 1988, pp. 17–18.

[15] Dag Anckar, 'Finland och VSB-pakten', *Finsk Tidskrift*, Vol. 106, 1982.

fact, most commentators had not even bothered to read the paper they were repudiating. The very idea of someone questioning the functionality of Finland's central security policy instrument was considered offensive, almost profane. However, when similar views on the Finnish-Soviet Treaty began to appear in the public debate on foreign policy at the end of the 1980s and the beginning of the 1990s, the reaction was quite different and expressed understanding, as well as a readiness to engage in a serious discussion about the place and the role of the treaty in Finland's future foreign policy. In fact, when it was announced in 1991 that Finland's future interpretation of the treaty would exclude the explicit reference to Germany as a potential enemy, this met with general and unreserved approval. The context of the foreign policy debate has changed. The Soviet influence has disappeared, the Soviet card is no longer there, pleas for self-censorship have lost their justification and credibility.

As an outcome of this change, the foreign policy culture in Finland has regained much of its challenging and pluralistic nature. One element in this development is a growing, although still not dramatic, discrepancy between the cautious official line on the one hand, and public opinion on the other. The restrictive attitude adopted in 1991 by President Koivisto and others with regard to the striving for independence of the Baltic Republics provoked widespread irritation, and the Finnish people were more inclined than their leadership to accept Finnish participation in European economic integration on a full membership basis. In Finland, public opinion has generally had only a weak impact on foreign policy; it remains to be seen whether this pattern will change in the future. However, one thing is clear. The disintegration of the Soviet Empire has altered conceptions of how the supreme national interest of Finland should be defined and has brought forward—as well as legitimised—a new variety of opinions and attitudes. There are now defenders, as well as challengers, in the debate on foreign policy and security policy in Finland, and there is a new kind of interaction and communication between the two camps. In this important respect, the country's foreign policy culture is drawing nearer to the culture that has come to mark other sectors and segments of Finnish political life.

POLAND'S TRANSITION TO DEMOCRACY: HOW MUCH PLURALISM?

WLODZIMIERZ WESOLOWSKI*

A TOTALITARIAN regime has a monocentric system of power. This is one of its constitutive characteristics. In opposition to monocentrism stands democratic pluralism, as a system of power relations within the state. In this paper the discussion of the transition from communism to liberal democracy in Poland will focus on the emerging pluralist structures. It will also stress the weaknesses of these structures. Particular features of the emerging new democracies may hamper the further political development of Eastern Europe.

I assume in this paper that the political process, understood as an ongoing interaction of various political groups, is the most outstanding feature of a contemporary 'pluralistic' democracy. Thus the existence or non-existence of the plurality of autonomous group-actors who have the potential for influencing governmental policy serves as the simplest criterion for distinguishing the liberal, pluralist political system from the communist one.

Liberal concepts of pluralism

In liberal democracies, pluralism has its own intellectual foundation. It is derived from the English empiricist philosophy and from the liberal creed of John Locke, John Stuart Mill, and Jeremy Bentham. In this philosophy one finds three basic axioms on the formation of economic interests and political goals (broadly defined as interests). These axioms are fundamental to understanding the pluralism of modern democratic regimes.

The first states that economic interests and political goals stem primarily from individual needs and individual perceptions of reality. The second states that there is a great variety of interests, which may change. The third states that there should not be any factual or legal restrictions on the articulations of interests or political goals. This implies that new articulations should always be accommodated.

The third axiom, with its emphasis on the dynamic character of interests, must be properly understood. It has a hidden aspect, pointing to relative stability and definiteness, as well as dynamism and changeability.

* The author is at the Institute of Philosophy and Sociology, Polish Academy of Sciences and is Visiting Professor at The Wilson Center, Smithsonian Institution, Washington, DC.

At any given time society has a relatively stable division of labour, stratification system, branches of industry and services and occupational groupings. Thus, it has an objectively predetermined set of economic interests.

Likewise, within a given society only some political orientations have currency. Society never represents an infinite combination of political demands or an infinite composition of individual interests. The relative stability of social structures and political orientations makes economic and political articulations converge into more or less definite clusters, which is why in a modern, democratic society, one sees a definite number of parties and interest groups.

This fact leads a researcher to pose a very difficult, although not hypothetical, question: Is there, in a given society, an adequate, insufficient or excessive pluralisation of interests and orientations? That problem, among others, will be addressed in my paper.

Economic order and material interests

There is a common wisdom in post-communist countries that these countries should move toward a free market economy, privatisation of the means of production, political pluralism and parliamentary democracy. There is a belief that the formation of pluralist structures ought to precede, or occur simultaneously with, the emergence of a democratic government.

However, it is overlooked that in some East European countries, pluralist structures in politics and economics are slow in forming, while the parliament and the government already operate democratically. Democracy has managed to outrun the Western model of the political pluralism of interest groups and political parties. Governmental democracy works without a proper socio-political infrastructure. Why?

One dominant feature of the Polish economy is the slow pace of its transformation. Although the old economic system has disintegrated, the new one has not yet emerged. The institutional bases of the economy are suspended between the principles of the state-owned, centrally controlled economy, and the mechanisms of the privately-owned, market-regulated economy. An important factor was the prolonged debate on how to privatise industry and commerce. Although parliament passed the privatisation law in late spring 1990, there are no practical attempts to experiment in the privatisation of state factories that could yield exemplary results.

The situation exerts a profound influence on employees and wage-earners and it affects the formation of normal interest groups. People know that their interests will be shaped by privatisation and new market mechanisms, but they find it difficult to see what precise shape those material interests will take. Therefore they stick to the old perception of their interests, as linked to state ownership, and they remain uncertain

131

about future possibilities. No new way of thinking about their interests has yet emerged.

The strike of railway employees in May 1990 offers an insight into how existing industrial conflicts belong to the 'old' system rather than to the emerging 'new' one. The state and the hired work force were involved in the industrial dispute. Nobody expected—indeed expects—any great change in this sphere, as railways will, in all likelihood, continue to be state-owned. Underlying the dispute was an assumption by both sides that the status quo would persist. The fear of bankruptcy was not a factor, nor was the prospect of being dismissed by new owners. The railway employees' feeling of community, and of a group interest *vis-à-vis* the state, had existed under the old regime. This is why they have simply demanded a larger share of the state budget, pointing to their functional importance.

The situation in commodity-producing industry is different. Enterprises may become privatised or bankrupt. The future interests of the employees will depend on the form of privatisation. It is not clear yet which of the possible forms are profitable for which particular groups of employees. Two basic forms may be adopted and will, in consequence, shape employees' perceptions of their interests. One possibility is a transformation of state-owned companies into employee-owned companies; the other, their transformation into regular joint stock companies. Each will form the basis for distinct combinations of interests, and the proportion of the two types of ownership in the overall economy will impinge on the global structure of economic interests of the society at large. In a sense, it is too early to expect the formation and crystallisation of new interests, taking into account the delay in the practical instrumentalisation of the idea of privatisation.

Privatisation also implies an increase in the number of small and medium-sized enterprises owned by families. This may serve to foster the traditional 'middle-class values' of personal responsibility, dutifulness, and thrift. One can fairly assume that under free market conditions entrepreneurial classes will develop their own concepts of group interest, distinct from the concept of interest of small craftsmen and businessmen within the system of 'real socialism'. The development of various 'middle-classes'—bourgeoisie, shareholders, owners of small work-shops—will shape the interest structure in the future. Today, however, even long-standing group interests such as those of the private craftsmen, are not clearly articulated.

As a final example, a look at Polish farmers shows that the articulation and the structure of new interests is in an incipient stage. Farmers still perceive their interests as they were in the previous economic system, focusing on prices set by state-run, highly bureaucratised agencies. This type of undifferentiated interest of the whole stratum of peasants will lose its significance in the coming years. The necessity of modernisation and the introduction of market mechanisms will create a growing division of farmers. One group will expand and increase its income, another will go bankrupt, while yet another will desperately strive for financial assistance. There is no clear indication that farmers, or their political or economic organisations, clearly perceive the coming changes or are reorganising themselves in preparation for them. These changes will require a restructuring of their interests, including the association and dissociation of various 'fragments' of their former interests.

The illustrations presented above allow me to draw some conclusions. The old structure of interests, linked to a state-owned, centrally planned economy, is gradually disintegrating. A new structure has not yet emerged. There are certain obstacles to the full articulation of the diversity of group interests that are a normal attribute of a capitalist market economy. The slow pace of economic reform is mainly responsible for this. On the intellectual plane there is a connection between the vagueness of the privatisation debate and the difficulty of providing various groups with the proper clues for discerning their interests, particularly as those interests may evolve in the near future.

Politicians, who might find some merit in providing the potential interests with organisational frameworks, are passive in this respect. The pressure from below is from traditional interests, organised along the 'industrial branch' divisions. The extent to which the trade unions will be intellectually prepared to help crystallise the new emerging interests or help transform the old ones, remains an open question.

Party structure and political scenarios

In a typical system of parliamentary democracy, there are several competing parties which present their programmes to the electorate. In Western Europe these programmes are rooted in the material interests of large segments of the population, or in some broad socio-political idea, or even in both interests and ideas. A comparison of the functions of political parties within a democratic system with the present-day political life in Poland shows clearly that the latter is not organised on the basis of 'party structure', i.e., on definitely composed parties with competitive programmes. Although political parties exist, they do not play a significant role in articulating programmes or promoting ideas; nor do they form the cabinet.

A more detailed description is necessary to explain the 'party system' in Poland today. There are three types of political units which resemble parties. First, there are the three parties of the old communist regime, one of which, the restructured farmers' party, represents a viable and still active entity that has visible support. It aims to represent the farmers' economic interests and appeals to the Polish peasants' traditional values. But, as I have already said, peasants—and the peasant party—comprehend their interests in a traditional way, as interests of an undifferentiated

133

stratum. The former communist party, although it still retains a few thousand members, is trying to survive after undergoing a politically weakening division. Nobody knows which groups it is going to represent in the economic conflicts and political battles. The Democratic Party, allegedly representing independent craftsmen and intelligentsia of the old regime, is searching for a new programme and constituency.

Second, there are numerous small parties organised primarily during the 1980s, either underground or shortly after the second victory of Solidarity in 1989. Some of them claim ties to the pre-World War II parties, while others are created by 'would-be leaders'. Their number is very high: the official figure is approximately 100. While some play a real, if minor, political role, they fail on the whole to formulate practical and workable programmes, and they remain on the fringes of the political processes.

Finally, there is Solidarity, a loose political movement that performs many political functions but is not a party. This kind of substitute entity cannot articulate and serve diverse political orientations. Thus, the transmission of the society's orientations, demands and needs, in all their complexity and specificity, is limited and restrained. It is relatively easy to explain the reasons why this situation has evolved. The exceptional role Solidarity played in overthrowing the unwanted regime is well known. As the victorious political and social power, Solidarity designated the government after its—and society's—electoral victory in June 1989. The parliament and the government led by Solidarity intellectuals shaped the programme for economic and political reforms. This programme has been successfully implemented.

Thus, Solidarity played an indispensable role in the breakthrough of democracy. It did so as a unified national force seeking universal national needs: independence, democracy, personal freedom. Experience has certified that the initiation of a democratic process can be achieved without political pluralism. However, the persistent question is: Can the next stage in the building of democracy be completed without a normal, pluralistic political structure? During the winter and spring of 1990, the validity of this question was debated. Many leaders of Solidarity thought that their loose movement would be able to carry out its political role without internal pluralisation—or without being formalised into a political party. Since the summer of 1990, the prevailing mood has changed. Walesa's political manoeuvres have provoked this new approach.

It is impossible to refer to all of the ideas espoused by political leaders in the period of August 1989 to October 1990. I will try to summarise them by presenting several possible scenarios. They are my own constructs which attempt to clarify certain unvoiced assumptions and predictable consequences.

In the autumn of 1989, the simplest and most obvious scenario was the formation of a normal political party under the name of Solidarity, of centrist orientation and with democratic internal regulations (statutes).

The party would be completely separate from the Solidarity trade union, although the two entities would cooperate in certain areas of politics. The Solidarity party would build strong social support for governmental policy. This scenario has never been seriously considered for at least three reasons.

Solidarity did not consider it necessary to formalise the political movement of Solidarity; it already functioned satisfactorily as the 'Solidarity' faction in the parliament (the Civic Parliamentary Club). Moreover, secondly, the trade union leaders saw a formal political party as a potential challenger to the already weakened Solidarity trade union. Thirdly, there was an aversion of many Solidarity leaders to political parties. They believe in a unifying power and in the uniqueness of Solidarity as a social movement. They believe that Solidarity is destined to lead the Polish people through the difficulties of a new social development. Some even hint that their movement represents a new type of socio-political entity that will replace political parties in the coming era.

Another scenario which was debated but never enthusiastically supported was the division of the Solidarity movement into three political parties: a Christian-democratic, a social-democratic, and a liberal party (in the European sense). Within the parliamentary Solidarity faction, these three trends have been slowly emerging, each with potential leaders of national standing. The scenario was rejected by the majority of Solidarity representatives, who considered a unified effort by all three orientations a better strategy for the effective passing of new legislation, for reconstructing the country, and for ensuring greater political stability. In addition, it was emphasised that Solidarity, as a loose movement, could form citizens' committees in localities without antagonising anyone except the former local élite. Citizens' committees seemed to provide the ideal instrument for winning local elections and thus completing the Polish revolution in the countryside. In their campaigns, in fact, the committees exploited Solidarity symbols and its vaguely defined 'ethos', while in their programmes they referred solely to local problems. They won the election. In this respect, staying unified and undifferentiated proved to be effective.

A third scenario has been abruptly proposed by Walesa's close advisors from Gdansk. The advocates of this proposal view it as an instrument for promoting pluralism. However, the suggested practical measures indicate the authors' inclination toward a more personal rule. The project started with the slogan: 'Walesa for President'. The plan's architect, Senator Jaroslaw Kaczynski, editor of the influential weekly *Tygodnik Solidarnosc*, has been systematically undermining the prestige of the government and of the Solidarity parliamentary faction. As a measure of preventing 'monopolistic' tendencies of the Mazowiecki government he founded an organisation called the Centre Alliance. This is a formal party, but it also builds strong links with small parties existing on the fringes of the present political system. The leaders of the small parties receive seats on the governing board of the Centre Alliance. Furthermore, the Alliance creates strong links with the local citizens' committees, which are the real political centres of influence in towns and regions. It also forms alliances with Solidarity's trade union organisations in factories.

The initial pronouncements of Senator Kaczynski, the chief proponent of the Centre Alliances' platform, were rather vague. However, the political actions of the Alliance bring definite associations to the sociologist's mind. They remind one of Edward Shils' thesis on centre and periphery. Mr. Kaczynski's project proposes to introduce patronage relations between the Alliance and other political parties and social organisations. It looks like a project for establishing a strong presidential political block which would penetrate the texture of the society. It is difficult to say whether Walesa endorsed the centre-periphery scenario and whether he was aware of its political implications. Since August 1990 he has been gradually distancing himself from the Centre Alliance, claiming that he is above factional divisions. In relation to that, he has been emphasising the need for further 'political pluralisation'. Walesa's appeals for pluralism, however, evoke the threat of a very fragmented political structure. For example, publicity was given to his receiving a couple from a small town in western Poland who had founded a new association. During the meeting, Walesa praised the founding as progress in pluralisation. Nothing was said in the press communiqué about what the assocation planned to do, leaving the impression that creating the association was enough in itself.

Creating associations and political parties for the sake of pluralism, and not for a definite action, seems to be a great danger for Poland. Polish history provides many lessons of the dangers of excessive pluralism. It may hinder the democratic process of reaching public decisions. Marshall Pilsudski imposed his personal rule in the 1920s, when the fragmented and quarrelsome parliament was unable to pass laws. To be workable, pluralism needs to be anchored in the structure of real economic interests and defined by political orientation. If it is not, an authoritative president may indeed be necessary to overcome the vices and spurious plurality of political actors.

However, in response to the Centre Alliance's action, there emerged a party called Democratic Action (or Road) and a new fourth scenario has become feasible. It will materialise if two or three normal parties emerge with their own relatively stable base. Several well-known leaders of Solidarity joined Democratic Action. They have liberal, Christian-liberal or social-democratic inclinations. They denounced the nationalism and populism of the Union of the Centre. They supported Mazowiecki's government and Geremek's leadership in the club of Solidarity parliamentarians. They seek to gain the support of the intelligentsia stratum.

The political split of Solidarity has become a reality. Under new circumstances, Walesa is postulating the formation of a strong 'right' as well as a strong 'left' wing in the political spectrum. Now it seems that his intention is to preside over a Western type, multi-party system. What is still not clear in his pronouncements is the relative strength of the parliament (in consequence, the political parties) *vis-à-vis* the president, in the future political system in Poland.

Is, then, a strong political party structure evolving in Poland? An optimistic and firm answer cannot be given yet. Neither the Centre Alliance nor Democratic Action meet the criteria of fully-fledged parties. They have been slow in formulating programmes, and their leaders have tended to concentrate political discussion on slogans or on very general issues. They have not elaborated programmes to change and improve the functioning of particular spheres of life. They are reluctant to say which version of privatisation they favour or what role the trade union should play in the privatised sector.

Debates reveal the tendency to define political choices in supposedly antonymic pairs: national interest versus European integration; popular activism versus professional competence; the rule of law versus extraordinary measures to speed up change.

Thus some analysts rightly see the cleavage between the two wings of Solidarity as the division into two types of cultural mentality rather than of pragmatic options. That situation suggests that in Poland the new party structure may have a heavy 'ideological' component. This could create unfavourable conditions for the development of definite links and interactions between the party structure and the structure of economic interests. Battles over vaguely defined 'national interests' or the 'European identity of Poles' will dominate over articulation of whose interests each party aims to promote by a specific set of policies.

In October 1990, a month before the presidential election, ideologisation was coupled with personalisation. Prime Minister Mazowiecki reluctantly accepted the nomination to run for president against Walesa. Campaigners of both contending candidates focused on their personal qualities and general philosophies, pushing into the background the pressing issues awaiting consideration. Walesa was presented as a strong man who possessed all the political qualities required to lead the nation. When elected he would know what to do and how to do it. He would motivate ordinary people and, when necessary, make personal authoritative decisions. Mazowiecki was portrayed as a candidate who symbolised the rule of law and respect for the parliamentary democracy, a man of reflection, knowledge and integrity, who opposed Walesa's shortcuts and acceleration, and who assured gradual and steady progress in reforming the country. On both sides only little was said about specific policies candidates would follow.

For my discussion of pluralism, one question is important: Whose presidency would have created better prospects for the formation and institutionalisation of adequate and workable pluralist structures?

Mazowiecki obviously favoured pluralistic democracy. Whether the economic policy of his government would foster conditions for stabilised pluralist structures remained to be seen. Several economic failures could undermine democracy's institutionalisation. The slow pace of economic transformation, mismanagement of projects, and unfavourable international conditions for the country's economic recovery may cause an outburst of dissatisfaction, provoke political changes and hinder the processes of building pluralist structures.

Walesa's presidency could evolve in several possible directions. Two threaten pluralism. The first would be fusion of all organisations under one umbrella to secure maximum power for Walesa and marginalise his opponents. The second would be a continuation of fragmentation combined with attempts by the strong leader to control contending groups and factions. This would be a politics of *divide et impera*.

The third, rather less likely, possibility would be for Walesa, as President, to accept democratic mechanisms for the articulation of economic and political interests—and their aggregation into politically significant units. In this case Lech Walesa would be satisfied with a less authoritarian, less controlling, and less powerful presidential role.

It is less likely, but, as Max Weber noted, charismatic leaders make unexpected turns and even miracles. If Lech Walesa is a truly charismatic leader, he is capable of doing both.

GREATER EUROPE: INTEGRATION OR ETHNIC EXCLUSION?

MARIE MACEY*

EUROPE—both west and east—is currently undergoing change on an unprecedented scale of a magnitude which has far-reaching consequences not only for Europeans, but for the rest of the world. In the west, the Single European Act of 1987, which will in effect abolish borders between the twelve member states of the European Community in 1992, carries with it the danger that the new 'open' west Europe will be closed to the rest of the world. In the east, the fall of communist regimes has led to the opening up of east European societies which, followed by the dismantling of the USSR, has laid the foundation for dramatic changes in existing (and future) east-west relationships. It is now impossible to discuss change in western Europe without at least some reference to east Europe, since the future of the two seems set to become ever more closely linked. The impact of a *united* Europe, not only on its members but on the rest of the world, may give a whole new meaning to the concepts of 'a new world order' and 'the north-south divide'.

This paper concentrates on issues of democracy and human rights with particular reference to identifiable minorities, especially those of ethnic origin who are highly visible in terms of skin colour. Within both east and west Europe, the new spirit of openness has been less than universally applied to the people who live there, let alone those who would like to do so, such as refugees.[1] For large numbers of European residents, changes in both government policies and public attitudes have been negative, as xenophobia, racism and nationalism escalate in Europe.[2] To understand the scale of the issue, we need to examine the numbers and status of minorities in Europe, their treatment within different states at the present time and the likely future impact on them of widespread change.

* Lecturer in Sociology in the Department of Social and Economic Studies at the University of Bradford, Director of the MSc in Race Relations and Director of the Christian Urban Resources Unit.

[1] Changes in west European policy towards asylum seekers and refugees constitutes a huge topic of discussion which is not dealt with in this paper, other than in passing. Refugees are viewed as one of the major problems confronting Europe in the 20th century and EC countries are progressively tightening their policies towards them with the distinction between 'economic' and 'political' refugees being ever more stringently enforced.

[2] Evidence is most comprehensively documented for the European Community itself; see, for example, the report of the European Parliament Committee of Inquiry into the rise of Fascism and Racism in Europe, Strasbourg, 1985, and that of the Committee of Inquiry into Racism and Xenophobia, Document A3–195/90, Strasbourg, 1990.

Western Europe

Membership of the European Community (EC) currently consists of twelve countries—France, Belgium, the Netherlands, Luxembourg, Italy, Germany, the UK, Ireland, Greece, Portugal and Spain. Austria expects to be a full member by 1995; Sweden and Turkey have both applied to join; Hungary has expressed a wish to do so and Norway, Iceland, Finland and Switzerland have signalled that membership may be an option for them. The former Baltic States of the Soviet Union—Estonia, Latvia and Lithuania—have applied for associate membership and may well be future full members. The combined population of the EC as presently constituted is around 327 million (not counting the unification of Germany), a number considerably larger than the USA with a population of 240 million or the USSR whose population (prior to independence) was 274 million (Commission of the European Communities, 1990). It is likely that membership of the Community will continue to expand as east and west Europe, however haltingly, come closer together. It is not, of course, only its size in population terms which is significant, for the European Community is one of the wealthiest areas of the world, one of the most technologically advanced and one whose sphere of power and influence in geopolitical terms is extremely wide. The combination of these factors gives the EC phenomenal potential power, for good or ill, and this alone should alert us to the need for constant vigilance in the preservation (and extension) of human rights and democratic institutions.

Minorities in the EC fall into three categories: (1) citizens of a member state who share, in theory, the same rights as other European citizens; (2) migrants from one EC country to another EC country who are protected by EC law, and (3) third country nationals who are highly vulnerable, having no rights or protection under EC law. Estimates of the number of people in this group vary between six and fourteen million,[3] the highest proportions living in France, Germany and the UK (Commission of the European Communities, 1990).

In addition to third country residents, western Europe has long been home to large numbers of people whose origins lie elsewhere in the world, including Africa, Bangladesh, India, Pakistan and the West Indies. The origins of such minority populations are related to Europe's history of colonisation, so that different countries have populations of different

---

[3] The Commission of the European Communities gives an estimate of six million (1990), but other sources put the number much higher. See, for instance, P. Gordon, *Fortress Europe? The Meaning of 1992*, The Runnymede Trust, London, 1989; A. Dummett, *Europe and 1992: Focus on Racial Issues*, Catholic Association for Racial Justice, London, 1990; and P. Müller, 'A Home to Refugees' in 'The Other Side of 1992: a Special European Edition', *Christian Action Journal*, Summer 1989. There are an additional two million third country nationals who come from industrial countries (the USA, Canada, Japan or the EFTA countries). These people do not generally intend to settle in Europe and are not regarded as problematic in terms of human rights.

geographical origins. For example, Britain's minorities come mainly from India, Pakistan and the West Indies, Portugal's from Cape Verde, Sao Tome and Principe, Guinea Bisseu, Angola and Mozambique and France's from Algeria, Morocco, Tunisia, Senegal, Martinique and Guadeloupe. Official status is the key determinant of human rights in the EC, and this ranges along a continuum from full citizenship carrying civil, political and social rights, as in the UK, to guestworkers with few, if any, rights, as in Germany. The possession, or otherwise, of citizenship will assume critical importance post-1992, when changes in legislation mean that non-EC citizens could face deportation from countries in which they have lived for twenty years or more and in which their children have been born.

1992—and people?

In the count-down to the completion of the single market in 1992, laid down by the Single European Act (SEA), it sometimes seems as if the only parts of the Act of which western European governments are aware are those relating to the free movement of goods and capital. In fact, the single market is defined in the Act as 'an area without internal frontiers in which the free movement of goods, *persons*, services and capital is ensured' in accordance with the Treaty of Rome which established the Community (my emphasis). The SEA also calls for the 'promotion of democracy on the basis of freedom, equality and social justice'. But on the human rights dimension, western governments seem to share both a highly developed selective perception *and* a form of collective amnesia about the origins of the EC, which lie in the anxiety of post-war politicians to avoid future European wars and to safeguard democratic institutions against dictatorships and the evils of fascism and Nazism. At its inception, then, economic integration was not seen as an end in itself, but as a vehicle for the preservation of social peace and human rights, including the elimination of discrimination based on nationality.

One of the most fundamental human rights enshrined in the SEA is that of free movement within the European Community. But here there is a tension between the EC's commitment to human rights *per se* (including the right of free movement) and its concern to protect its own citizens relative to non-EC nationals. For what seems to have been overlooked by most people is that with the move towards the abolition of *internal* frontiers, there will be concomitant tightening of control at *external* borders, and this highlights a further problem with Europe's planning for 1992. Although the SEA compels EC states to develop common policies towards third country nationals, it has so far failed to produce its own coherent policies to which member states must adhere, leaving individual countries to take whatever measures they deem necessary to control immigration.

A standardised European policy on immigration may, or may not, be a positive step towards equality of treatment of people in general and third country nationals in particular, but its absence has led to the establishment of undemocatic, if not downright sinister, 'informal' decision-making bodies. These include the Trevi and Schengen groups, the Working Group on Immigration and the Group of National Co-ordinators on the Free Movement of People.[4] Because such coalitions operate outside the official Community framework, the EC plays no part in preparing proposals and the European Parliament has no opportunity to scrutinise or amend them. Such secrecy and lack of either informed public debate or accountability is totally against the spirit of the EC, and poses a major threat to the democratic process. Of particular concern is that these groups operate at the supra-national level, making decisions which determine the life chances of people such as migrants who are not generally in a position to exercise political or civil rights.

The signficance of groups such as Trevi and Schengen assuming responsibility for the development of common EC migration policies should not be underestimated. The fundamental point of 1992 is free movement between member states of the EC which means that, in principle, after 1992 it should be as easy to travel between, say, Britain and Luxembourg as it is between Lancashire and Surrey. But state frontiers are *not* the same thing as county borders and all states regulate entry to, and exit from, their countries. And this is where Trevi and Schengen assume crucial importance with respect to human rights and free movement, not only for third country nationals, but also for the Community's visible minorities:

> Citizenship may open Europe's borders to blacks and allow them free movement, but racism which cannot tell one black from another, a citizen from an immigrant, an immigrant from a refugee—and classes all Third World peoples as immigrants and refugees and all immigrants and refugees as terrorists and drug-dealers is going to make such movement fraught with difficulty.[5]

---

[4] The Trevi group was set up (at Britain's suggestion) in 1976 with a mandate to examine terrorism, radicalism, extremism and international violence (hence its name). That such a group is now charged with harmonising policies on immigrants, refugees and asylum seekers can be said to convey the message that the two groups of people are synonymous, thereby negating the human rights issues involved in the latter cases.

The Schengen countries (France, Germany, Belgium, Luxembourg, The Netherlands and Italy) have agreed common policies on 'firm' border control and visa policies. They exchange computerised information on asylum seekers, 'undesirables' and people under official surveillance, again juxtaposing asylum seekers with terrorists, etc.

Membership of these bodies, which are making key political decisions, includes civil servants, police and customs officers, immigration officials, security and intelligence agencies and military chiefs. The main contributing bodies from the UK are the Home Office, MI5, the Association of Chief Police Officers and the European Liaison Section of the Metropolitan Police Special Branch (see T. Bunyan, 'Towards an Authoritarian European State', in *Race and Class*, Special Issue, Institute of Race Relations, London, January 1991.

[5] S. Sivanandan, 'UK Commentary: Racism 1992' in *Race and Class*, vol. 30, no. 3, January–March, Institute of Race Relations, London, 1989.

Ethnic minorities and external border controls

Potentially adverse effects may accrue to identifiable minorities if external frontiers are fortified to compensate for the dismantling of internal ones. One only has to observe an airport to appreciate the accuracy of Sivanandan's comment (above), i.e. that black European citizens are perceived *en masse* as 'aliens'—that possession of citizenship is no protection against deeply ingrained public prejudices and stereotypes. Nor is there any doubt that groups like Trevi and Schengen project a distorted image to the public by making the equation between black people, illegal immigrants, terrorists and drug dealers. This image has also been popularised by politicians of both right and left wing persuasions, and though European governments have ignored the human rights dimension of the EC, they have not been slow to develop negative policies towards minorities, particularly black ones.

An analysis of west European governments' policies on immigrants, refugees and asylum seekers shows that external borders are being systematically strengthened. Since 1973, there has been a developing European convergence towards increasingly stringent immigration and deportation policies in relation to non-EC peoples with Sweden, the Netherlands, the UK, France, Germany and Switzerland showing remarkable homogeneity.[6] Cohen refers to this as the 'external policing' of frontiers; in more restrained language, the European Commission notes that exclusion from free movement will be a major contributor to structural discrimination against ethnic minorities and the Human Rights Division of the Council of Europe expresses grave concern over the tightening of policies on asylum seekers and refugees.

Each state within the EC defines its own nationality laws which tend to build on past elements of national policies evolved between 1960 and 1980 to regulate entry. These were not developed with the aim of excluding non-EC peoples, but were connected with changing labour market demands. An expanding post-war labour market led to the need of most economies in western Europe to draw on non-indigenous labour supplies, often—as with Britain, Germany and the Netherlands—from former colonies. By the 1960s this need no longer existed and black people were perceived as not only redundant but a 'problem'—a view which dominates public discourse to the present day.

The development of the EC, then, did not so much bring about racist immigration policies as build on existing trends. Nevertheless, from the point of view of third country nationals, refugees, asylum seekers and ethnic minorities, the situation over the last twenty or thirty years has been one of ever more stringent controls. In Britain, for example, successive

---

[6] See R. Cohen, *The New Helots: Migrants in the International Division of Labour*, Gower Publishing Company, Aldershot, 1988; and T. Hammer, *European Immigration Policy: A Comparative Study*, Cambridge University Press, Cambridge, 1985.

pieces of immigration legislation have defined citizenship in ever more narrowly prescribed ways. The 1968 Commonwealth Immigrants Act was held by the European Commission on Human Rights to be in breach of the European Convention on Human Rights, to be racially discriminatory and to constitute degrading treatment. The 1971 Immigration Act excluded right of entry to people from British ex-colonies; it also withdrew rights of appeal against immigration decisions, leading to more than 2,500 people per year being deported. The 1981 Nationality Act removed unqualified right of entry from anyone who could not claim patriality which meant, in effect, that the majority of black Commonwealth citizens lost their rights whilst the majority of white Commonwealth citizens retained theirs. The Act also removed the ancient right of birth on British soil (*jus soli*) as the basis of citizenship and replaced it with that of descent (*jus sanguinus*) so that children born here no longer have automatic citizenship rights. The Carriers Liability Act of 1987 imposed fines on airlines which transported people without full documentation and the Home Office is currently proposing doubling the fines for offences under this Act as well as removing legal aid from immigrants and asylum seekers. The 1988 Immigration Act made deportations even easier than was previously the case, a step which led to a 50 per cent increase in deportations that year. The imposition of visa requirements has also increased in recent years and Algeria, Bangladesh, Ghana, Haiti, India, Nigeria, Pakistan, Sri Lanka and Turkey are among countries which have been affected by this change.

Other western European countries have followed a similar trend in tightening immigration legislation. In 1979 France introduced a plan to reduce the immigrant population by 200,000 per year and brought in increasingly restrictive immigration controls during the 1980s, together with harsher measures against illegal immigration and increased use of deportation. In 1986 measures were introduced to make it more difficult for foreigners to obtain residence permits; the 1981 law which required court sanctions for the expulsion of immigrants was repealed and new laws gave local prefects the power to order expulsion. Rights of appeal against deportation orders were abolished and within two months of the implementation of the law, some 1700 people were deported. France also imposes visa requirements on all non-EC countries other than Switzerland. Germany imposed a ban on all worker recruitment from non-EC countries in 1973 and in 1982 introduced a scheme for repatriation. Foreigners face a strict system of internal control through the Foreigners Law of 1965 and other measures which give the authorities extensive powers, including deportation. Nor is it simply a matter of more stringent immigration controls: in Greece, for instance, the Ministry of the Interior deprived 544 ethnic Turks of their citizenship over a three week period in February 1991. Countries which have traditionally had relatively lenient immigration policies have recently shown signs of tightening up in line with general EC immigration policies. Spain has adopted strict controls to stem the 'flow' of immigrants from North Africa and now requires visas from Moroccans, Algerians and Tunisians. In Italy, the 1990 Martelli Law signalled a hardening of attitudes to immigration, and its treatment of Albanian refugees in 1991 likewise denotes its determination to halt asylum seekers.

In sum, over the last two decades or so, increasingly stringent controls have been implemented at the external borders of western European countries, and these have had a disproportionate impact on black people. This is not due to the establishment of the EC, but is, rather, a function of changing labour market demands. It can, in fact, be argued that the community offers an opportunity to reduce the scale of injustice currently experienced by third country nationals and ethnic minorities under the domestic laws of member states. Institutions such as the Council of Europe could develop positive policies at community level and community law overrides domestic law. Whether or not this opportunity will be seized remains to be seen, but there is little evidence at the moment of the existence of the political will necessary to developing a humane, racially just Community respectful of human rights. In fact, there are frightening intimations that the reverse could be the case when the Italian Diplomatic Consul can state that the Schengen Agreement is a progressive move, since it will enable people to be moved from one country to another according to the needs of the labour market (BBC2, 16 July 1991). Under this scenario, a sort of stockpile of workers will be created to be moved around the EC as required—a reserve labour force which is disposable and for whom no-one need assume social, political or moral responsibility.

Ethnic minorities and internal social control

Racism *within* west European societies has not been caused by membership of the EC any more than has the development of discriminatory immigration controls. In the case of internal controls, however, the relaxation of external borders may contribute directly to the development of policies which operate in a racist way. Instead of immigration or citizenship status being checked only at a frontier checkpoint, practices may develop which lead to checks operating any and everywhere. In Britain, there is already evidence of raids on homes and workplaces by police and immigration officers, of checks by the police on individual black peoples' immigration status and of the linking of public services and benefits to citizenship status. However, although this kind of internal 'policing' already takes place, it is not, as yet, systematised in law; post-1992 it may well become so, as is already the case in other west European countries where minority rights are either non-existent or are not defended in law.

Notwithstanding the above, and despite an erosion in their citizenship rights over time, most minorities in Britain *are* citizens with concomitant civil, political and social rights. The caveat that possession of citizenship is no protection against discrimination and subsequent marginalisation was noted above, but does not negate the importance of this legal status. In a number of other west European countries, minorities are not accorded citizenship, so have few rights but many restrictions placed on their participation in society. In Germany, for instance, guestworkers face extensive restrictions on political activity and cannot vote or stand for public office. They and their families, together with refugees, face a system of institutionalised discrimination which bars them from a wide range of occupations in the public sector, including teaching, the post office and public administration. In reality, foreign workers were never intended by Germany to become permanent residents, so that despite the fact that over 70 per cent of them have lived in Germany for ten years or more, with over 80 per cent of their children being born there, guestworkers face a life of legal and psychological uncertainty and their children are denied citizenship. The instructions on implementing the 1965 Foreigners Law illustrates the situation graphically:

> Foreigners enjoy all basic rights, except the basic rights of freedom of assembly, freedom of association, freedom of movement and free choice of occupation, place of work and place of education and protection from extradition abroad.[7]

In France, nationals from Martinique and Guadeloupe are French citizens and, like their British counterparts, theoretically have the same rights as their white counterparts. Those from former French colonies such as Algeria are now defined as foreigners, are denied free association, obliged to observe political neutrality and have only limited rights to form voluntary organisations. When immigration legislation was tightened in 1979, the police were given wider powers enabling them to hold immigrants for up to forty eight hours without charge and to summarily expel anyone whose papers were not in order. A system of computerised record-keeping was established which brought together residence and work permits in one unforgeable document containing 40 items of information on nationality, residence, employment and dependents. Later legislation extended police powers to check peoples' identities, including their right to be in France.

In the sphere of human rights, the general tendency in the EC has been to move in the direction of the 'lowest common denominator', i.e. towards adoption of the most, rather than the least, austere systems of control and surveillance. The relaxation of external border controls is not likely to reverse this trend in terms of the imposition of constraints within the various countries. And any such moves are likely to result in a higher level of racial harassment than already exists.

[7] S. Castles with H. Booth and T. Wallace, *Here for Good: Western Europe's New Ethnic Minorities*, Pluto Press, London, 1984.

The growth of intolerance in Western Europe

It is not, of course, only formal controls which impact upon peoples' lives; informal attitudes and actions play a major part in determining the quality of life, particularly for identifiable minorities. On this dimension of human rights it can be suggested that not only does western Europe's record leave a great deal to be desired, but that it is significantly deteriorating. There is considerable evidence that the traditional 'isms' of intolerance in Europe—fascism, racism, anti-Semitism and neo-Nazism—have expanded in recent years to encompass nationalism, chauvinism, extremism, xenophobia and religious bigotry. That the situation is critical is demonstrated by the fact that the European Council, the Commission and Parliament felt the need in 1986 to jointly publish a Solemn Declaration Against Racism and Xenophobia. The findings of the recently published 'Report on the findings of the Committee of Inquiry into Racism and Xenophobia' (1990)[8] would seem to indicate that the Declaration has had little impact.

Discrimination takes different forms in different west European societies and is practised against different groups, but in almost every EC country, minorities suffer systematic discrimination of an order which places (and keeps) them on the lowest rung of every ladder—housing, health, education and (un)employment. Increasingly, hostility towards minorities has manifested itself not only in structural inequality and personal prejudice, but in overt and organised violence. In Britain, which has the most highly developed race relations legislation in the EC, racially motivated physical assaults on Asians and Afro-Caribbeans have increased dramatically and are now everyday occurrences of a life-threatening order with some 700,000 racial attacks taking place every year. The escalation in racial violence in Scotland, including arson attacks, has been linked to the establishment of a base in Glasgow by the British National Party. Antagonism towards travellers remains high—it is not uncommon to see notices in public houses saying 'Gypsies not welcome'—and continual struggle is needed to maintain such rights to camp sites as the law currently provides. Overt anti-Semitism has grown in recent years, with Jewish graveyards being vandalised and Jewish school children physically attacked. Antagonism to Muslims is growing and this extended to the burning of mosques during the war in the Gulf.

In France, the level of racially motivated violence is high, and growing, and has been linked to extreme Right political parties such as the Front National which campaigns on an anti-Semitic, anti-black, anti-foreigners ticket. Extreme Right parties have attracted growing support in recent years and have lent a spurious respectability to racist behaviour. In the last

---

[8] European Parliament, *Report of the Findings of the Committee of Inquiry into Racism and Xenophobia*, Strasbourg, 1990, *op. cit.* Much of the evidence cited in this section comes from this source.

four years about twenty foreigners have been killed, all but one of North African origin, and numerous other violent incidents have resulted in amputations, paralysis and physical and mental handicap. Anti-Semitism has manifested itself in similar form to that in Britain; Jewish cemeteries have been vandalised and in 1990 over thirty tombstones were desecrated and the remains of a man buried two weeks earlier exhumed and mutilated. The high number of Muslims in France has been used by right wing politicians to stimulate anti-Islamic hostility which has included bombings and physical assaults on Muslims.

In Belgium, there has been a resurgence of anti-guestworker feelings in recent years and the neo-fascist party, the Vlaams Blok, made significant increases in the 1988 local elections. In addition to support for electoral parties of the far right, the 1980s showed a disturbing rise in levels of racism and hostility to foreigners, manifested at times in physical attacks on North Africans and Turks who are the most disliked and discriminated against groups in the country. Referring to immigrants as 'barbarians' has become acceptable and commonplace and is not unconnected to the Belgian Interior Minister's use of the term in 1988 when he talked of the country being 'invaded by barbarian peoples such as Arabs, Moroccans, Yugoslavs and Turks'.[9]

In Denmark, where open neo-Nazism is stronger than in any other Scandinavian country, there have been violent attacks on refugees and people seen as supporting them. In 1986, 2,000 'rockers' instigated a concerted attack on a hostel containing Iranian, Sri Lankan and Lebanese asylum seekers. The extreme right Fremskridt Party almost doubled its share of the vote in the 1988 elections, campaigning on a ticket which promised to expel all refugees and Muslims.

Even in countries with a long-standing reputation for good majority–minority relations, such as The Netherlands, there has been a growth in racist attitudes since the mid-1970s, and institutionalised racism is demonstrated in such facts as that black people (mainly Surinamese) have the highest unemployment levels in Europe, running at four times the rate for whites.[10] The level of actual racial violence remains low, but such far right political parties as Centrumdemokratea are making electoral gains.

Since 1990, Italy has witnessed an eruption of racial attacks directed mainly against Moroccans and Africans from Senegal and the Ivory Coast. In 1990, 200 masked people arrived at a carnival armed with baseball bats and iron bars with which they beat black people and Roma (Gypsies). Arson attacks have taken place on immigrant reception centres and new racist groups are circulating inflammatory literature urging 'vigilance against the blacks and Gypsy pigs and the drug traffickers and the filthy Bolsheviks who protect them'. Anti-Islamic feeling is increasing, and in 1990 the Archibishop of Ravena issued the warning that Europe was

9 *The Guardian*, 27 December 1988.
10 British Broadcasting Corporation, Channel 2, *Black on Europe*, London, 1991.

being Islamicised, adding that it was not possible for people of different cultures, languages and religions to live together.

In the light of projected closer east-west European relations, developments in Germany since unification merit close scrutiny in terms of minority rights. Unfortunately, it would appear that the 'new' Germany has followed the same trend as the rest of western Europe. There has been an upsurge in hostility towards migrants, especially Turks and other non-Europeans which has expressed itself in physical violence. Neo-Nazi organisations have become increasingly active, directing much of their recruitment activity towards young former east Germans. Violence is inflicted particularly on black people, but also on homosexuals, lesbians, perceived left-wingers and eastern bloc refugees. Poles have been attacked and robbed whilst travelling between Poland and Germany and there is increasing hostility between citizens of the former two Germanies. Right-wing extremism and neo-fascism did not emerge with the collapse of the Berlin wall, but was noted in the east as early as 1981, though neither formally acknowledged nor acted upon. Attacks by right-wing skinheads, Nazi-punks and self-styled 'Faschos' occurred in the 1980s in the east, as they did in the west. Nor is anti-Semitism dormant in Germany; in the former east Germany, Jewish cemeteries were vandalised and in the united Germany extremists are openly denying the existence of the gas chambers and forging links with like-minded groups in Britain, Germany, France and the USA.

In sum, it would appear that western Europe is confronted by a form of highly virulent pan-European intolerance which embraces racism, anti-Semitism, religious bigotry and right-wing political extremism. Furthermore, there are worrying signs of the forging of international links between far right groups, particular young 'skinheads' whose networks extend across Britain, Germany, Belgium, France, The Netherlands, Scandinavia, Hungary, Poland and the USA (where it is linked with the Ku Klux Klan). Furthermore, German unification has demonstrated that this is not only a western phenomenon, but one which has its counterpart in the east. Since the dismantling of the USSR and the democratisation of other eastern bloc countries means that the futures of the 'two' Europes are likely to be ever more closely aligned, we need to examine the extent of discrimination based on ethnicity which exists in eastern Europe.

Eastern Europe

If recent years have brought massive change in western Europe, the extent and speed of change in eastern Europe has been little short of astounding and certainly of an order which few in the west could have predicted even a few months ago. The unification of Germany referred to above pales into insignificance in the light of recent events in the USSR and becomes only a minor element of what amounts to the total transformation of eastern

Europe on social, political, economic and ideological dimensions. Much of this change is viewed by the west as representing a highly positive move towards democracy and hands are rubbed in glee at the 'death' of communism. But the disintegration of official Marxism–Leninism has left an ideological vacuum which is currently being filled in many areas by nationalism and it is not beyond the bounds of probability that it will be filled in the future by fundamentalism, whether Christian or Islamic. As the authority and power of the state in a number of eastern European societies has declined, so has the expression of sectional interests—frequently constructed around ethnic or national differences—grown.

As in the west, ethnic minorities—and their treatment—varies from country to country. Though we have far less comprehensive information on majority-minority relationships in eastern Europe than we do on those in the west, it is clear that structural discrimination and prejudiced attitudes are widespread. Poland, for example, demonstrates intense antagonism towards Roma (Gypsies) whose homes were attacked during 1991. There is also intense anti-Semitism (despite the tiny number of Jews in the country) which, for the first time since the 1940s, took the form of physical violence during the Presidential election. Anti-Semitic publications are now openly on public sale and graffiti are widespread.

Hungary, too, is antagonistic to both Gypsies and Jews and the leading political party, the Democratic Forum, contains leaders who are openly anti-Semitic. Jewish property has been vandalised and there is a significant spread of 'skinhead' far right groups.

In Romania, the Hungarians claim that they are discriminated against to the extent that they are being forced to leave the country. Likewise, after six centuries away from the Ukraine, large numbers of Ukrainians are seeking to return as a result of structural discrimination. The registration of the Greater Romania Party as an official political party has led to renewed fears of fresh outbreaks of anti-Semitism and violence against the country's ethnic minorities. There is a growth of extreme right-wing organisations which are openly racist and proclaim their intention of waging bloody war against Hungarian, German and Gypsy minorities who are viewed as being 'racially impure'.

At the time of writing, Yugoslavia remains second only to the Soviet Union on the world stage as Serbs and Croats do battle in what is generally labelled an ethnic dispute. Religion plays a role in the conflict, with tension not only between Christian and Muslim, but between Catholic and Orthodox. As in Ireland, history is re-lived: in Yugoslavia during World War II some 1.7 million Serbs, Jews and Gypsies were massacred by the pro-Nazi Ustasha, yet Serbs and Croats have intermarried and lived in peace in the recent past. In the Serbian-Croatian crisis there is a tendency to forget that there is, in fact, no part of Yugoslavia which is ethnically or socially homogeneous, so that it may be simplistic, convenient or downright cynical to refer to the apparent break-up of Yugoslavia as an 'ethnic' conflict.

Since the Soviet Union has now been formally dismantled (and the communist party suspended) any discussion of the future of human rights, particularly those of minorities, must contain a large element of speculation. On the principle that human beings do not shed their cultural constructs either quickly or easily, however, it is legitimate to assume that certain attitudes can be inferred from the current and pre (second) revolution period. And the most dominant force at work at the moment is nationalism as independence is claimed by Azerbaijan, Lithuania, Latvia, Estonia, the Ukraine, Byelorussia, Moldova and Georgia (and formally granted to Estonia, Latvia and Lithuania). In turn, the mainly Armenian region of Nagorno-Karabakh has declared itself independent from Azerbaijan, and the Russian speaking region of Dniestr in Moldova has declared independence. Moldova is dominated by ethnic Romanians and is likely to press for union with that country.

Russia is the biggest and least homogeneous of the Soviet republics and is divided into republics, regions and districts, each created to cater for a distinct nationality, none related in ethnic terms to Russians. These include Tatars, Chuvash, Dagestanis, Bashkirs, Chechens, Burvats, Yukuts, Kalmyks and Chuchi, many of whom expect to be treated worse in the future than they were under a Soviet government. Every one of the Russian republics has declared its sovereignty over the last year, despite a number of them actually consisting of Russian majorities (Buryatia, Karelia, Mordovia, Udmurtia and Komi). A recent increase in anti-Semitism in Russia has included physical violence and murder. This has been linked to the growth of the Pamyat (Memory) Party which blames the ills of the country on the Jews. In 1990, the Pamyat went into an alliance with four other groups, renamed itself the Republican People's Party of Russia and received recognition as a legal organisation. It has links with extreme right-wing groups in London.

Some 25 million ethnic Russians currently live outside the Russian republic and have done so since before the first revolution (in the Ukraine, Byelorussia, Moldova, the Baltics and parts of central Asia). In many republics there is intense hostility towards Russians, extending as far as the application of the pejorative terms 'aliens' and 'half-castes'. The situation has worsened dramatically in recent times and many Russians are being forced to consider retreating to the centre.

Nor are the majority of other Soviet republics free from ethnic strife. There is a long-standing conflict between Azebaijan and Armenia in which religion is a mobilising force between the Muslim Azerbaijanis and the Christian Armenians. In Uzbekistan the local Muslim majority (which has shown growing evidence over the last two years of a developing Islamic consciousness) has clashed with ethnic Armenians. In 1989 the homes of Turks were burned down and the people lynched in an explosion of ethnic violence for which no-one seems to have an explanation. The Ukraine has a long history of ethnic discord with its Polish minority, as has Lithuania. In Georgia ethnic strife is endemic, especially in Transcaucasia which has a fiercely nationalistic administration. Only Byelorussia is relatively homogeneous and free from ethnic conflict.

As the tyrannies of eastern Europe collapse, it appears that old territorial and ethnic conflicts are re-appearing in stark and shocking form. However, this may be less to do with ethnic conflict *per se* as the fact that resistance to totalitarianism often manifests itself as nationalism. On the other hand it may be that the current level of nationalistic fervour will be maintained and, if this is the case, the prognosis for Europe as a whole, and ethnic minorities in particular, is ominous. Nationalism and respect for minorities are not usually compatible, and systems of domination tend to feed off each other. The fusion of the rampant nationalism of the east with the virulent racism of the west is too horrific to contemplate, but the atmosphere in Germany militates against complacency.

Towards a greater Europe?

For people who believe that the founders of the European Community were right in their aims of promoting closer collaboration between people, the expansion of human rights and democracy and the elimination of warfare, fascism and Nazism, an examination of Europe today makes depressing reading. Totalitarian regimes in the east are crumbling, only to be replaced by rampant nationalism and renewed territorial and ethnic strife; frontiers are being dismantled in the west, only to be replaced by ramparts heavily fortified against the rest of the world. In both east and west, ethnicity and religion are being mobilised as organising frameworks within which power struggles are taking place.

The situation holds many dangers, both for Europe and the rest of the world. The attempted coup in the Soviet Union alerted western Europe to the fact that its destiny is inextricably linked with that of eastern Europe and there is now considerable pressure to re-think our policy on aid to the east. But this will not come cheap and money directed towards eastern Europe is likely to be so at the expense of the so-called Third World, in many parts of which people are struggling to survive. Our policies on migrants, refugees and asylum seekers will also have an adverse effect on third country peoples and we need to be aware that the gap between north and south is rapidly assuming the proportions of a chasm. In their rush towards capitalism, east Europeans are not yet aware that the global economy is a cruel place for weak countries; the Third World has known this for a long time and former east Germans are currently learning the lesson the hard way.

As far as racism, xenophobia, chauvinism, fundamentalism and nationalism are concerned, it is the *trend* which is of concern, and even more worrying is the fact that this reactionary shift to the right is not restricted to Europe, but seems to be taking place on a global scale. The ruin of the hope held out by communism, not only in Europe but in the Third World, has created an ideological vacuum which religious fundamentalism has already rushed in to fill. In Europe, we are highly conscious of the threat of Islamic extremism but are blind to the dangers of Christian fundamentalism. The death of communism coincides with the Christian decade of evangelism in which Europe has been targetted by certain extremists as 'the new dark continent' and we need to be alert to the threat this poses to human rights. On a more pragmatic level, young European-born ethnic minority people are not willing to tolerate the indignities which their immigrant parents suffered; if we do not act forcefully and quickly against racism, the very cohesion of the European Community could be under threat.

There is, however, a positive side to the situation. Ethnic conflict is *not* innate and therefore *not* inevitable. Ethnic identity is neither static, nor all-encompassing, but is situationally specific. We *can* learn to think in terms of human dignity, rather than in narrowly nationalistic ones; to respect and value difference, rather than adopt ethnocentric or xenophobic attitudes. The fact that this will require a massive effort of political will which is not readily apparent at the moment should not paralyse us. Change can be brought about by individuals and groups, as demonstrated recently in the USSR, and the very existence of the EC offers real possibilities for progress in the field of human rights.

Extreme right-wing groups have organised themselves not only across Europe but across the Atlantic. A similar process has begun from the opposite stance and human rights activists have begun to network across national boundaries; there is a need to increase the momentum of this. The Council of Europe, which is responsible for the functioning of the European Commission of Human Rights and the European Court of Human Rights, has already been mentioned. The Netherlands Institute of Human Rights, the Joint Council for the Welfare of Immigrants, the Refugee Forum and Migrant Rights Action Network, International Alert and Kairos Europa are other co-ordinating and pressure bodies which are working towards a more equal and just community. For at root, this is what it is all about: not only combating racism and other forms of discrimination based on ethnic, religious or cultural differences (important as that is in itself), but the fight to maintain and extend human rights which '... arise from one's humanity and not from citizenship of a particular State, inside or outside the EC' (European Parliament, 1991). It would indeed be ironic if, at the very time that east Europeans are ceding fewer of their rights to the state, west Europeans were to adopt a passive, pessimistic attitude to their own possibilities of influencing the course of events.

THE POLITICAL ECONOMY OF
A 'MID-EUROPEAN REGION':
THE ALPE ADRIA
COMMUNITY

PAOLO PERULLI*

'Only the largest states now have an importance of their own ... Gone are the days when countless shepherds drove their flocks in confusion across the pastures of Europe.' [F. NAUMANN, *Mitteleuropa*, Berlin 1915.]

NAUMANN's prophecy of a mid-European *Gemeinschaft*, a federation of States in the central zone of Southern Europe, has been one of the recurrent utopian ideals of this century (together with Rathenau, Troeltsch, Meinecke and Mann, Naumann was a key figure of early twentieth-century German culture). The idea of privileged, even federal, relations between the states of this crucial area on the boundary between East and West (a territory stretching from the Vistula to the Vosges, from Galicia to Lake Constance but destined to attract other central and southern European nationalities) was, however, destroyed by the rigid demarcation of blocs after the Second World War.

These preliminary remarks are necessary as they put recent developments into a clearer context following the collapse of the Soviet bloc, the reunification of Germany and the consequent strong attraction which the European Community represents to the new post-communist structures emerging in Eastern Europe.

What relations are established between the Community and the countries of Central and Eastern Europe, and what form these relations take is still the object of speculations and hypotheses and even dramatic conflicts (as seen in the war in Yugoslavia). But, paradoxically, Naumann's prophecy could once again become topical, provided that it were somehow 'turned around'; that is, not an *opposition* between the principle of one 'largest State' (in this case the European Community) and that of 'countless flocks' (small states, autonomous regions, ethnic minorities etc.) but a reasonable coexistence between them. In fact the very evolution of the European Community into a 'super-state' currently appears unlikely—

* Paolo Perulli works at the department of regional economics and social analysis, University Institute of Architecture, Venice. His article has been translated by Christopher Stevens.

it seems far more likely that we shall witness the formation of new 'federations', 'confederations' or 'condominiums'. In these types of organisation 'there is no single identifiable sovereign—just a multitude of authorities at different levels of aggregation, territorial or functional, with ambiguous or shared *compétences* at the head of overlapping and diverse organisational hierarchies'.[1]

In this hypothesis the European Community will not only tend to establish forms of agreement, association or 'weak integration' with external civil units, but will also acknowledge a certain autonomy for its own internal sub-national units. These (regions, metropolitan areas, cities) will strive to increase their own 'competitive advantage' above all by establishing relations, various sorts of alliance and partnership, with the aim of widening their own influence and their own economic and commercial penetration. This activism of the sub-national units will seek to outflank the monopolistic control of their own respective national states in areas such as social and economic policy, and even diplomacy and foreign politics. Indeed, the success of efforts within economic competition is ever more closely linked to the ability to control agreements made with other sub-national units across national boundaries. It is very indicative that individual European regions or cities are opening representative offices or businesses in other important European regions and cities, and in the rest of the world. Equally significant is the formation of 'clubs' of international cities, associations of regions from different countries in search of an individual identity and of forms of co-operation independent of their own state of origin. Sometimes the development of these forms of trans-national co-operation depends on the pre-existence of traditionally autonomous tendencies, especially in the case of border regions.

Since the 1970s a certain number of bodies for inter-regional co-operation have begun to be formed in the south-eastern area of Europe involving various regions (or Republics, *Länder*, autonomous provinces) of Italy, Switzerland, Germany, Austria, Yugoslavia and Hungary. The first to be formed was the *Comunità di Lavoro Arge Alp* (central alps), in 1972. It was promoted by the head of the Tyrolean government and made up of the free State of Bavaria, the Canton of Graubünden, the Autonomous Province of Bolzano, the Region of Lombardy, the *Land* of Salzburg and the *Land* of Voralberg. Other regional units joined subsequently: the Autonomous Province of Trento, the Canton of Sankt Gallen and the Canton of Ticino (as an observer). This group of alpine regions, gathering together in free association public organisations with accomplished managerial abilities, intends to tackle common needs and problems in collaboration, especially in ecological, cultural, social and economic fields. The *Comunità di Lavoro Arge Alp* is recognised by all the federal or central governments of the regions which comprise it, and it

---

[1] P. C. Schmitter, *The European Community as an Emergent and Novel Form of Political Domination*, Stanford University, April 1990.

is also recognised by the institutions of European co-operation. In particular *Arge Alp* is part of the *Gruppo di Lavoro delle Regioni di Confine* (AGEG) and of the *Ufficio di Collegamento delle Organizzazioni Regionali Europee* (made up of the AGEG and the *Regioni Pereferiche Costiere*) which develops liaison services between the member-regions and the European Organisations (EEC, Council of Europe).

The second association operating in the alpine arc is *Cotrao* (*Comunità di Lavoro della Alpi Occidentali*) which is of a similar nature but will not be included in this study as it is devoted to the western border-regions of the alpine arc (France, Italy, Switzerland).

Through the initiative of the Venetian Region the *Comunità di Lavoro Alpe Adria* was formed in 1978. This was initially joined by the Region of Venetia and the Autonomous Region of Friuli-Venezia-Giulia (Italy), the Austrian *Länder* of Burgenland, Carinthia, Styria, Upper Austria and Salzburg (the last with the status of 'active observer'), the Socialist Republics of Croatia and Slovenia (Yugoslavia), and, also with the status of 'active observer', the Free State of Bavaria (Federal Republic of Germany). They were subsequently joined by the autonomous Italian Region of Trentino Alto-Adige (1981), the Lombardy Region (as an 'active observer' from 1985, becoming a full member in 1988), and the Hungarian Committees of Gyor Sopron and Vas (as 'active observers' since 1986).

It is worth noting that, since 1982, the three Communities (*Arge Alp*, *Cotrao*, *Alpe Adria*), whose members are in some cases duplicated, have carried out a practice of joint meetings which led to a conference which established their official collaboration in 1988.

Returning to *Alpe Adria*, the basis of the association is certainly historical and geographical homogeneity but there are also economic and strategic considerations. Some of these regions, indeed, belong to the strong economic zone of the Community—in particular Lombardy, Triveneto and Bavaria have registered the highest economic rate of growth in Europe in recent years. It is because of this very dynamism that they have not been included in the national and community support programme and they therefore intend to increase their own ability to apply pressure on international organisations through infrastructural and structural means. In particular, the member regions emphasise in their documents the 'common problems of marginalisation with regard to their respective political and administrative decision-making centres', and the 'possibility of influence within their respective governments' across the *Alpe Adria* zone. Due to their geographical location these same regions consider themselves the prime candidates for penetration of the new markets of Eastern Europe.

On the other hand the 'weak' regions of *Alpe Adria* are striving for the advantages of having at their disposal a quantity of information and technology (above all in the field of high technology) possessed by their 'strong' fellow regions. This allows them to make the transition from a state-planned economy to a market one more easily and to appear competitive in the future panorama of a single European market.

The organisation and international activities of Alpe Adria

In the 1978 protocol of entente the *Comunità Alpe Adria* arrogated to itself the task of 'dealing in common in areas of information and technology and of co-ordinating problems which are in the interests of its members' (article 3). It was foreseen that the following problems would be considered in particular: 'transalpine communications, harbour traffic, production and transportation of energy, agriculture, forest use, water use, tourism, protection of the environment, conservation of the cultural and recreational landscape, territorial structure, urban development, cultural links and contact between scientific institutes.'

The management of this long list of problems requires an adequate organisational structure. In reality, the *Comunità Alpe Adria* is endowed with a decision-making body, the Conference of Presidents of the Regions and *Länder*, in which the representatives of each region meet annually and where the programmes to be followed, resolutions to be undertaken and financial decisions to adopt are decided. It should be underlined that the Community makes 'recommendations', in the sense that these are not legally binding documents.

Equally, it is no accident that it has no assembly or parliament because there is no legislative activity. The discussion stage is prepared by the activities of the *Commissione Alti Dirigenti*, a sort of permanent executive which makes use of the studies and research carried out by six Commissions and by sub-groups in specific fields.

The technical commissions deal respectively with: territorial structure, transport, culture, economy, agriculture, and health and hygiene. They are each stationed in one of the member-regions, following a principle of rotation. We can thus observe that, as the jurisdiction is diffused in all the regions, and as each division has the responsibility for a single area, no specialised bureaucracy is created in the Community. They are simply appendices to the single regional governments. Even less is there any hierarchy of the political centres: Munich, Venice, Milan, Zagreb, Ljubljana etc. assume the presidency in turn following a biannual rotation. The picture is one of a network of responsibilities which avoids centralisation in a similar way to the territorial, institutional and infrastructural organisation of the *Alpe Adria* region. For an appraisal of the type of activities developed from 1978 to the present, the initiatives of three of the commissions can be summarised.

The Commission for territorial structure has produced various joint reports. It first produced the First Common Report on Territorial Planning (1982) which was above all a document with information about the respective systems in force in the regions. This was followed in 1983 by a Glossary of the Terms Used in Territorial Planning. A Common Report on the Management of Waters was produced in 1983. This was dedicated to a comparative examination of the problems of Regions, *Länder* and Republics and an early identification of common tasks. A Common Report on the Protection of the Environment followed (1985) and an Observatory of Marine Pollution was constituted while specific groups of experts examined areas such as urban and industrial discharges, the impact of urban infrastructure on the environment and the pollution of the Adriatic. A second Report on Territorial Planning appeared in 1988. It concentrated more on questions of mobility, commuting and transport.

The Economic Commission developed plans of action for tourism with the promotion of initiatives for a common image and the establishment of a data bank on economic, social and territorial aspects. It promoted collaboration between banks to support commercial interchange, energy saving and the use of alternative energy sources, development policies for small and medium-sized enterprises and scientific and technological co-operation.

The Transport Commission (probably the most important) concentrated on the elimination of various obstacles existing in the field of transport of both people and goods. The First Common Report on Major Communication Infrastructures was produced in 1987. A decentralisation of goods traffic toward rail transport was foreseen, for which development concentrating on the doubling and scaling of lines was projected which would favour increases in speed and capacity. Here in play are relevant decisions regarding the European high-speed rail system, the motorway network and new transalpine tunnels. The questions of reinforcement of inter-regional air transport and north Adriatic harbouring (Venice, Trieste, Fiume, Capodistria) have also been worked on by the Commission.

As is evident, the activities have been more on a level of information than real definition of strategies or common area policies. It can be considered that this work is active in the breaking down of barriers of knowledge between members, and in the creation of a common image at an international level. This 'strategic marketing' activity is, however, accompanied by early evidence of 'orientation', lobbying and the application of pressure on the European Community with regard, for example, to the community 'master plans' for specific areas. The *Alpe Adria* seems to want to turn its recent activity in this direction. Increased international recognition, either on the part of the EC or of its member states, is essential to this aim. The first results were achieved with the declaration of Millstatt (1988), on the occasion of the tenth anniversary of *Alpe Adria*, when the foreign ministers of the five countries to which the Regions, Republics and *Länder* belong recognised the successes achieved by the initiative and declared themselves willing to 'support and provide incentives for international collaboration in the *Alpe Adria* framework'. Equally significant was the formation, in 1989, of a 'Quadrangular

Initiative' between Austria, Italy, Yugoslavia and Hungary, designed to favour these early experiments in co-operation in the light of the events taking place in Eastern Europe. These relative successes are, however, very much provisional, as they are subject to political evolution and to the fate of the push for independence in progress, in particular (but not only) in the Yugoslavian Republics.

The political resistance to, and scepticism about, the effective practicality of a *'Comunità di Lavoro'* between the alpine-adriatic regions are, moreover, very strong. *Alpe Adria*'s activity has, on one hand, been severely criticised in recent years by the Polish, Czechoslovakian and, obviously, Yugoslavian press, and, on the other hand, almost ignored in the concrete actions of the Italian, German and Austrian governments.

How similar are the alpine-adriatic regions?

Until the 1960s the alpine-adriatic regions were in a relatively backward condition in the European panorama. With the exception of Lombardy, the other Italian regions (Venetia, Trentino Alto-Adige, Friuli-Venezia-Giulia) were very backward with regard to industrial development. In Germany, Bavaria was still a predominantly agricultural state.

Since the 1960s, however, the economic growth rate of the Italian and German regions of the *Alpe Adria* has been above their respective national averages. This accentuated growth has continued in the seventies and eighties: at the end of the eighties the per capita product of these regions was above both their own respective national averages and above the EC average. This spectacular growth has essentially been due to a strong development of small and medium-sized enterprises with flexible specialisation in traditional and advanced fields, to a huge expansion in the fields of new production technology and research and development activities, to greater economic flexibility and to the construction in these regions of 'network economies' and 'economies of scope' as alternatives to the traditional 'economies of scale' typical of regions of long-standing industrialisation.

A parallel and converging phenomenon has been the re-emergence of regional economies.[2] Whereas areas based on mass production and the Fordist model have encountered severe reconversion problems (above all Turin and Piedmont in Italy and Bremen, Hamburg, the Ruhr and the long-industrialised *Länder* in Federal Germany), specialised and flexible regional economies are emergent in the most recently industrialised regions, most commonly located in Southern Europe.

As has been emphasised by specialised literature,[3] and by Bianchi in

[2] C. F. Sabel, *Flexible Specialisation and the Re-emergence of Regional Economies*, in P. Hirst and J. Zeitlin (eds), *Reversing Industrial Decline? Industrial Structure and Policy in Britain and her Competitors*, Oxford, Berg, 1989.

[3] Reclus/DATAR, *Les villes 'européennes'*, La Documentation Française, Paris, 1989.

this volume, the European economic panorama is characterised by an early central band of historical industrialisation, which stretches from South-East England across Belgium and the Low Countries as far as Northern and Central Germany and to the old Italian industrial triangle (Piedmont, Lombardy, Liguria). Set against this axis of early industrialisation there is a southern band which stretches from Catalonia through Southern France to the Po Valley and modern Italy (*'la terza Italia'*) and to the Southern German *Länder* of Baden-Württemberg and Bavaria. It is this axis which has seen the highest rates of economic growth in recent years.

The *Comunità Alpe Adria*, therefore, seeks an ideal extension of the strong new Southern European axis towards the East and especially towards those Eastern regions which are already, either culturally or economically, easier to integrate with the countries of the EC.

If the countries of Southern Europe currently hold a competitive advantage (especially due to their technologically advanced and flexible industrial structure), they must nevertheless overcome some handicaps, particularly with regard to their communications infrastructures.

The regions of South-East Europe in fact have little horizontal integration at their disposal (with the exception of the Po Valley). The obstacle represented by the alpine arc, from Switzerland as far as the Bavarian and Austrian Alps and the regions of Yugoslavia, could seriously disadvantage these regions in favour of other communication axes. For this very reason, one of the main points of the agenda of *Alpe Adria* is that of communication. This includes the creation of new transalpine links between Germany, Italy, Austria and Yugoslavia, the completion of the high-speed railway network along the Lyon-Trieste axis, the reinforcement of the port system in the Northern Adriatic and of waterways etc. The hypothesis of strengthening relations with Eastern Europe is at least partially helped by the presence of Yugoslavian Republics and Hungarian Committees in the *Alpe Adria* Community which from the point of view of economic development are relatively integrable with the Western regions and *Länder*. As can be seen from Figure 1, the composition of the gross regional product (which largely corresponds to the zonal composition of the active population) is not too dissimilar. Indeed, Croatia and Slovenia in particular have a very different structure to the overall Yugoslavian composition and are therefore much more similar to the Western European regions (it is considered that the two Republics supply 40 per cent of Yugoslavia's Gross National Product).

On the other hand the data on the banking and financial structure of the different regions show that the Yugoslavian Republics and the Hungarian Committees are naturally on a clearly inferior level: see, for example, the notable difference in per capita deposits, which range from less than one million Italian lire for the Hungarian Committees to 24 million for Bavaria (Table 1). Co-operation between banks and financial institutions is not currently among the activities of *Alpe Adria*. Some lines of international credit are currently open between some banks in the different regions and

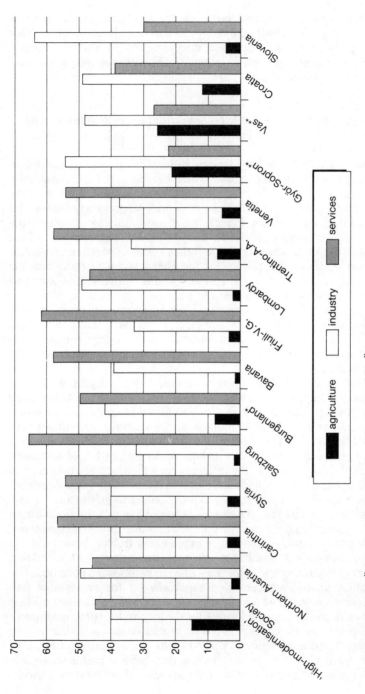

* 1985 figures, from Ö.S.Z., *Statistisches Handbuch für die Republik Österreich.*
** 1988 figures, from Központi statistiszkai hivatal, *Statistiszkai Eukönyv.*
Source: Alpe-Adria, *Indicatori economici,* maggio 1988 and Alpe-Adria, *Secondo rapporto comune sulla pianificazione territoriale* (versione preliminare).

FIGURE 1   Composition of Gross Regional Product, by Region (1986).

countries of *Alpe Adria*. These, however, are only used as counter-items for real exchanges, otherwise they lie unused in inter-bank accounts. This weakness presupposes, in order to set up an integration, a strong penetration of Western capital into the economies of Eastern regions, an increase of contracts and transactions.

Forms and limits of economic co-operation: the role of the special interest groups

The strong attraction the Yugoslavian Republics and Hungarian Committees feel towards border-regions which belong to the EC is naturally more a political problem than an economic one. The development of the Yugoslavian Republics' push for independence is at present uncertain and threatened by serious violent events. It is clear that the as yet fragile co-operation with Western European regions is shown to be impotent where these events are concerned, but should they result in partial or complete recognition of the independence of the Republics it is clear that the attraction of the sphere of the Community would be greatly increased and would lead to a stronger economic integration.

Limiting myself to a consideration of the economic aspects of integration, it can be seen that the principal objective identified by the *Comunità Alpe Adria* for the moment is to encourage forms of co-operation and technological transfer from the strong regions of the group to the weaker ones.

The first results of this preliminary search for integration are the formation of a 'suppliers' exchange' and of a 'technology exchange', and others are being planned such as a 'handbook of investors' which would improve awareness of opportunities for economic investment. An Economic Bulletin published periodically by the *Comunità Alpe Adria* in its various languages continually brings up to date a list of institutes, centres and organisations of the different regions which are prepared to collaborate in the fields of applied research, diffusion of technology and, above all, in the field of medium-sized and small enterprises. Since 1984, when new laws partially freed relations between Yugoslavia and Western Republics, a significant increase in joint ventures and direct foreign investment has come about. Joint-venture agreements trebled between 1984 and 1985 alone, and simultaneously the promotion of state bodies, Chambers of Economy and some Yugoslavian banks was intensified. The liberalisation process concentrated especially on the creation of free customs zones (towards which end internal and coastal Yugoslavian cities strove), which would act as platforms for the localisation of joint ventures designed primarily for exports to Third World countries. If the path of collaboration and joint ventures should continue, the eastern regions of the *Alpe Adria* Community, which show they have available space, low labour costs (as little as one-fifth of the average of the western regions) and economic incentives for the movement of goods, could be transformed into types of large 'free enterprise zones' for the use of Western investors. Here we touch on a crucial point in the whole question. It is indeed noted that the model of free enterprise zones is based on what particular conditions are offered to companies by the host country: good infrastructure and services, low labour costs and social peace, non-interference. The model has been succesful, as we know, in Hong Kong and in Singapore, and has since been used for the revitalisation of de-industrialised urban zones.[4] The same strategy has been adopted by the countries of East Europe to maintain their own independence by setting themselves up as free production zones. This strategy is partly based on the pre-existence of sub-supply relations in the Western economies: this is the case for the outsourcing German production in Slovenia and for that of France and Italy in Romania. But the speed and flexibility of operations in free enterprise zones is such that they offer appreciably superior advantages to foreign companies than direct foreign investment or joint ventures with local companies. Nevertheless it should certainly not be taken for granted that the adoption of possible free enterprise zones would be compatible with forms of partnership and integrated co-operation.

Despite their advantages, the offer of free enterprise zones to the East has not up till now been favoured by Western Europe; it is probably felt that political uncertainty may still increase, and that the conditions on which free enterprise zones are based (control of salaries and social and fiscal non-interference by the host-country) are not achievable in these countries, especially in the long term.[5]

Given the absence of any government policies within the *Alpe Adria* Community, all these prospects are currently entrusted to the initiative of the economic institutions and the interest groups organised by the Regions. Since the beginning of the eighties *Alpe Adria* interest groups and area organisations (such as the Chamber of Commerce and the Economy, the Conference of Presidents of Banking Institutions, organisations of University Vice-chancellors, of Directors of business fairs, and the Trade Unions) have begun to operate on a stable basis. But even the interest groups seem to suffer from the same operational weakness which characterises political governments. In fact the Conference of Presidents of Chambers for the Economy of the *Alpe Adria* Region, which meets annually, does not seem to do more than make recommendations, supply information and co-ordinate contacts. More effective phases would have to be run by 'effective intercameral groups' employed in specific fields, such as that of technological innovations and applied research.

In reality, a group of truly connected policies and actions capable of moving *Alpe Adria* past the stage of 'recommendations' and promotional

---

[4] P. Hall, *Cities of Tomorrow*, Basil Blackwell, Oxford, 1988.
[5] S. Boba, 'Le ricche merci e i salari di fame delle "zone franche"', *Politica ed Economia* 9, 1991.

TABLE 1   BANK DEPOSITS AND INVESTMENTS IN THE ALPE ADRIA REGION
(a) Composition

Alpe Adria Regions	Residents	Surface Area (km²)	No. of Banking Counters	Deposits lire (MM)	Investments lire (MM)
Bavaria	10,959,203	70,546	9,768	263,950	311,479
Burgenland	269,771	3,965	266	3,844	2,368
Friuli-V.G.	1,233,984	7,845	444	12,337	6,977
Györ-Sopron	421,742	4,012	74	355	547
Croatia	4,601,469	56,538	732	8,320	6,209
Carinthia	536,727	9,533	442	8,843	6,573
Lombardy	8,891,652	23,856	2,862	121,872	80,614
Upper Austria	1,269,540	11,980	955	19,601	13,001
Salzburg	442,301	7,154	354	9,379	6,784
Slovenia	1,891,896	20,255	295	3,123	3,335
Steiermark	1,186,525	16,387	716	10,497	15,671
Trentino-A.A.	873,413	13,613	603	6,447	3,545
Vas	280,465	3,337	49	225	279
Venetia	4,345,047	18,368	1,257	42,426	25,275
Alpe Adria Total	37,203,735	267,389	18,817	511,220	482,655

(b) Ratios

Alpe Adria Regions	Residents/ No. of Banking Counters	Surface Area/ No. of Banking Counters (Km²)	Deposits/ Residents (mil.)	Investments/ Residents (mil.)	Deposits/ No. of Banking Counters (MM)	Investments/ No. of Banking Counters (MM)
Bavaria	1,122	7.2	24.1	28.4	27.0	31.9
Burgenland	1,014	14.9	14.2	8.8	14.5	8.9
Friuli-V.G.	2,779	17.7	10.0	5.7	27.8	15.7
Győr-Sopron	5,699	54.2	0.8	1.3	4.8	7.4
Croatia	6,286	77.2	1.8	1.3	11.4	8.5
Carinthia	1,214	21.6	16.5	12.2	20.0	14.9
Lombardy	3,107	8.3	13.7	9.1	42.6	28.2
Upper Austria	1,329	12.5	15.4	10.2	20.5	13.6
Salzburg	1,249	20.2	21.2	15.3	26.5	19.2
Slovenia	6,413	68.7	1.7	1.8	10.6	11.3
Steiermark	1,657	22.9	8.8	13.2	14.7	21.9
Trentino-A.A.	1,448	22.6	7.4	4.1	10.7	5.9
Vas	5,724	68.1	0.8	1.0	4.6	5.7
Venetia	3,457	14.6	9.8	5.8	33.8	20.1
Alpe Adria Total	1,977	14.2	13.7	13.0	27.2	25.6

Source: Figures provided by credit companies and central institutes of the Regions belonging to Alpe Adria.

activities to that of achievements seems as yet undefined. Interest in the creation of such new instruments is not lacking. Recently, for example, the National Council of Italian Economy and Labour, which unites employers' organisations, trade unions and government experts, proposed the creation of one of these instruments:[6] a 'regional development fund for the countries of the quadrangular' (Austria, Italy, Yugoslavia, Hungary) modelled on the EC regional development fund. The fund would aim to support specific shares of a communal or interregional nature among the different member countries with the help of non-interest-bearing funds in capital accounts and interest accounts. The fund would in particular enable the completion of studies and works which would further the integration of single countries into the network of infrastructures to be financed and should give financial support to the less developed countries and regions of the quadrangular. It would be a 'regional finance company for the *Alpe Adria*' funded equally by the regions and by private economic institutions (large banks, savings banks and insurance companies). The finance company would have to operate as a 'group investor' (with a system of rotation of funds) reducing the economic risk of the investment by the concession of loans destined to have a deferred economic return to initiatives such as infrastructures and services in which public-private co-operation is possible. The significance of these proposals is that they would create new capitalist institutions and partnerships in which groups currently outside the market economy would operate (the regions and republics of the East). These new institutions would have to aim, among other things, to encourage these groups to 'learn' the mechanisms and the working principles of the capitalist market, even before they could be fully included in the institutions of the European Community. The EC could take part, albeit without direct commitment, by 'using' the new institutions as a form of interface with the regional economies of the East. Moreover the EC, through the General Department for External Relations, is already promoting co-operative interventions with the individual countries of the quadrangular which are outside the community.

Conclusions

The *Alpe Adria* Community, whose experience we have briefly outlined here, currently seems to be in a rather ambiguous situation. Although it is far from being a 'strong' federal experiment between homogenous regions in a position to develop joint policies, it nevertheless represents something more than a simple 'co-ordination centre' for studies and research between different regions.

---

[6] Consiglio nazionale dell'Economia e del lavoro-Commissione per i Rapporti Internazionali, *Alpe Adria*, Rome, April 1990.

This ambiguity is partly due to the very uncertainty of its own promoters about the possible results of its actions. Whilst *Alpe Adria* was pioneering in the seventies, it risks falling behind the precipitous course of events since 1989. Moreover *Alpe Adria* was conceived more as an 'axis' between northern and southern alpine regions and it is only recently, somewhat carried by the wave of events, that it has emphasised its role as a gateway between East and West. These developments in the importance of the alpine-adriatic initiative can be traced back both to internal causes (changes in the membership of *Alpe Adria* and the evolution of its member-regions) and to external factors (changes in the East and the phases of European unification).

With respect to its original structure it should be stressed that in the eighties, with the expansion to Lombardy, *Alpe Adria* has ended up identifying itself with some of Europe's strongest regions (Bavaria, Lombardy, Venetia) on an economic level, while the support of the Hungarian Committees has strengthened its Eastern membership. The initiative has thus modified some of its original characteristics as a 'club of border-regions' in order to take on new ones; on the one hand, that is, an association between strong and weak regions, and, on the other, a mid-European area where East and West are integrated. In the words of one of its founders (at that time the President of the Venetian Region and now the influential Italian minister for transport), 'the entry of Trentino-Alto Adige, Lombardy and the Hungarian Regions has progressively caused *Alpe Adria* to assume the borders which correspond to the original history of that part of Europe'. Meanwhile the birth of other experiments in regional European clubs (in North-West and North-East Europe, but also in Mediterranean Europe) has resulted in an increased level of competition between the different initiatives. This has shown that the process of European unification is being carried out in the strengthening of regional and sub-national dimensions, thereby confirming the original intuition of *Alpe Adria*. Within the competitive atmosphere between networks of European regions it has also caused *Alpe Adria* to identify its own distinctive role in East-West co-operation in its unique position as a network of regions belonging to these two large areas. But will this vocation fully involve the strong regions of the Community? Lombardy might still be more attracted by partnership with other strong European regions (as is seen in the club of 'four motors for Europe' consisting also of Baden-Württemberg, Rhone-Alp and Catalonia) and Bavaria might be attracted by integration with what was East Germany.

Leaving these uncertainties to state the main components of the *Alpe Adria* experience thus far, it seems possible to identify the following:

(*a*) *The will of local political élites* which, seeking their own national and international legitimation, see a possible place for themselves in the formula of the *Comunità di Lavoro*. It should not be forgotten that the western regional élites which began the initiative are politically homo-genous (the Christian Democrats have constantly been in power in

Bavaria, Venetia, Lombardy, Friuli-Venezia-Giulia and Trentino Alto-Adige) and that they saw the Community as an opportunity for reinforcement and lobbying which would strengthen their national role.

(b) *Autonomy* as an integral element of the club of regions. It should be remembered that not only have the Yugoslavian Republics of Slovenia and Croatia claimed independence for a long time, but also that two of the Italian regions (Trentino and Friuli) are autonomous and that the other two (Venetia and Lombardy) show strong autonomous and anti-centralist urges. From an institutional point of view the Bavarian *Land*, like the Austrian *Länder*, is given strong autonomous powers by the central state. Despite national constitutional differences autonomy therefore plays a most important role.

(c) *Interests of areas or of economic élites*. Although it does not show, clearly a constellation of economic interests is at work. Right from the start, important interests in the field of communications infrastructure identified favourable opportunities for the development of the motorway and railway networks (the project for the creation of a new Brenner railway tunnel alone is worth eight thousand billion lire). More recently, a strong thrust of companies towards the East has been seen, above all of small and medium-sized enterprises concentrating on export. Unlike large multinational groups which have greater and more direct access to national and international foreign policy, these small and medium-sized enterprises have to make do with regional policies for promotion and commercial and technological penetration.

(d) *Para-diplomacy*. Among the ingredients of local development policies administered by municipal or regional governments in Europe is that of diplomatic initiative. This is no longer limited to what are marginal actions from an economic viewpoint, but directed at genuine marketing of respective economic resources: local industrial production, especially production of a technologically sophisticated nature, and also tourism, culture and services (real expansion areas on the international market). Especially in the case of the export of services, it is not a matter of providing a flow to consumers in other countries so much as the establishment of subsidiary bases in other regions (such as banks and insurance companies) or the creation of networks among several regions in different countries. This dimension of city or regional marketing, often the vehicle for the multiplication of business opportunities, has had an important role in the initiative. Economic marketing relies ever more heavily on forms of political marketing which allow the regions and local governments to take direct part in forms of partnership without the mediation of nation states or traditional diplomatic channels of representation.

If these seem to be the principal ingredients of the *Alpe Adria* experience thus far, it is now time to consider what might be the future contribution of other factors which have emerged in the meantime, and which will increasingly be affected by the process of European integration which is in progress. First and foremost, there is the problem of transition from a 'forum' of regions to a genuine *orchestration* of regions. In order to have true orchestration, the main development choices made by participating regions would have to be discussed and agreed by institutions with powers of representation. If only as a 'second level' request, the *Comunità Alpe Adria* would have to be granted some delegation of functions by its member-regions. Currently, however, the exclusively technical nature of the commissions, as we have seen, makes it obvious that a decision has been made to keep a low political profile so as not to 'disturb' any region or create problems for their respective national governments. On the other hand, not only politico-institutional problems, but also economic strategy will be resolved if *Alpe Adria* acquires autonomous powers. Might the dominant strategy be to create a large 'free production zone' in the East which would receive the sub-supply of less specialised output from the adjoining high technology German and Italian enterprises? And how would such a strategy stand in relation to the German unification, for example, which has led Germany to burden itself with the colossal industrial reconversion of the former DDR? Above all, could the European Community justify such a strategy whose upshot would be an increase of social dumping, stigmatised by the Community as 'recourse to working conditions and social norms which are substandard with respect to the productivity levels that the economy could normally justify'?[7]

The solution of these dilemmas is linked, at least in part, to the evolution of *regional community policies*. If the EC put the integration of Eastern economies at the centre of its own agenda, *Alpe Adria* would be singularly well-placed to receive a constant flow of finance since it already has some of the key East European countries among its members. The EC has already decided to increase the structural funds destined for less-developed regions, in Southern Europe as well as Ireland and some areas of Great Britain. These funds, among other things, could be sent directly to regions, bypassing national governments. In competition with weak European areas it is certain that partner-regions of Eastern regions would be treated preferentially, even when compared with more inadequately developed areas; and this is probably the wish of the active local élites of *Alpe Adria* today.

---

[7] *Observatoire social européen*, 1990.

INDEX

INDEX